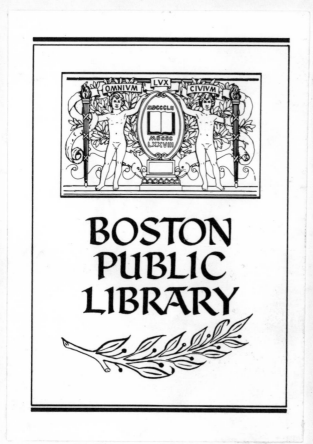

To
Challenge
a Distant
Sea

To Challenge a Distant Sea

James Tazelaar & Jean Bussiere

HENRY REGNERY COMPANY · CHICAGO

Library of Congress Cataloging in Publication Data

Tazelaar, James.
  To challenge a distant sea.

  1. Gau, Jean, 1902-   2. Atom (Ketch)

I. Bussiere, Jean, joint author. II.   Title.
G530.G332T39   910'.45 [B]   76-46490
ISBN 0-8092-7935-5

Photo credits

Ph. Amy, M. Ancel, Jean Pierre Causse, Robert Clements, Joe Cordonat, Jean Gau, Andree Pierret, Robert Price, Michel Thibault, Government of Tunisia, United States Navy, Louis Vernette, Jean Villemagne, Stephanie Wooten.

Copyright © 1977 by James Tazelaar
All rights reserved
Published by Henry Regnery Company
180 North Michigan Avenue, Chicago, Illinois 60601
Manufactured in the United States of America
Library of Congress Catalog Card Number: 76-46490
International Standard Book Number: 0-8092-7935-5

Published simultaneously in Canada by
Beaverbooks
953 Dillingham Road
Pickering, Ontario L1W 1Z7
Canada

To

Carmen Von Bose

Whose
spirited encouragement
enabled
one of us
to cross
his own distant sea

     and

Gilbert Bussiere

whom the sea hath taken

Acknowledgments

Without the enthusiastic and generous help of the following individuals and agencies this book would not have been possible.

Argonaut
James Bruha, American Vice-Consul, Tunisia
Howard Cady
Frank Casper
Robert Clements
Joe Cordonat
Norma Millay Ellis
Moulton Farnham, Editor-at-Large, *Boating*
Sumner Gerard, American Ambassador, Jamaica
David Getchell, Editor, *National Fisherman*
Dorothy Hasty
Beverley Holle
Charmaine V. Keyes, American Consul, Tunisia
Mark Parris, American Consul, Azores
Joe Pettus
Andree Pierret
Betty Rigoli, Editor, *Chesapeake Bay* magazine
James Rockefeller
Bill Robinson, Editor, *Yachting*
Henri Sauzet
Talcott Seelye, American Ambassador, Tunisia
J. D. Sleightholme, Editor, *Yachting Monthly*
Duncan Spencer, *Washington Star*
Mahommet Traish, Peyton Place Bar
Ministry of Interior, Government of Tunisia
Neal Walker, Secretary, Slocum Society
Hein and Siggie Zenker

Contents

Salah Ben Hamida El-Ouni rapidly blinked his eyes.

Staring at the body sprawled on the rocky reef far below, the shepherd dropped the firewood he carried and began searching for a path that would take him down the windswept, jagged face.

He paused, startled by a movement of one of the man's arms.

Quickly he sought footholds along the cliff's naked surface and began to descend. Minutes passed before he reached on outcropping ledge below which he could not safely climb. He was close now. The man below, bleeding from cuts on his head and limbs, made an effort to rise, his strangled gasps somehow audible over the waves crashing against the rocky fingers of land that pointed into the sea.

Salah the shepherd removed a rope he used as a belt. Gathering closely the folds of his burnoose, he wrapped the rope tightly around his hand. Then he knelt and leaned over the wet lip of the ledge to lower it within the man's grasp.

"Monsieur!!" he called. "Monsieur!"

White hair matted with salt water and blood, the man below painfully raised himself on one elbow. His thin shoulders shook as he labored to breathe. The surf withdrew and then returned, sloping briskly onto his trousered legs. Slowly, at the sound of Salah's voice, he rolled his head.

After several attempts he took the rope and made a small loop around his thin wrist. He nodded. Struggling, Salah gradually pulled the exhausted man up onto the sloping ledge. His brown hand gently wiped away the sand and blood that streaked the drawn face. Placing an arm around the sailor's scrawny chest, Salah raised him to his feet. One of his legs, he noted, seemed useless. They began to climb.

Pausing repeatedly in their arduous climb across the fissured rocks, the men finally reached the top of the cliff and crawled over the edge. Shaking from the effort, Salah Ben Hamida El-Ouni whistled wearily. A small sad-eyed donkey, its ears flicking at flies, trotted to where the men lay.

They did not look back at the distant sea, where restless swells mourned the death, several days before, of a Mediterranean gale. Nor did they look down at the beach, where gray waves relentlessly broke into spray and small stones, tumbling, returned to the sea; nor at the pathetic hulk pounding against the jutting rocks nearby. Sprung by the pounding, several hull planks twitched with each slap of the waves like the antennae of a wounded insect. A plastic name board, wrenched from the tortured hull, floated bravely in the lifting surf. The name board read "ATOM New York."

To
Challenge
a Distant
Sea

1

The Tender Blue Sea

"As a youth my favorite readings were sea stories," Jean Gau wrote in his sixty-seventh year, "and my dreams only of shipwrecks, gales and voyages." These youthful fantasies were not in keeping with his place of birth, a busy village in the sun-soaked vineyard that is southern France. It was here, in Serignan, Department of Herault, in a modest Roman-tiled house close to the wintry banks of the river that skirts the village, that the future dean of singlehanded navigators was born, on February 17, 1902.

Several miles below the village, in the river's estuary, its fresh and placid waters mingled with the salty, often boisterous Mediterranean. This was where he first heeded the call of the sea. In a sense this mingling of waters was symbolic of the turbulent life of Jean Gau, for the name of the river was Orb.

There was little in Serignan, however, that did not reflect the sole industry of the entire region, the growing of grapes. Its link with the sea was a tenuous one, the frequent visits of the fisher-

1

men and their families who lived a short distance away in the seaside village of Valras.

There, the chief occupation was fishing. In Valras's small harbor, off the majestic Orb, the gaudy, double-ended fishing smacks provided endless movement and color. Along the village's sandy shore and on its net-webbed walls, young Jean discovered the pulse of the sea. Sweeping inland, the sea breezes stirred the growing mind and spirit of the lad who stood tossing sticks at the restless waters.

At the time of Jean's birth his father was the manager of the Bistoule estate. Just before the beginning of the Great War, through hard work, fiscal acumen, and single-minded purpose, Pierre Gau acquired his own vineyard. In time he even bought a small hunting preserve. Though he lived but six miles from the sea, he had never thought of it as a suitable livelihood, certainly not for the Gaus. They had been small vintners for generations.

His wife's father, however, was a fisherman. During family visits he held the child in his great arms, telling him rough stories of the sea. Thus he was nourished, on the one hand by the sun and earthy toil of the vineyard, on the other by the salty croonings of his grandfather.

Jean ventured out onto the river's slowly moving surface in a variety of craft. According to Jeanne Sirri, a town clerk in Serignan, "Jeannot served his apprenticeship on board abandoned trunk lids, patched canvas canoes, and other dead dogs." Once the boy made a leaky raft by tying together several purloined bundles of his father's firewood. Poling the sluggish craft along the tree-bordered banks, he explored its sun-warmed rushes and cool marshy reeds, keeping as his landmark the serene tower of the village's fifteenth-century church. With other boys he fished for mullet and carp along the river's banks, or, from the tall bridge, watched silently as its waters flowed to the distant sea.

Devout, honest, respectable, the Gau family's status in Serignan was that of the hard-working independent vintner. It was inconceivable to Jean's parents that their only child would not succeed to the family's modest holdings and, through industry, native cunning, and a good marriage, increase them. Inconceivable!

Pierre Gau was not a large man, but, for his size, stout and muscular. Village gossip said he was something of a Don Juan; he had eloped with a strong-featured girl of Serignan, Marie Louise Tabarie. Pragmatic, phlegmatic, and staunchly conservative, he had little interest in either the impractical or the unconventional. Through his cunning and labor the family was comfortably established on Moliere Street.

Jean's mother appears from her photographs to have been plain featured and short in stature, her countenance typical of the French petite bourgeoisie. She was said to be easygoing and generous, with a pleasant personality.

As a child Jean was spoiled and pampered, especially by the mother he adored. He and his father never really understood one another, and there was often conflict. But the father's love for his only son prevailed, and he eventually forgave the boy's follies. In his later years Jean resembled his mother, especially the fine, pale gray eyes, the color of light steel, accented by tiny hazel spots. But his pragmatic and independent spirit he probably inherited from his father, a simple man of the earth.

The strenuous life of the vineyard never appealed to him. The dusting of the growing vines with copper sulphate after each rain permeated his consciousness; he too felt stunted. Whenever an opportunity arose to visit his grandfather in nearby Valras, the boy's bicycle was not to be found.

Sweating from the exertion, Jean whooped and whistled with delight as, beyond the central marketplace, he came upon the blue sea and the white beach that linked the pretentious casino and the mouth of the River Orb. On days when the Mistral or the Tratamonte winds blew, he could see the massive blue Pyrenees in the distance, by shading his eyes with one small hand. The wiry lad bicycled the six miles between the villages on many a summer night "just to look at the sea." In the sights and salt smell of the harbor at Valras, he found not only escape from parental tyranny but an expanse of blue water that stirred his appetite for excitement and adventure.

At school young Jean was often truant and, except for his final year, an indifferent, even lazy pupil. "Jeannot," recalled his favorite schoolmaster, Paul Callas, smoothing his thick red moustache, "was a strong-willed child. He had an *extraordinary* interest in solving difficult problems." But he studied only the two subjects that appealed to him, mathematics and geography.

Interested in the sea and ships, the red-haired schoolteacher often took Jean for outings on his small sailboat or for long walks along the windswept beach at Valras. Days at school were enlivened by furtive drawings of boats and crayoned seascapes. At home the boy often locked himself in his room to read the adventure stories of Verne, Stevenson, Conrad, and London.

In Valras, Jean absorbed much of the fisherman's practical involvement with the sea. Although the Valras fishermen were hardly models for learning how to navigate the world's oceans—the town has no naval traditions, only the simple ways of men who live by the wind and weather—their rough, colorful existence, strange jargon, and spritsail boats with big lateen sails inflamed his imagination. On occasion the son of the Serignan vintner was allowed to go out to the fishing grounds aboard one of the pungent, heavily-built smacks. He grew up to be comfortable with the fishing folk of the world.

As a youth he often visited the Perrone shipyard in Valras, and there the sight of a boat's skeleton or the smell of Stockholm tar deepened his inarticulate gropings for identity. Although he observed the lofting and building of fishing boats and an occasional sailboat, he never developed an interest in boat design. He was, as he said, "content with drawing them for their beauty."

"Jeannot's *only* interest, even early in life, was the sea and boats," said Margot Panisse, a friend of many years and the daughter of a former mayor of Valras, when reporters sought information in later years about the elusive sailor. "He lived just for the sea."

A relative in Serignan, Louis Roumagnac, recalling facets of his nephew's youth, said, "Jean has always been passionate about the sea." He shook his head for emphasis. "Always!"

Jean had friendships with other children, but he always seemed distant. His sense of justice and of equality developed early; he once beat up a school bully who had mistreated a weaker child. At his first communion, distressed by the sight of a poorly dressed boy, Jean complained to the priest that it wasn't fair for the other boys to be well dressed. Except for the fact that he fainted easily, possibly as an indirect result of a high level of albumen in his blood, his health was good.

He had a strong sense of romantic curiosity, which explains the calls he made years later on his great voyages at such unusual and out-of-the-way places as tragic Pitcairn Island. Even in his last years this sense of adventure was evident: while watching an Amazon television documentary Jean sighed repeatedly, obviously *involved* with what he was viewing. He was then seventy-three.*

In his sixty-fourth year, in a letter to the manager of a newspaper, Gau revealed his deep and lasting interest in exploration and exciting travel. From Port Moresby, New Guinea, he wrote that he was "very glad to quench (his) insatiable curiosity. . . . Believe me, I will enjoy myself to the fullest." Twice he eagerly ventured into the awesome New Guinean jungle when it would have been natural for a sea-weary voyager to prefer the companionship of dockside bars to the foul and steaming bush.

Jean's independent and detached nature would have been completely out of step with the prosaic procedures of the typical scientific expedition. His was the spirit of wanderlust, and it fed on such words as *head-hunter, skull, snake-infested swamp, Indian* and *bow and arrow*, Gau, we now think, crossed oceans just to visit New Guinea's jungle, to travel across New Zealand's tortured landscape, to lay a course for the center of the equally mysterious Sargasso Sea. His hunger for adventure in the raw labels Gau as a man born one century too late.

Among his classmates he displayed a flair for eccentric behaviour, a desire to startle. Acquaintances later recalled how they sensed that as Jean was animatedly relating an incident he also appeared to be studying their reactions.

---

*Asked in his seventieth year, "Why visit such places?" Gau replied, "No tourist's islands for me!" Three years later, reading a book by a prominent world sailor, Gau tossed it aside, saying, "It is not interesting. He had no adventures."

As an only child, he also seemed uncommonly interested in privacy, with all its accompanying freedom. "Having gotten used to solitude over the years," he wrote many years later, "I no longer felt its weight." As a boy he often spent many long nights alone, studying the Mediterranean constellations. Locked in his room, his long thin legs scissored across the bed, he was never lonely; he read and drew and devised new pranks. But though his father forgave many of his boyhood antics, such as teasing the family cat with an electric probe, the strains they caused never completely healed.

What was perhaps the most important single break between father and son came about over an apparently minor matter. By the age of thirteen (some accounts say ten), Jean had decided that he wanted to become a naval officer. But to enter the Naval School at Brest he would need good grades. In his thirteenth year, therefore, he improved his studies dramatically, attaining the rank of first, with honors, in the school district. One day, the family story goes, Johnny approached his father, his thin shoulders trembling, and said:

"Papa, I want to enter the Naval School."

Pierre Gau thoughtfully smacked his lips and put his half-emptied glass of red wine down on the table. "Jean, you little scatterbrain, never has a Gau exchanged the vine for water!" He paused, looking directly at his small son. "You, a sailor? *Non!*"

Young Jean, struggling to justify his interest, cried out, "The sea, Papa, is so—nice!"

The old man cleared his throat, "Ya, nice. But it's not worth money like the nice vineyards we'll leave you one day."

Innocent as this exchange was, it so affected Jean that he never returned to school. But its real significance was that his mind was set on a seafaring existence of one kind or another.

Two decades later, seeking information about the man who had just completed his first Atlantic crossing, a *Paris-Soir* reporter described the father's recollection of the incident: "The wooden stairs creaked as the father, strongly built and wearing Gallic moustaches, entered the room. He spoke immediately. 'My son is a sailor, but I am not. When he was ten he handed me a paper saying, 'Papa, just sign it and I leave for the Naval School at Brest.' It was a genuine call and I refused! Had I signed the paper today he would perhaps be a famous captain."

But what little discipline Pierre Gau extended to his son ceased when the father was conscripted for the Army. Their relationship, always difficult, reached an ugly point. The excitable teenager, angered in a confrontation with his father (then on furlough), threw a rock at Pierre's passing automobile, breaking the window.

Like most men who must break firmly their family ties, Jean never lost touch with his parents; he wrote letters over the years hoping to heal the breach. After one of his Atlantic crossings Jean posed proudly with his father, whose years of disappointment at his son's failure to follow in his footsteps are clearly evident in the photograph. But on each Atlantic crossing, as long as his parents lived, Jean returned faithfully to the whitewashed, thick-walled house on Moliere Street.

If his father's no-nonsense attitude and sense of personal achievement subtly influenced the boy's character, his mother gave Gau his easygoing, insouciant personality, an acceptance of things as they were. But the extent of her contribution to her son's principal psychological characteristic, his air of total detachment, can only be conjectured: photographs of her suggest a placid acceptance of whatever life has to offer, an impersonal relationship with people, place, and time.

As the boy matured he became more conscious of his appearance. Friends still recall how, in his late teens, Johnny ordered and wore the latest Parisian fashions. With a personal magnetism that ranged from serenity to alarm, he was, said one childhood friend, "well liked by the girls, who identified him as a Byronic figure, romantic but aloof." He was also a good dancer, especially in the waltz and tango.

Jean's relationships with women were, for them, exciting but irregular and trying. But if his attitude towards women was detached, it was often chivalrous:* in Tahiti, for example, he

---

*His gallantry never ceased. Years later, as a friend's wife, angrily complained about a domestic matter, her false teeth slipped and fell to the table (she had bitten a towel in her anger). With admirable aplomb Jean retrieved them and handed the teeth to the startled lady, saying, "_____, you dropped these."

carried his wahine's fruit and fish on a shoulder pole, to the vast amusement of native men in the marketplace. Women have always found the wiry and muscular Frenchman highly attractive, even in old age, probably because in him they sensed adventure. The comment came again and again: "Johnny never sought women. They sought him!"

His slight build and mobile face with large pixieish ears, his startling hazel-flecked steel-gray eyes, and his *presence*, a kind of serene vitality, caused fellow Serignans to joke about the youthful Gau as the village rooster, a play on the Provençal word for cock. There is a story, still current, that in his late teens Jean used to leave his girl friend in the early morning hours, escaping by a window to visit a young widow who needed consolation. At that time his body was so white that his darker-complected girl friend nicknamed him *Le Blanc*, Whitey. "Jeannot," said Jeanne Sirri, "could have remained the village rooster. But no . . . he had his dream."

The boy was clever and worked well with his hands; he built the first radio in Serignan, an early model with earphones. This persuaded Pierre Gau to have him trained as a mechanic. And as an apprentice, he mastered a trade that, like the swimming learned long ago in the River Orb, would one day prove vital to his survival.

His interest in mechanics often manifested itself in pranks. Once he startled his mother in a manner that shows both electrical skill and psychological insight. "Mother," he said one day, "don't go into my bedroom anymore. Promise!" Marie Louise goodnaturedly reassured her mischievous son, but her curiosity overcame her reserve and she quietly entered the boy's room when he was away.

The next day young Gau, beaming broadly, announced, "Mother, you disobeyed me!" He held before his astonished mother a photograph of her in the room. He had rigged a hidden camera above the door, using a trip and a silent shutter he had invented.

On another occasion Jean rigged an electrical apparatus under the dining room table. To Madame Gau's consternation and alarm, the bouillabaisse suddenly stirred in its bowl!

But not all his pranks were family ones. Once the young mechanic constructed a device employing dynamite; he and a friend blew up a village dike. His fascination with electricity was shown the night after a dance hall manager had refused the dapper young teenager admission! Jean short-circuited the dance hall's wiring system.

Despite the family's respectable status in the community, Jean appears never to have accepted his native village's conservative and orderly existence. One senses that his youthful impression of Serignan's inhabitants was that they were too limited in their contact with life and with the world. After all, did not the River Orb empty into a larger body of water? Was not Serignan but part of a greater whole?

Much of this period Jean spent in a desultory and idle fashion. Refusing to work in the vineyards, preferring to dabble in painting and inventing, the restless teenager began to associate with the village's worst elements. He remarked sixty years afterwards that he might well have become "a gangster." But his early religious training had made him aware that, good being better than evil, his restlessness might find satisfaction in another form of escapism—perhaps art, or even travel? The quiet, intense mechanic began to dream, and to plan.

At eighteen, having displayed a talent for drawing and painting, Jean and a friend spent six months studying the masters in the Louvre in Paris.* But even here his father's practical outlook dominated, and Jean never developed a liking for Impressionism. He did develop a drawing technique that was uncommonly accurate and photographically realistic. Many years later, an expert in photography, upon examining reproductions of Gau's drawings, stated, "He has done *everything*

---

*They lived in a studio attic, their fare cheese, sausage, and bread, and, for dinner, a bowl of soup. A waitress, liking them, gave them a second bowl free. Appreciative, the lads entertained her with, among other things, a Sunday movie. Their first painting brought 300 francs. Celebrating, they drank four bottles of champagne and landed in jail. Later they showed in Barcelona, selling sixty paintings in a month's time. Head cocked, mouth twisted, Gau later said, "We were *good*." They also avoided paying customs on the paintings (copies after Rembrandt, Corot, Delacroix) by crossing the border into Spain on foot.

that a camera can do." Satisfied with his training in art, the young mechanic returned to Serignan.

In time his ability to draw reached the point where his sense of line and precise detail suggested the possibility of forgery. As a result of his Louvre studies Jean had perfected his talent for reproducing details of masterpieces; now he decided to try his hand at reproducing bank notes. It would be, he reasoned, a challenge of his superior ability to copy. If the first bank note was not detected it would prove that he was at the top of his art, that there was nothing more to learn.

He competently engraved and etched the necessary plates. On a printing press that he designed and built, Jean printed several twenty- and fifty-franc notes. This illicit enterprise was discovered; one village anecdote is that a pimp, a police informant taken in by one of Gau's forged notes, turned him in. Bank of France officials, incidentally, later unofficially attested to the excellence of his work.

Jean's emergence into early manhood received a severe jolt when the two gendarmes arrested him before his startled mother. Drawn by the surprising presence of a police cart, a small crowd of curious neighbors quickly gathered before the Gau house. They stood whispering and pointing as the ashen-faced boy, handcuffed, head bowed, was brought out of the house and placed roughly in the horse-drawn cart. Beside him sat another man falsely accused as an accomplice.

Jean's incorrigible spirit, fostered and strengthened by parents too lenient with their only child, brooded and suffered during his three-month pretrial imprisonment in Beziers's ancient prison fortress. There, behind cold steel, he heard of his mother's sleepless nights. Gossip raced through the villages as the family priest tried to console his humiliated parents. The meaning of life and death, man's struggle with good and evil— these thoughts were his sobering companions. But he had other companions as well.

"Johnny learned how desperate men communicate in jail, how they conceal small items in their assholes," said a boyhood friend matter-of-factly, years afterwards. "But for him, jail was redeeming. Jean decided to seek a life beyond civilized life. . . . You could say that he was determined to leave civilization whenever he could."

Sixty years after the forgery, Gau, standing before the old prison, his mobile features twisting with recollection, said, "I thought then my life was broken."

Although details of the incident are not clear,* it is certain that Pierre Gau again came to his son's rescue. By selling off a part of his estate, Pierre managed to persuade village officials to drop the charges inasmuch as his son had not attained his majority. The trial never came to pass. Had Jean been convicted he could have been imprisoned for several years on notorious Devil's Island.

The police confiscated the printing press and part of the forged money. The remainder, hidden under a false mantelpiece, they failed to find. Local gossip, in time, would say that Gau used this money to emigrate, but this is untrue.

Many of the villagers had been victimized by false currency before, and the forgery incident would not soon be forgotten in Serignan. Seventeen years later, Henri Cordouret, head chef at the Hotel Taft in New York, wrote to Pierre and Marie Louise Gau:

". . . For six years I've been Jean's friend and boss. Our relationship is indestructible. Equally sound is an urge to write and tell you that *despite what has been said* Jean is truly a good and honest person. . . though at times his character is difficult to understand. But if this is a defect it is vanquished by his other qualities. Jean has always known what he wanted, a virtue that few men ever possess."

The unending disapprobation of the village is evident also in the fact that although an official function was held in the city hall (attended mostly by his closest friends and admirers from little Valras) at the end of his first circumnavigation, Serignan never sponsored a communitywide reception to honor her native son on his return from his great voyages. In time Jean's relatives

---

*Confronted at the informal hearing by a long-whiskered Bank of France official, who held examples of forged and real bank notes demanding, "Which is false?" the shaken youth admitted that certain notes could not be forged. The official advised the judge, "We don't want him prosecuted. We want to know *how* he made those notes!"

stopped talking to him. Serignan, drowsily blinking in the grape-tart air, would never forget—never.

The even but dull tenor of village life exacerbated Jean's discontent as the days passed. Then, at twenty, he was conscripted for military service. He was assigned to the Army, an event that, though it did not affect the village's poor impression of him, inflamed Jean's smouldering impatience for action.

The River Orb had served its purpose. On the threshold of young manhood, his imagination no longer in step with the routine of daily existence, the restless vintner's son sought excitement far beyond the dust of the grape-heavy vineyards, far beyond the river's placid limits.

2

The Cadiz Affair

Jean's disillusionment with civilized order was growing. As Private Gau, he had been posted to Alsace-Lorraine for several months, and had there taught himself to play the accordion. Then an ugly incident occurred. A close Army friend, carrying secret documents, was killed by German agents and his body thrown from a train into a river.

Transferred to Algeria, Gau was stationed in Blida, a bleak military post in the northern foothills of the Atlas Mountains. But Army life had its compensations. Free from the nagging of his father, the twenty-year-old mechanic experienced for the first time the enchantment of travel. It was a strange and largely desolate land with exotic people and sun-blistered ambience, and his latent desire for excitement burst into flame. Never again would he settle for an ordinary existence.

In Blida, Jean borrowed a copy of Alain Gerbault's book, *Alone Across The Atlantic*. Gerbault, France's major tennis figure of the '20s and something of a mystic, had forsaken a career on the courts to set sail in an aged cutter, the *Firecrest*. Years later, having established himself in the South Pacific, he was imprisoned by the Japanese in World War II. He died while captive.

Readers of his book usually weary of the endless difficulties Gerbault experienced with his cranky boat, its rotted canvas and weak rigging, But the idea of a national hero renouncing all for the discomforts of total freedom strongly appealed to Jean. Three decades later, captain of his own boat, Gau called at Bora Bora to honor the memory of his "master," Alain Gerbault.

One passage in Gerbault's book may have been a deciding factor in convincing Jean that he too would one day own a sailboat capable of crossing distant seas. Chancing to look out a train window, Gerbault saw a young beggar running beside the train. The ragged boy seemed to him the epitome of freedom. "I felt I should have liked to have been in his place . . . I who am always roving in quest of youth. At any rate I felt I was master aboard my own boat, and could go on roving round the world looking for the open air, the great spaces and adventure; leading the plain life of a seaman, and bathing in the sun a body and mind not content to inhabit the houses of men." Stirring words—yet years later, Jean confided that he preferred Dumas, Slocum, and Day to Gerbault, whom he considered "stubborn,"—a typical southern France indictment of all Bretons.

During his tour of duty in Blida, Jean rode a camel into the mountains and the rolling desert hill country of the Sahara, whose pervasive, pristine solitude etched onto his mind the beauty of a hidden world. His deep-sea logbooks, years afterwards, mention the topographic analogies between the oceans and the world's largest desert; at one point he writes that his boat was like "a camel crossing a strangely moving desert."

Alone in the immense splendor of great deserts, no man escapes being deeply moved by his insignificance. In the isolation of the great oceans this awareness, for Jean, was confirmed. It became the fundamental premise of a fatalistic philosophy.

Discharged, Gau returned to France and exchanged his uniform for a mechanic's overalls, taking a job in Beziers, a moderately large city six miles from Serignan. For a while he settled down, trying hard to improve his status in the community. To make more money, he quit the mechanics job and went to work in a distillery.

Always popular with village girls, Jean now met and fell in love with a pretty dressmaker, Honorine Armengaud. In time their love matured, and on March 26, 1926, they were married in her hometown, Valras. Jean was twenty-four and for the first time in his life he had willingly laid aside his hunger for adventure. Love had conquered—but not for long.

True to the conventional French wisdom of live and let live, the villagers did not openly display their antipathy for the young couple. Nevertheless, Jean smarted from the memory of the forgery scandal six years before. Part of his disquiet may have stemmed from his ambivalent feelings toward his native village, and part from an eagerness to prove that Pierre Gau's son was not a scoundrel but, in fact, a local hero. The desire to be recognized locally is not uncommon in men of drive and ambition. With dream-haunted men it is inextricably tied to achievement of their goals.

At any rate, several months after the marriage Jean's restless nature surfaced when he startled his young wife with the blunt announcement "Let's try our luck in America!" Vastly more reserved but still in love with her vital, somewhat erratic man, Honorine agreed. His parents were astounded. But, reluctantly, Pierre Gau provided the money for their passage.

Jean saw the journey as an adventure. And, he argued, it might also save a marriage already deteriorating. But behind his manly argument and reasoning, the River Orb quietly flowed.

Honorine did not share her husband's energetic enthusiasm for boats and the sea. Whenever he mentioned the subject, she shrugged. Her simmering resentment finally boiled over one day when, accompanying Jean in a small sailboat in the harbor at Valras, Honorine screamed hysterically as the boat heeled to a puff. Villagers still recall the scene: Jean, intense anger disfiguring his face, suddenly luffed, tore the sails off the mast, and rowed heatedly back to the harbor landing. Had Jean revealed to his wife his real reason for emigrating—to buy a boat—she would never have agreed to go.

Still conscious of the community's silent treatment, the young couple emigrated to America in 1927. Jean, unable to get a mechanic's job in pre-Depression New York, went to work as a dishwasher at a brand-new kitchen in an apartment house on East 86th Street.* In time the young couple found lodgings on 72nd Street in Jackson Heights and settled down for what was to have been a profitable stay in the New World. Jean continued to draw in his spare time.

Fortunately, one of the apartment's telephone operators was a native of Valras, Margot Panisse. Jean had known Margot years before when her father had been the village mayor. Through her the young couple met two fellow countrymen, Joseph Cordonat and Eli Agnel, both chefs and both natives of Marseilles.

Cordonat soon introduced the athletic Serignan to kayaking,† and on weekends the young expatriates went sailing around Manhattan. "At that time," recalls Cordonat, "there was a small beach under the Queensboro Bridge, subway fares were a nickel, and men wore derbies." Honorine, however, still did not share her husband's enthusiasm for boating. Both of them grew lonely.

To overcome his lack of English Jean enrolled in a night school language course, a gift of his employer. But before long the village rooster was dating his instructress, who taught Spanish as well. Impatient at the half-hour wait before her class was over, Jean enrolled and learned to speak another language. In time they became lovers.

Time and the demands of an unfamiliar land, the limited social life, and the difficulties of Jean's exasperating changes of mood accelerated the erosive process. The quarreling and anger grew. One day, arguing at a friend's house, Jean slapped Honorine violently. Soon afterward, he returned home one

---

*He was paid $25 a week, food included. Interestingly, the first week's salary went for clothes, except for $5 placed in a bank.

† Once Jean and two sisters made an overnight kayak trip. The weather was freezing so the girls suggested all three sleep in the same bag. "The only way anyone could turn over," said Jean, "was for all to do so. I didn't sleep that night, and you can imagine the fun I had!"

evening to find that she had left him. A note, pinned to a living room lamp, said, "Good-bye, Johnny. Have fun."

For the twenty-six-year-old Jean there were no emotional scars, only relief. Now nothing stood in the way of his eventually owning a boat, especially since he was not burdened with alimony. Asked many years later why he had never remarried, Gau replied, "I realized that, for me, marriage would be a major drawback to my love of sailing."

Eventually he was hired as a "vegetable man" at the Gateway Restaurant. Although he would never become attuned to the preparation of dishes—a skill almost innate with the French—in time Gau became Chef Entremetier (hors d'oeuvres) and, in later years in other jobs, Chef Saucier.* But whenever he was asked to name his favorite dish, the former chef, mouth twisted in mock seriousness and eyes smiling, replied, "French fries and steak, of course!"

Now more solitary than ever, young Gau began saving his money. He was determined to own a boat. About the long hours and mundane work in various kitchens, he wrote, "I don't complain . . . because it is the only way I can realize my dream."

From 1927 to 1934 "Le Blanc" had several affairs, a reasonable development in the light of Honorine's desertion and Jean's appeal to women. One of these affairs is said to have developed into love, but determined to follow his star, Jean escaped marriage. Since he had received little parental discipline in his formative years, a strong streak of egocentricity had developed.

---

*While he was still a dishwasher, his boss approached him. "I want you to learn roasting, Johnny."

"But I don't know anything about it! *Mon Dieu!* I can't cook."

"Yes, I know. But you'll get ten bucks more a week."

"OK, I cook."

Much later the chef spoke to Jean. "Well, Jean, the only position you haven't held is Chef Saucier. . . "

Gau (who liked telling this story because it cast him as a cunning Frenchman) protested. "No, no!"

"My assistant is leaving and you will do the job."

". . . How much you give me for that, boss?"

"Twenty dollars a week more."

"OK, chef, I make the sauces!"

In time it would flourish and grow into a singular devotion to self-fulfillment.

In 1931 his three-year search for a boat ended at De Quincey's Boatyard near Boston, where he found a beautiful schooner for sale. The yacht's owner, one of Boston's wealthiest yachtsmen, was impressed by Joe Cordonat's businesslike air ("Johnny cried for fear he'd lose that boat!"). He lowered the price to $2,000, and Johnny was now the owner and skipper of a "terribly run down" sailboat, *Onda II*. Happy and confident—although his sailing experience then consisted only of boyhood jaunts with his schoolmaster, Paul Callas, and with his fisherman grandfather—Gau managed, with Cordonat's skilled help, to return the badly fouled boat to New York.

Because *Onda's* engine wasn't working properly, they couldn't take the Cape Cod Canal, and had to sail "outside." On the first day out each man ate eight fried eggs and half a loaf of bread. But to the skipper's dismay, the ancient coal stove caught fire and had to be tossed overboard. On the second night at sea Johnny, still hungry, began feeling around in the unlighted cabin for food containers. "Jam!" he whispered, loud enough for Joe, sleeping in the forward cabin, to hear. Grabbing a loaf of bread, Gau ran topside to tend the helm and ease his hunger. After one enormous bite he sputtered, "Goddamn! Mustard!" Cordonat's eyes twinkled at the memory: "Johnny was so hungry he ate the whole bottle!"

The two eventually reached an exclusive boatyard on Long Island, but as they approached, the manager ran out and yelled, "Get that damned wreck outa here!" *Onda's* bottom was so foul, recalls Cordonat, that under full sail in light breezes the schooner wouldn't move! Finally they found a yard that would accommodate them and the boat was hauled. But when *Onda* was out of the water, "she smelled so bad the yardmen put her back. They actually scraped her underwater."

Jean was promptly fired from his job, the chef refusing to believe that he had been at sea. "Why didn't you telephone?" he demanded of the dumbfounded Gau. Johnny immediately found work as vegetable man at the Hotel Roosevelt, where Cordonat was the Executive Chef.

Now began a long period of carefully refurbishing the boat. It was while Johnny lived aboard *Onda*, to save rent, that he met an ancient mariner (and former gunrunner) whose "glittering eye" and long-held secret figured largely in his subsequent world voyages. But just now the young chef's yearnings were for an Atlantic crossing, a feat that would impress his Serignan peers and elders and possibly even all of France.

But even on land Jean was seldom without adventure. Once, when the club's winter snows had melted, Jean discovered a body in a wooded area nearby. At another yacht club, he slept through severe winters in a small room at the clubhouse. But whenever the harbor froze over while he was aboard, he had to smash the ice with an axe to make a path for his dinghy to get to work. This always provoked laughter from club members.

"In the late thirties," recalled Joe Cordonat, "there was a particularly severe winter. Johnny woke up one morning with his bedclothing frozen to the cabin sides. He escaped only by forcing his way out of a stiff sweater."

In the thirties, when times were hard, Jean belonged to a gang of gregarious sailors, including a dentist, a building contractor, an architect, and a burlesque singer. One of the members leased a piece of land near Whitestone landing. There they built a shed with a big stove and a huge anchor that served as a lamp. To outfit the shed the members "borrowed" certain items from nearby moored boats.

Such as? "Mattresses, you know, knives and forks. Housekeeping stuff." Joe's voice trailed off. He chuckled and leaned forward in his chair.

"The members were . . .," he paused, smiled, and said, "friendly. *Very* friendly. Now, Johnny somehow managed to steal the president's gal away . . . " Laughing at the thought, he shook his head. "We used to order bootleg whiskey a week early. I swear it contained essence of dead cat, potato peels, bits of shoe leather, and caramel for color! But we were glad for it, mixed it with orange juice the government gave away free!"

The neophyte skipper did not spend his weekends handing, reefing, and steering his sailboat on Long Island Sound to develop the seamanship skills he would need for his first long voyage. The time aboard *Onda* was for refitting, for building and installing a looped aerial radio. Amazingly, Jean never thought of his lack of experience as a pressing matter. He simply reasoned that once clear of the land he could manage. And for nearly four decades, although he heard ten-ounce canvas explode in gale winds, watched as storm waves climbed aboard his boat, or wore ship to avoid beating in the far-off Indian Ocean, he did.

One of Jean's favorite New York haunts was the Hayden Planetarium. With library books he taught himself the rudiments of celestial navigation in his spare time. Although he never developed more than a competent layman's knowledge of the subject, four decades later Captain Jean Gau lectured at the United States Naval Academy on his methods of navigating at sea.

Refitting *Onda* took four years, and then Jean informed his startled employer that he was leaving for a one-month cruise to Nova Scotia. This, his first long voyage, was fraught with the difficulties of handling a large sailboat in nice weather and rough waters. But Jean, determined, had an essential knowledge of tides, currents, and heavy-weather sailing. He had also learned that a beautifully appointed boat of large size, no matter how lovely its lines, is not necessarily suitable for deep-sea sailing.*

In three brief paragraphs, Jean Gau's youth, early manhood, and first long cruise (in at least one way, the most instructive he ever made) are summarily presented in what must be among the world's most economical introductions by an author to his own writings—and one of the most revealing:

---

*Among the important persons Johnny and Joe met and became friendly with in this period was the Secretary of the Treasury, Andrew W. Mellon, who appears to have liked the two affable Frenchmen. "Jean," Mellon said one day, "I'm going to Bermuda to fish for bonefish." To this day Gau isn't certain if their legs weren't being pulled. The three men often had coffee aboard *Onda*, prepared by Joe in a "dirty old pot," relaxing and sharing sea stories. On one occasion, Jean was aloft painting Onda's mainmast with aluminum paint. Mellon appeared for his usual cup of coffee. The paint can slipped, fell, and splattered a large area of deck. The distinguished seventy-seven-year-old Secretary of the Treasury asked for a rag, bent over, and helped wipe up the mess.

I have often wondered how the call of the sea was born in me. As a youth my favorite readings were sea stories and my dreams only of shipwrecks, gales and voyages. The story of Alain Gerbault roaming the oceans in his small sailboat was, for me, a revelation. In time I realized that the only way I could make my dreams a reality was to own a boat. It was with this thought that I emigrated to the United States in 1927 to make and save money.

With the money saved I spent three years poking about harbors searching for a boat that would defy the Atlantic's wrath. In 1931, in De Quincey harbor near Boston, I discovered a rare pearl, the pocket schooner *Onda II*. I bought her and sailed her back to New York, and for nearly seven years lived on board.

Completely refinished, such that her previous owner couldn't have recognized her, *Onda* was ready for an extended cruise. In 1935, accompanied by a young and fearless American girl, I sailed to Nova Scotia and returned, richer for the experience, which included sailing in impenetrable fog. Betty, my companion, was sick five days out of five days. In short, I vowed never again to have anyone along because for this sport one needed to sail alone.

Not mentioned in Gau's account is that Joe Cordonat and his wife went along to pick up their newly built French pilot boat, *Ouida,* at Harvey Gamage's famous boat yard. On the return trip the Cordonats motored through the Cape Cod Canal; *Onda,* because of her erratic engine,* sailed outside. After four days of waiting in New York for the *Onda,* a worried Joe called the Coast Guard. "Don't worry, sir," he was dramatically informed. "We'll comb the ocean!" A day later *Onda* arrived. When told of the Coast Guard's heroic effort, Jean mumbled, "Funny. I never saw 'em, even once!" *Onda,* out of gas, had drifted onto the dangerous Georges Banks, where his companion, using her charm, had talked several frugal Maine fishermen out of their surplus gasoline supplies.

More significant is the fact that "Betty" (her real name was Peggy), a friend said recently, "was never sick in her life. Peggy was a tough egg. I mean she was bright, feisty, able to take care of

---

*Onda's converted engine, which never functioned properly, was worked on by a "crazy" mechanic. To stop the engine he placed both forefingers on the spark plugs, thereby short-circuiting it.

herself." The speaker leaned over the desktop, brushing aside an old sepia photograph of the couple. "She once fought with her sister in the middle of a harbor. Now, fightin' with relatives is perfectly all right." His mouth opened to reveal tombstone tilted teeth. "But *not* when the relative is one of four persons in a six-foot dinghy! I think Johnny was afraid of her."

But why the misstatement regarding Peggy's condition? Most probably it was Jean's way of providing a simple answer to the annoying question, "Why do you sail alone?"

The cruise over, the thirty-three-year-old, wavy-haired cook berthed *Onda* and returned to his pots and pans at the Hotel Roosevelt. He was promptly fired for being late. Through Cordonat, Johnny found a chef's job at the elegant and prestigious Hotel Taft.

As he stood in the great kitchen, half-heartedly slicing and chopping small hillocks of glistening vegetables, Johnny decided that as soon as his bank account was adequate he would again put to sea, this time bound for Europe and his first Atlantic crossing. He paused to wipe perspiration from his brow with the tip of his apron. His heavily-lidded eyes concealed the images that flooded his mind: of *Onda,* cloudlike against a blue sky, of a sail's fluttering leech. And he would sail alone. A smile crossed his face, and he laid down the chopping knife. With his right arm he swept a pile of chopped vegetables into a pan. But ahead of the dreaming cook lay a series of mishaps, any one of which would have destroyed most men's infatuation with boats and the challenge of distant seas.

Onda, completely refinished and glistening in a new coat of paint, her extensive brightwork shining in the late morning light, slipped out of Long Island Sound on July 7, 1937. In a letter to his parents written just before leaving, the skipper mentioned that in *Onda*'s hold were "forty gallons of water, sixty tins of condensed milk, five kilos of tobacco, etc." He did not mention *Onda*'s malfunctioning engine.

"Johnny never poormouthed anyone," said a friend, recalling the departure for Europe. "So he never mentioned in his manuscript that a photographer, so laden with cameras and light meters that he resembled a bunch of grapes, begged Johnny to let him go along as far as Montauk. Sensing that the guy needed a scoop, he agreed. Halfway there, Johnny casually mentioned that he had to pump the bilge. 'What!' the man cried. He ran and looked down in the bilge and saw moving water. 'Oh, my God!' he cried. 'I've got kids, and a wife. Please! You gotta let me off!'" The speaker smiled crookedly. "Old Johnny didn't say anything. Just turned the boat over to me (I left in Montauk) and rowed the nervous guy ashore."

The handsome schooner worked her way to the open sea, and her skipper, "anxious to climb the waves," elated and confident on his first voyage off-soundings, grinned broadly. He often broke into a song, a catch in his raspy voice revealing deep satisfaction. At hand, Jean knew, was real adventure—around him was nothing but sea and sky, and in his sunburned hand was the helm of a sturdy boat. But he sang mostly because he was alone—completely alone.

Ahead lay his first encounter with absolute solitude and with the unsettling effect of seemingly endless fog on the human spirit. But the adventurer in him also burst forth. "I reveled in my misery," he wrote after his first storm at sea. Now Jean Gau, for the first time, was entering *his* world, one in which he had as much freedom as any man could want, and all the beauty his eye could capture. Like William Blake, who saw "a world in a grain of sand," Gau found in the oceans a world he could understand.

The New York papers did not report his voyage. His friend, Henri Cordouret, wrote Jean's parents castigating the media for being "mute," but he admitted that Jean's "true character" cared nothing "for flourishes and trumpets." Jean, his boss declared happily, "is to his fellow workers a pure hero in the best sense."

The sympathetic citizens of little Valras saw him in the same light. They made plans to welcome Jean and his beautiful *Onda*. After all, only a few men had previously sailed the Atlantic single-handed. Now old Pierre Gau's son was to become one of them!

For his part, Jean no doubt felt that his feat would be a dramatic demonstration to fellow Serignans of his superior talents and uncommon abilities. By this means he would also restore himself in the eyes of his aging parents. Although his marital problems had delighted the village gossips, his position as chef at the prestigious New York address had given him a more favorable image in the decade since he'd left Serignan. And now—he smiled richly at the thought—he was returning as the owner of a magnificent forty-foot yacht! Moved by her beauty and great heart as she breasted each threatening wave, the lightly clad sailor suddenly bent over and passionately kissed *Onda*'s glistening coaming.

But he would return to France also as the man who had single-handedly challenged the Western Ocean's harsh realities, a feat that only the intrepid achieve. One day, Johnny mused, as he had often done behind the hotel's hot stoves, Serignan would value the name of Gau as France revered the name of Gerbault.

Stirred, he gripped *Onda*'s varnished oak and bronze wheel harder as she lunged ahead. Beneath his bare feet, meanwhile, *Onda*'s engine lay silently seizing up with rust. And along the still distant Spanish coast, harbor lights were being extinguished because of the Civil War. Had he known, that too would have stirred his thoughts.

As the solitary and ingenious Robinson Crusoe is the island hermit par excellence, Jean Gau became the sea hermit nonpareil. Answering the call of the spray, his devotion to roaming the seas, alone, began with his first transatlantic crossing. The account that follows, from his manuscript, is pure Gau. Terse, maddeningly deficient in details, terribly impersonal and detached, this account, compared with the famous Anita letter of the next chapter, gives the impression that two different authors are involved.

Those who heard Captain Gau lecture in later years about the Cadiz Affair will recall hearing slightly differing versions. We have tried to cull out the patently false and present what we believe to be the most accurate version. Admittedly, some of the variations are interesting: that he was imprisoned in the tower that saw Columbus depart for the New World; that a woman living near the beach, seeing his nakedness, hurriedly brought him a blanket; that he was imprisoned and later visited by Franco; that *Onda*'s iron keel was melted to make bullets for the

Nationalistas—these variations we find absorbing. But they must, for the present, be placed on the shelf.

We admit, however, to being stymied by Jean's matter-of-fact, prosaic description of this, the second most traumatic incident of his life. For from this searing event would come a seven-year period of astounding creativity.

I worked hard preparing *Onda* for another cruise. This time I laid aboard a four-month supply of food. Of course, four months I felt not long enough to quench my thirst for freedom and adventure, the leaving behind of the weariness of shore life. But on July 7, 1937, I took the leap!

Onda, loaded so that her Plimsoll line was submerged, proceeded in nice weather to Montauk Point, where she took on fresh water. From there I took my departure five days later.

As the land merged with the horizon I eagerly inhaled the breezes fresh off the ocean. I have never been able to describe that first feeling of being totally alone. I can say only that I was *happy*. On July 14 I spent the morning fixing the bilge pump. That afternoon the *Normandie* crossed the horizon, a reminder that I was in the shipping lanes. Later, mounting a masthead light, I shot the polar star and got my position. At dawn the next day I had a big bowl of coffee before going on deck; a northeasterly was blowing. *Onda,* her wheel lashed, steered herself all that day. I was terribly happy!

Forty days after departure, August 24, I sighted the Azores, pleased with my navigation. My plans were to stop at Horta, take on fresh water, and send news to Serignan.

This leg of my voyage hadn't been without troubles, however. For several days there had been a hopeless fog, the noon sun nothing but a pale halo. Visibility was less than half a mile. I was exhausted from having to stay awake, sounding the foghorn constantly. It was, for me, a period melancholic and gloomy, and the sound of the horn was almost too much. But on the fourth day the fog lifted.

But then crossing the Gulf Stream wasn't fun, either. Nighttimes I hove to and slept, exhausted. But there were nice days as well. Often I saw mirages. I once hailed a boat but it flew away! The sharks, dolphins, and seabirds kept me from being bored.

At Horta I was greeted effusively and many persons showed me souvenir photos of Gerbault, who called there many years before. The photographs of this worthy sailor moved me and I kept a copy in my wallet.*

September 2 I weighed anchor, and by nighttime the next day the Azores had vanished, lost in the brooding seas. My speed at that time averaged 120 miles a day, and with little to do, I speared fish, hauling them aboard with difficulty. At times *Onda* flew over a sapphire sea that lay, mysteriously, between the islands and Portugal. Trouble was brewing, however.

On September 25 the wind drew forward, causing the swells to smash into one another. The season was well advanced, as they say, and any day I expected violent gales. The next day the barometer began falling jerkily, the anemometer read 35 knots, and the seas were swollen, confused, and dangerous. I could see but the glittering crests of waves. The next day the wind blew fearfully and the lovely *Onda* scudded before it under a topmast fore staysail.†

The day after, the wind was stronger and the seas terribly swollen. I set the storm jib and struck the staysail. But even with the jib *Onda* made seven knots! She behaved wonderfully and I was excited. Of course, we needed this speed to keep ahead of the seas astern. Between successive waves I dashed down to the galley for a cup of coffee and some sea biscuit. Then on September 29 I spied Cape Espichel, and at midnight anchored behind a hill after a crossing of twenty-seven days. Good enough! *Onda* later rode to two anchors while I ate a huge meal. Outside the anchorage a hurricane was howling.

Impatient, two days afterwards I departed for Gibraltar . . . the gale was still raging. Outside, the seas were magnificent! *Onda* would climb to the top of an enormous wave and pause, I swear, ready for flight. Seconds later she lay . . . in the abyss of the sea. I was living my boyhood dreams!

Finally *Onda* passed Cape St. Vincent and entered the strait proper, only to be becalmed for ten days. Ten full days with not a breath of air! But currents caused us to drift seventy-five miles south of the strait to the vicinity of Fort Larache. This was the beginning of my misery.

---

*In Horta's Cafe Francais, Gau met the Duchess of Guise, mother of the Count of Paris (exiled pretender to the French throne, then visiting Horta). Introduced by the duchess to her son, Gau asked, "Who is he?" The duchess answered, petulantly, "The future king of France!" The Americanized Gau responded, "Boy oh boy!"

† Not reported by Gau was the fact that lightning struck *Onda*'s mainmast at sea, flattening the top (trucks). In later years Gau hauled a chain overboard, fastened to the mizzenmast foot.

At ten o'clock on the evening of October 15 the wind rose and I began to work my way back towards Gibraltar. While hove to that night, lights burning, I was startled by a hissing sound. "The wind?" I wondered, when suddenly I was thrown to the cabin floor. *Onda* was shaken crazily.

On deck in two jumps, I saw the diminishing lights of a trawler in the thick darkness. My lights had gone out, and the hissing sound I'd heard was from the trawler's steam engine. The shock, I discovered, was *Onda*'s bowsprit being torn off. The forward deck had been ripped open. I repaired the damage the best I could, fearful that foul weather would sink us by the nose.

My anxiety was honed several nights later when the huge black carapace of a submarine materialized in the blackness. In the dark my small size was not discernible, or else the officer sensed that I was harmless, possibly a joke, when I said that I was from New York. The U-34 roared off into the night.

Again I began an approach to the strait, but it wasn't in the cards. This time a Levante or easterly met me, and on October 17 it was raging. Every minute I felt the wind was at its peak, it was that ugly. That night, at one o'clock, the anemometer read sixty-three knots in the gusts. As though melted by the storm, the clouds were a leaden gray. Spindrift cut my face as waves, mounted by other waves, roared out of the east. *Onda* was seldom on her feet. That same night, lashed to the helm, I was repeatedly submerged by waves as they swept her clean.

But, frankly, I thrived on my misery, for I was living the gales and shipwrecks of my youth! I was too fascinated to be afraid.

On October 20 I sighted Cape St. Vincent as the storm let up. I had been blown 150 miles off course, and I still had to pass the Strait of Gibraltar. But after ten days of painful beating I sighted Cadiz, Spain, to my tired eyes a fairyland. I decided to put in to repair the trawler-caused damages.*

That night I had sailed into the broad Bay of Cadiz, preparing to land at dawn, when, without warning, an enormous blast of wind burst across my boat, splitting the mainsail completely. I jumped to the

---

*Points not mentioned in Gau's manuscript: the U-boat captain had warned him of the Civil War in Spain, and Gau, not expecting to land there, carried no large-scale charts of Spanish harbors (years later he recalled seeing city lights and the masts of ships in Cadiz harbor). This meeting at sea with the U-34 deeply impressed both skippers; they met ashore subsequently on one or two occasions. One version of their meeting has the German skipper, learning of Gau's plight, visiting him in Cadiz. The two seamen reportedly boarded the submarine, where they drank schnapps.

halyards and got the crazed and shredded canvas down. *Onda,* under reduced canvas, began drifting swiftly toward some rocks about half a mile to leeward . . . although I couldn't see them, I knew they were there.

I started the engine, although I didn't trust it. Twenty minutes later, it quit! Near panic, I gathered certain items from the cabin, placed them in an oilskin, and went topside in the dark to await the inevitable. Suddenly *Onda* knocked* onto the sands and listed immediately. I dove overboard and began to swim.

Dragging myself ashore, grateful that I had reached the beach and not landed among the rocks, I managed to start a fire. While I danced to get warm, several carabinieri, with drawn bayonets, as startled by the sight as I by them, approached. I explained the situation in Spanish but it was pretty obvious they weren't going to accept the tale of a man in Adam's clothes, who claimed he'd crossed the Atlantic alone and who now was jumping around a beach fire outside Cadiz harbor! *Loco, muy loco!*

I was remanded to the house of a frigate captain, Don Carlos de Pineda y Soto, in nearby Puerto Santa Maria. The next morning a tug arrived to salvage *Onda* but, because of the heavy weather, could do nothing. On the fourth day *Onda* became part of the shoals and rocks in Cadiz harbor.

I will say nothing more of my misery.

I began to think about my next boat.

Spain was then having its Civil War. But eventually I was interrogated by the French consul, Moreau, in Seville. After examining my log book and identification, he said, "What strikes me, Gau, is that they didn't shoot you next to the fire on the beach. You deserved it!"†

The American consul, on the other hand, was very considerate, but could not help me to return to France. My only hope, he said, was to return to America. But after ten years absence I wanted badly to see my parents. My father, in the meantime, had asked the mayor of Serignan

---

*To protect himself against Morocco Coast pirates, Jean carried a stolen .38 Police Special revolver aboard *Onda.* Earlier, back in New York harbor, he had practiced shooting at several ducks, telling his friends, "Tonight, we eat duck!" He'd missed. "Oh hell!" he'd said. "Fish again tonight." Now, when a policeman started toward the wreckage of *Onda,* Jean swam out, climbed aboard, and threw both gun and ammunition overboard.

† Gau has consistently stated that *Onda* first struck the rocks, to be thrust back onto the sands later. His drawing of the stricken *Onda* is inconclusive. Part of his "jumping," Johnny later humorously explained, was from stubbing his foot against driftwood, his "teeth chattering like castanets."

to intercede. In time I was notified by the American Embassy in Paris that I would be embarking on the liner *Britannia* from Gibraltar, bound for France.

I arrived in Gibraltar, boarded my ship, and was cheered and given champagne. I even received an invitation to continue to India. But after a while I saw the coastline of France and shortly thereafter the skyline of Marseilles. But, sadly, I saw them from the sooty deck of a giant liner, not from dear old *Onda*'s.

What better example of Jean's detached nature than this simple flourish—admittedly written thirty years later—to what must have been the onset of a lengthy and deeply emotional experience? The loss of his magnificent *Onda* must have caused him countless hours of unease, even depression. Lamenting the loss of less handsome and luxurious yachts, other sailors have spoken of guilt-heavy nightmares, of waking wet with sweat, of seeking relief from going mad with grief. Why then view Jean as less tormented by gruesome visions of a lovely ship he had seen destroyed as he stood by, impotent, in shock?

While in Spain, Gau wrote to his worried parents. The letter, dated November 4, 1937, suggests the tenseness of the times. More important, it reveals for the first time Jean Gau's total commitment to the sea.

> My dear parents:
> I am sorry to tell you that I cannot reach France because the French Consul simply dropped me—I am no longer a French citizen. For the present the American Consul in Seville is doing what's needed for my return to New York. *Onda* is buried in the sands. I could rescue a few navigation instruments but, *believe me, I will do it again, for now the sea has taken me forever. I love that life!*

Ignorant of *Onda*'s loss and of Gau's difficulties with Spanish officialdom, Serignan was beginning to wonder at the delay. A reporter, visiting the village in anticipation of Gau's arrival by sea, filed this account of "Gerbault's disciple" on November 8, 1937:

> The Autumn sun gilds the red-roofed houses and narrow streets of the village, asleep now that the grapes are gathered. As the vintage distills in vats old men sit beside the whispering fountains in the

small, shady village square and ask, "Will he arrive today?" The extraordinary adventure of their young neighbor has kept the village busy; their only source of information the newspapers and scanty remarks by the young man's parents.

A more inquisitive reporter might have concluded differently.

Grim-faced, more withdrawn than ever, restless from inactivity, Gau pondered as the *Britannia* neared Marseilles. Pained by the unbelievable outcome of his first major challenge of the sea, he was decisively strengthened, nevertheless, in his belief in himself. Had he not survived the insensate cruelties of nature? Had he not confronted, bare-handed and alone, the imponderables of life? Had he not almost succeeded in breaking with civilized life?

Jean, detached, his features sunburned and deeply creased, reflected also on the vagaries of life, the death of his friend, the specter of war—and with the deepest depression, the glorious thing that had been *Onda*.

As the stately *Britannia* neared her slip a pensive Gau tossed his cigarette into the dirty harbor waters. He was aware, vaguely, of having crossed more than one barrier.

3

Dreams in a Brownstone Flat

In his thirty-fifth year, deeply chastened, his natural ebullience at its lowest in ten years, Jean returned to the little house on Moliere Street. There, whatever their misgivings or convictions, his parents enthusiastically received their errant son.

But the villagers, shrugging a shoulder over an evening anisette, dismissed Jean's debacle as another, middle-aged, forgery. "Where is this yacht, eh?" they asked one another. "But of course, on the *other* side of the mountains!" When the French newspapers, probably because of the geopolitical aspects of his landing in wartime Spain, falsely reported that Gau had been imprisoned, the villagers' ugliest suspicions surfaced. Besides, they eagerly pointed out, the border was closed. How *did* Jean Gau manage to cross it, eh? Perhaps there was, you know, *money** in *Onda*'s hold, *n'est-ce pas*? After all, had not old Pierre Gau's son

---

*Money wired by his parents while he was in Spain was deposited in a Spanish bank. It is reportedly still there, Gau having been unable to withdraw it.

repaid his father for his and Honorine's transportation to America within one year? And now he buys a fabulous yacht! *Mon Dieu!*

Unable to accept their tangible disbelief, puzzled by their reluctance to acknowledge his feat of having sailed single-handed across the Western Ocean, Jean smouldered. He ached for the impersonal and tolerant existence he had found at sea. While he fretted in Serignan, his friend Cordouret wrote to Jean's parents that "their son's mastery of the ocean erased the unfair opinions held by many evil-tongued persons." He couldn't have been more wrong: the subtle pressures were too much, and Gau booked passage for the States after only two months ashore. He did not return to France for nine years.

The following incident, one of the most delectable in Gau's life, is not mentioned in his manuscript, except as a passing reference to a "cargo ship." Its absence illustrates the depth of Jean's escalating desire for privacy. But it shows also how determined "Gerbault's successor" was that his manuscript contain only nautical matters.

Attractive, confident, mature beyond his years, Jean had a love affair aboard the returning ship. In a long letter to his confidant and aunt, Claire Gau, he describes the affair. This letter, begun on his thirty-fifth birthday, sheds light on the reclusive sailor's essential makeup. Aside from its humor and human interest, it affords a rare view of Gau's natural confidence, tempered by an attractive modesty that overlies a rebelliousness against established order. At a deeper psychological level it underscores his most singular trait, a detached relationship with life. Here, then, is the famous Anita letter.

Thursday 17 February, 1938
On board liner President Roosevelt

As I stated in my last letter, our Frontier Security Police (whose job is nothing but hassling the poor passengers, tying them in red tape) felt obliged to prevent me from departing for the States because I lacked a passport! It was then three P.M. and the *Champlain* was weighing anchor at four.

After a lot of jawboning with a particular individual, I rushed off to the Le Havre administrative office to get results. I suggested that the head man there cable Beziers and ask permission to grant me a passport in Le Havre.

The next day, in less than an hour's time, I got one and went to the ticket office and had my ticket transferred to the American line. That same evening, at midnight, I boarded the *President Roosevelt*.

I can't describe the looks of that policeman puppet when I handed him, *without saying a word,* my new passport, issued that very day in Le Havre. And only after the mooring lines were dropped did I shout at him with all my lungs, "Fuck you!"

Friday 18 February

At eight o'clock we reach Southampton, England, where we stop. At noon we're at sea under a lovely sun.

Saturday 19 February

Early in the morning we are within sight of the Irish coast, and at seven A.M. sail into Queenstown harbor. Nice day, beautiful landscape. A large tug brings off five passengers, among them a pretty Irish girl about twenty to twenty-two years old, who is weeping bitterly, waving her handkerchief at someone on the tug. We leave at noon and by five P.M. Ireland has left us.

I'm the only Frenchman on board among Americans, English, Germans, Russians, etc. And I have to myself a large cabin with two berths, sofas, electric heat, etc. I am convinced that the *Champlain* could not have been better.

Sunday 20 February

Beautiful weather, but the dining room is crowded. From the day we left I've been sitting along at a small table. Today, however, the Captain was kind enough to ask me if the new passenger who boarded at Queenstown yesterday might join me. So here I am, tête-à-tête with this lovely Irish girl. She is very pretty but sad (perhaps she has left a lover in her native country?).

Monday 21 February

The sea is rising and the liner rolls like an old bucket. There are fewer people in the dining room at noon, but my neighbor is present. We eat with a good appetite under the approving eye of the Captain, who pretends not to notice. My neighbor is no longer sad-looking and begins to smile a bit. Her name is Anita.

Tuesday 22 February

Same weather, blue sky, but the sea is swelly. Many people are seasick. Fortunately my neighbor, Anita, is not. So much the better, because I'm taking her to the movies.

Wednesday 23 February

The wind, since we left, has veered to the east, then the northeast, and now to the northwest. In sea terms, we say the wind is drawing ahead. It's a bad sign—we're going to have bad weather. Fewer passengers are in the dining room. Anita is in perfect shape: she eats like four persons, and is no longer sad. In fact, at the movies last night she laughed until she cried.

Thursday 24 February

Heavy weather. During the night, about one o'clock, a huge wave struck the ship. She gave such a list that I thought she was going to capsize. Tons of water poured through a hatch and flooded the corridor. Women were shrieking like skunks. Everybody was up.

Anita, with her heart in her boots, took shelter in my cabin—and, of course, stayed there till the next day. We didn't shut an eye the entire night.

The next morning she woke me up with a pillow fight! (Now she has forgotten her native country.)

In short, we are good friends. She won't let me out of her sight.

Thursday noon

We're near the Newfoundland Banks. High seas, heavy gale. Anita, in a corner of the deserted deck, fearfully watches as I take snapshots of the gale. When I think how *Onda* and I fought these same seas for twenty days I am actually thrilled.

A young deck officer, seeing me from the bridge, hails me, saying that it's rash of me to be there taking pictures. I continue to snap pictures while he shouts.

Then Anita leaves her shelter, and, taking my side, shouts at him, saying that he would have little to teach me, that without a striped cap or white gloves I have crossed the Atlantic alone.

He comes up to me and offers his hand. "Oh," he says, "I bet you're Mr. Jean Gau? I read your story in the New York *Herald Tribune*. Please accept my apology." We go to my cabin, where I give him a picture of *Onda*.

Anita is proud of me and now everybody, more or less, knows my story. At supper there were seven men and a young girl. The charming girl was, of course, Anita.

No movies tonight, because the wind broke several panes in the main lounge. No dancing either, because the boat is rolling badly. Well, we'll spend the evening in my cabin.

With her artless look, Anita is nevertheless a little scoundrel. As I was watching her she burst out laughing. "What's the matter?" I asked.

"Oh, nothing."

"Why are you laughing, then?"

"Because I went to my cabin and undid my berth so the maid will think I spent the night in it!" And she started laughing once more.

Friday 25 February

Ominous date. The sea is peaceful. Yesterday we left the Gulf Stream and now sail in the cold Labrador Current. Very cold on deck. But in my cabin it's much warmer—specially near Anita. Now, she no longer laughs. . . . the trip is ending. Tomorrow we arrive in New York. We must part, for she goes to Boston.

Saturday 26 February

Up at five o'clock to view the New York skyline. At eight o'clock we sail into the harbor and immediately are boarded by officials, who check visas and passports.

I was recognized and journalists assaulted me with thousands of questions about my Atlantic crossing. Anita, who does not let me out of her sight, sometimes answered for me because she knows my story by heart.

At nine-thirty we're free. I take Anita to the station. She no longer laughs, but promises to write and to see me again. The train leaves. She calls out, "Good-bye, Johnny!"

At ten o'clock I'm at my best friend's house. I've found my New York again.

Best Kisses,
Jean

Jean's manuscript is less communicative. It relates his return to the States in this way: "After two months in France I decided to return to the United States. Because my funds were low I shipped aboard a cargo vessel. In New York I returned to my old hotel, where, with many friendly gestures, the chef welcomed me back and handed me an apron. I returned to the stoves and pans." That's all he wrote.

"But Johnny had no brains for the job," lamented his former boss. "He spent the whole work day talking about a fish he met in the ocean"—a reference to an incident also not mentioned in the manuscript.

"After every meal Johnny would wash his dishes in the sea over the side, using a large white dishrag. Once, about 500 miles off New York, a large fish grabbed the rag from him. Johnny looked and saw a large mackerel." His friend shook his head. "Day after day as *Onda* sped across the Atlantic the fish followed her, staying in the boat's cooler lee shadow. Johnny got mad, tried harpooning the fish and missed. But he raised a big blister on the fish. That damned fish actually followed *Onda* to the Azores!" The speaker's eyes rounded as though pulled by the suddenly lifted eyebrows. "When he left, the fish followed *Onda* clear to the Bay of Cadiz!"

His shipboard romance completely forgotten, Jean settled into an apartment on 39th Street, spending his days in front of the "damned kitchen stoves" at the Hotel Taft. He did not, however, return to an entirely Spartan existence. Although fiercely determined again to achieve his goal of owning a sea-worthy boat, the nattily dressed Gau spent money at the movies and at restaurants "nearly every night with one of my girl friends," most probably his former language teacher.

But on the job, in the hotel's great kitchens, Jean, Eli Agnel (not yet head chef), and Margot Panisse formed a group called The Three Musketeers, whose boisterous and disruptive doings often caused the head chef heartburn and difficulties with his boss. One of the kitchen workers was suspected of informing the chef's superiors, who then caustically scolded him for the Musketeers' uproarious doings in the kitchen and among the French-speaking staff.

Never attracted to the cold, reflective, introverted individual, Jean preferred for company the flamboyant, extroverted, and good-natured types, an interesting fact in light of his own secretive, hermitlike character.

Margot Panisse had a large voice to match her size and an ebullience that could not be put down. Although her father had been a professor and a town mayor, Margot was descended from (or had been involved with—the record isn't clear) circus people. "Good-natured, noisy. A female riot!" recalls one of her friends. He laughed, and told of the time when, accused by an angry boss of "being a Red," Margot had replied, "I'm not. I'm a purple!" During the forties, she began a letter to Eleanor Roosevelt, "Since you are the First Lady of the land and I am the Last, . . ." Its purpose was to seek government assistance in restoring her family home in Valras. Her argument, that Allied planes had destroyed the structure, reportedly carried conviction; the house was rebuilt, purportedly by American funds.

A gregarious and mountainous French-Italian immigrant, Eli Agnel became notorious through the years for his pranks and jokes among the kitchen help. Once a co-worker complained that his vision was getting worse. Assuming a perfectly straight mien, Agnel advised the man to eat carrots.

"But, chef, I don't like carrots." The man's voice carried conviction.

Agnel smiled gently as he whispered, with admirable concern, "But you must must eat them, *mon petite,* else your eyes will get even worse!"

"So for nearly six months the poor guy ate carrots—raw, garnished, boiled, creamed, sliced—and each day Agnel would politely inquire about his eating of them. "Finally," recalled Cordonat, "one day he curtly turned to Agnel, who towered above him, and demanded, 'Chef! Goddamn it, six months ago I could see over to New Jersey. Now, Christ! I can't see across the goddamn street!"

But not all was gay and carefree. Still embittered by his hometown's reception, distraught over *Onda*'s loss, Jean was determined to buy another boat. It would have to incorporate features he knew were essential for comfort and survival under all conditions. Now totally committed to the sea, he believed that such a boat, whenever he found one he could afford, might even become a permanent home. His search went on for seven years.

"Until 1945," he subsequently wrote, "my life was a succession of omelettes and steaks, cooked to order." It was an existence that even his employer, Henri Cordouret, felt "unworthy of Jean." Yet this was the most artistically creative period in Johnny's life, the period of the *Onda* drawings. As before, he failed to mention this significant event in his manuscript.

It is hard to explain satisfactorily Jean's renewed interest in drawing or the seven-year duration of it. Obviously this intensive effort was something to occupy his spare time, something relatively inexpensive to do. Psychologically, however, it is fascinating to speculate that the unbelievable realism of these seascapes, the superb precision of nearly every element—especially the restless energy of the disturbed waters*—could have resulted from a subconscious desire to redeem himself artistically for the not-forgotten period of forgery. Viewed in this sense, it was the making of plowshares from swords.

When asked to sell them, or why he had painted them, Gau always replied, "They are for my pleasure only. They are not for sale." But to accept this too simple answer, to view his drawings as pretty objects trotted out in every port to please and surprise visitors, is to overlook a special insight into Jean's emotional makeup. At any rate, whether Johnny had previously mastered his drawing technique does not matter. Now he did.

Upstairs in the cluttered attic of the modest brick house, in Jackson Heights, a man stood looking at the lightly penciled outline on a paper tack-mounted to an easel. A sepia photograph showing a clubbed jibsail lifting its belly to the wind was tacked to the easel frame. He jerked a cigarette from a pack, lit it, and turned to a small table beside the sunlit window. With mortar and pestle his short, powerful fingers deftly crushed the exposed leads from several ordinary drawing pencils. His lithe figure bent slightly as he poured the powdered leads into small heaps atop a palette on the table. Soon several pimples of color stood on the palette's flat surface.

Knocking ashes from the cigarette, he replaced it in one corner of his mouth. Then he methodically wrapped a piece of clean cotton cloth around the forefinger of his right hand.

---

*"Johnny admired and studied seascapes by Dawson and other great marine painters," recalls Cordonat. "He even went to Monhegan Island, Maine, to visit a well-known artist living there."

With very light and careful strokes he dabbed a bit of color onto the paper, concentrating intently on the chroma that arose under the wrapped fingertip. He worked slowly, never mixing the colors on the palette before applying them to the paper. Having placed a color on the paper, he carefully rearranged the cloth to obtain a clean surface. As he worked, ashes from the burning cigarette fell onto the unswept floor. The smoke rose sensuously through the shafts of sunlight penetrating the grimy attic window.

Intent now on achieving hue, he studied the remaining small heaps of color, often referring to a color wheel mounted on the inside lid of a large wooden artist's box. Then he began rubbing two colors together until the right combination of hue and saturation arose from the paper. His thick, short eyebrows suddenly rose like hyphens above the round eyes. Neither humming nor whistling to show his satisfaction, Jean Gau studied the paper. He had achieved what he wanted for the nonmarine aspects of the drawing.

Next Jean examined the open areas of water and sky penciled on the paper. Grinding out his cigarette, he lit another. He picked up a sharp-pointed eraser-tipped pencil and carefully wrapped the finger cloth around the eraser's edge. Bending over the paper, he searched the remaining white areas to ascertain distribution of color and mass. With short clean strokes he deftly placed color on the paper in fine, thin lines, achieving details with the cloth-covered eraser too small for his forefinger.

Quietly, softly, expertly, Jean blended colors until the waters began to move before his view. Spray flew, the ocean's salt tang arose from the paper, sunlight danced onto the curved surfaces of countless droplets; the winds blew across the horizon, and the ageless rhythm of God's oceans swelled, tumbled, broke, marched, *moved*! Wetting his thin upper lip, Jean blinked several times. He paused, hypnotized by the movement of the shadowed greens and blues and whites of the waters that swelled and heaved and receded before his hooded gaze.

Retreating to a broken-backed chair away from the shafts of light, he sat staring at the sight of the wind-angered waters and scudding clouds that swept across the drawing. Feeling the heat of the cigarette at his lips, he removed it, threw it onto the floor, and mechanically stamped it out with his shoe, his eyes never leaving the seascape. The first edge of shadow reached the drawing; it was late. He stood up and took a deep breath, then strode, grim-faced, from the darkening room. The weakened sunlight spotlighted an empty corner as the attic door was closed.*

From the *Onda* drawings it seems that the artist was attempting to sublimate his dreams and memories in a lasting way. Despite his 1953 pre-world-voyage statement that "I'll paint pictures that I can sell," Jean Gau never again painted so masterfully. But between 1939 and 1945, intensely unhappy without a boat, haunted by mental images—of idyllic sea days, of high winds in a dark rocky harbor and the labored death of a beautiful boat—like a child who produces his imagination on paper with crayons, Gau lovingly recreated the saga of *Onda* with simple lead pencils.

After 1945 he never painted again. Asked why, he always replied, "Well, now I have a boat." This disarming comment, said a close friend, "was absolutely true. Johnny really was busy with the boat."

If the paintings provided emotional relief, so did a set of boat plans ordered in 1945 from naval architect John Hannah. It is not difficult to imagine the little New York cook, "wearied after eight hours before the stoves," studying details of his "dream boat" by the light of a living room window in the brownstone flat on 39th Street.

Finally, satisfied with the design, he ordered a boat, to be built that summer for fall delivery. In a letter to his aunt and her adopted niece, Andrée Pierret, he compared its design with that of the beautiful *Onda*, now a memory in color.

28 June 1945

Dear Aunt and Dear Dedee!

I already have the plans, and am waiting impatiently for the government's permission to start laying the keel. Because the war

---

*Surprisingly, Gau did not use a medium to fix the colors to the paper.

isn't over, the Army and Navy get the materials first. But once I have the permit the rest will be easy, the actual building not taking more than three or four months.

My new boat will be a ketch. . . . The hull is round or pointed at the stern. This design has proved to be seaworthy. . . . two boats have already made long voyages in the Pacific, from San Francisco to Tahiti.

The architect lives in Florida and writes to me every month. He's a great guy. He also owns a boat from the same design, has sailed it single-handedly in the Gulf of Mexico.

In comparison with *Onda*, here are a few details. *Onda* was a magnificent cruising schooner, twelve meters long by two meters fifty centimeters, two meters draft. She belonged to an American millionaire, a Mr. Parsons* of Providence (he owned a nickel mine), who used to race each year from New York to Bermuda, 800 miles. Three men were required to handle her.

When he read of my Atlantic crossing he was astounded. On my return to the States he came to see me, offering to help me with building another boat. He died the next year.

With her slender lines, her mahogany interior, *Onda* the beautiful was the admiration of all the Long Island yachtsmen. But handling her single-handed was very hard work; I had 700 square feet of canvas to handle.

Once, in the Atlantic during a heavy gale, I waited too long before lowering the sails. They were stretched like iron curtains, ready to burst. It was impossible to lower them. I had to stay seventy-two hours at the wheel† to keep *Onda* as close to the wind as possible . . . to avoid Lost Ships Harbor.

So my new boat will be a little ketch thirty feet long, about nine tons (*Onda* was fourteen). Her lines will be full. A ketch is very easy to handle, the sail area not over 470 square feet, which means less fatigue for me. The engine will be new and always ready to start in

---

*Many years later Gau told individuals and audiences that "a Mr. Crowninshield" was the owner. Perhaps he was confusing names: George Crowninshield, of Salem, Massachusetts, built the first yacht in America, *Cleopatra's Barge*. Gau was an avid reader of nautical books; it seems likely that in later years he mistakenly recalled Crowninshield's name for that of Parsons.

†This was during part of his approach to the Strait of Gibraltar, October 17-20, 1937.

case winds or foul currents try to throw me towards the Spanish coast.

Having studied her lines for some time, I conclude that she really is the boat of my dreams. . . .

I kiss you both,
Jean

Two months later World War II ended, and American shipyards, freed from wartime restrictions, began building work and pleasure craft. But Jean's little ketch never materialized. Instead, he found the boat that he would forever be identified with. In a letter written in late October of 1945 he enthusiastically relates his journey from disappointment to discovery:

I have just arrived after a three-week sea trip *aboard the boat of my dreams*. My happiness is boundless! Here's what happened.

A few days after the war ended the government withdrew restrictions on the building of private boats. I lost no time getting in touch with the shipyard owner who had promised to build my boat. I was greatly disappointed when he told me he had four trawlers laid down and had work until the summer of 1947.

I applied to other yards and was even more discouraged by the prices they were asking, just for a hull! My discouragement can't be described. But then I recalled how I found *Onda*. So I wrote letters to ten brokers: "From 1924 to 1942 one hundred and fifty boats of the Tahiti ketch design have been built. If you have a boat of this type for sale please let me know."

A few days later I had two positive answers. In Nova Scotia a boat was available for $6,000. Another guy in New York had one for $4,500. I started to buy it but the next day I had an offer from Washington for $3,500!

There was something about its construction, the quality of the wood, and the completeness of its equipment that were most favorable. I decided to go and look at it. On October first my friend, his wife, and a broker left with me for Washington by train.

In the mouth of the Potomac River was my little boat. At first glance I found her perfect, exceeding all my hopes. Finely built of first-rate wood and materials, her ribs were of oak, her hull cedar, and her masts of Oregon pine. Her builder and owner was a Norwegian artist and tobacco farmer. Close to his farm there was a small woods where he'd selected the best wood for building his boat.*

It's funny but he began building her the same day that I lost *Onda* in Spain. Odd, isn't it?

We were guests of this good Norwegian for four days, visiting around his farm and the small boatyard where he's building another boat to the same plans, but larger. He has four children.

On October 4 we weighed anchor, set all our sails, and steered for New York, some 600 miles by open sea. We sailed down the Potomac River and into the Chesapeake Bay, which took several days. Then for forty-eight hours we stayed in a small harbor called Cape Charles. On October 8 we made for Montauk Point, a 400-mile trip out of sight of land. We reached Montauk in four days, having tested my boat in October winds. We rested there for another four days. The remaining 100 miles to New York we did in two days.

I can't describe my elation! I'm the happiest man in the world!

Because of the terrible situation in France I'm not planning to sail there, but I will in the spring of 1947. . . .

When I have pictures of my beautiful boat I'll send them to you.

> I kiss you tenderly,
> *Jean*

Gau's boat was first called *Lois,* in accordance with the time-honored custom among Chesapeake Bay watermen of naming their craft for their womenfolk. She was built at Shadyside, Maryland, in 1938. The "mouth of the Potomac River" referred to is actually St. Mary's River, a lovely arm of the Lower Potomac.

Tied to the river's clay banks, the fat-hulled ketch immediately caught the seasoned eye of the forty-three-year-old Gau. It was the story of Slocum and *Spray.* Dumas and *Legh,* Voss and *Tillicum,* all over again. But Jean didn't know this and, had he known, he wouldn't have cared. For he was struck by the magical word *Tahiti.*

---

*The "Norwegian artist" was Bjorn Egeli, portrait painter to the DuPont family. Egeli recently recalled buying a timber of Georgia yellow pine, 30' x 14" x 14", for $30 in 1930. The timber, which subsequently provided *Atom's* keelson and bilge stringers, "was taken from a dismantled brewery in Alexandria, Virginia, that was over 100 years old." He was, he says, "a bit skittish" in 1945 about selling the boat to Gau because at that time the government, concerned about smuggling, required clearances from the State Department on boats sold to registered aliens.

Tahiti! It is difficult now in an age of jet air travel to understand just how exotic and engaging a word this was. But one can still imagine how dream-filled Jean's gaze was that afternoon as he ran his sensitive hands over the planking. Tahiti!

Watching the small figure examine the ketch was the owner and builder, a former square-rig sailor, Bjorn Egeli. His blue eyes studied the quick movements as the man busily tapped the hull, examined the sails, slammed cabinet doors. Gau's solitary crossing of the Atlantic and grasp of the boat's seaworthy features impressed the quiet Norwegian, who was also a portrait painter and a tobacco farmer.

But while Jean hopped excitedly about the boat, his friend Joe Cordonat was arguing with the broker. "Johnny was close to tears for fear he'd lose the boat," Cordonat recalls. "He'd whisper in French, 'Pay him, Joe! *Please*!'" At last, the deal consummated, Cordonat discussed the boat's soundness with Egeli.

"She needs a new engine, so watch the oil. And when I cast the keel I forgot about contraction and expansion, but that won't hurt this boat," said the muscular, level-eyed Egeli. Joined by his wife, he then told the New York chefs that *Lois* was carrying a stowaway. He smiled broadly at their astonishment.

"But," Egeli laughed, "the stowaway is a living barometer. No need to worry!"

Joe and Johnny looked blankly at each other. Cordonat smiled wanly, trying to regain a businesslike mien. Johnny, however, blurted out, "What's that?"

The builder replied, "A mouse."

"But you said a barometer!" Jean's Adam's apple bobbed rapidly. "I mean, what's a *mouse* got to do with it?"

"The mouse—we call him Joe—when he drops his tail, don't go sailing, boys! But when Joe raises his tail, you can go sailing. OK? A mouse barometer, you understand, Mr. Gau?" Nodding and laughing, they joined Mrs. Egeli in the house for late afternoon tea. They left early the next day, observed from the river's grassy shore by the builder and his wife, by their gregarious and blond-headed brood, and by a pair of beady eyes in the boat's starboard locker.

Offshore, days later, the early October evening air was chilly. Seeking warmth, the boat's small stowaway crawled from his nest. He sniffed the salt air, and then quickly ran up Jean's trousers. He, busy at the galley stove, was startled by the movement of something crossing his chest. He quickly grabbed the mouse, ran up the ladderway, and threw it into the sea. "Even though it was a proper burial for a sea-going mouse," mused Joe Cordonat, "my wife cried openly."

Shortly afterwards the weather turned bad. Midway home Cordonat caught a large bonito. With one leg thrust against the galley side to compensate for the boat's heeling, Joe prepared the fish in olive oil and onions, "with a side order of French fries." Unfortunately, he was using a large frying pan with a loose handle. As he started for the cockpit with the heaped skillet, the pan flipped. The hungry skipper and crew ate from the cabin floor and the ladder.

The little ketch was berthed in *Onda*'s old slip in New York. But, as with *Onda*, Gau did not spend his weekends sailing on the nearby Sound. The ketch was his home. When he wanted to go, she would be ready.

Hiroshima was then only two months old, and Jean named his boat *Atom*. "She was so small," he later wrote, "yet so powerful!"

Johnny was happier now than he'd been for years, and he settled down to the familiar routine in the kitchens of the Hotel Taft. In the hotel bar, Charley Drew, a popular piano-vocalist, entertained crowds nightly with risqué songs, especially the popular "She Came Rolling Down the Mountain." In the ballroom, Vincent Lopez's orchestra played the popular tunes of the day. And in far-off Serignan, Jean's improved status at the hotel lessened slightly the stigma of his earlier years: perhaps, mused the older villagers, old Pierre Gau's son has "rid himself of those unconventional habits, *eh bien?*"

But if Jean was unconventional, he was also cautious where *Atom*' was concerned. During the nearly thirty years *Atom* was moored in New York, she made only *one* local cruise.

This was in the late forties, when a German millionaire badgered Johnny into taking him to Nantucket. Gau reluctantly agreed, but once underway he was "so careful, dropping the main whenever there was *any* wind," said a friend who went along, "and raising it when there wasn't any," that he antagonized both millionaire and friend. "We wanted to sail *Atom* to Nantucket, not drift!" The German finally got nasty to the point where Jean said, "Leave!" When they reached the island, the millionaire boarded a plane for New York—but not before provoking *Atom*'s normally mild-mannered skipper even further.

At that time well-made boat fittings were still hard to come by. The German, who had ordered the two small Frenchmen about unmercifully during the cruise, emerged from *Atom*'s small head carrying the head's bronze handle. He had used it too vigorously. Now, puzzled, he confronted the stunned skipper. "My God, the shithouse handle!" cried an amazed Gau. He never again made short cruises aboard *Atom*, in New York or anywhere else.

Two years after he bought *Atom*, Jean's bank account to outfit the ketch for a long voyage was adequate and his confidence as a skipper high. He sensed that the time was right for a return voyage. In early May, 1947, Johnny enthusiastically announced to the Musketeers and to the other kitchen help that he was soon leaving for Europe. He would, he said, "salute France for them."

The word soon reached France, and again little Valras made plans to welcome its adopted son. One month before his expected arrival by sea, *Midi Libre,* southern France's major newspaper, somewhat proudly informed its readers of Gau's Serignan boyhood and his nautical achievements.

Once more, figuratively speaking, the props were being hauled onstage, rehearsals scheduled, and tickets sold for a hometown drama. This time, surely, the show *would* go on, *n'est-ce pas?*

4

Two Failures

Jean left New York on May 24, 1947, bound for Valras, France. Ostensibly because of *Atom*'s inability to sail satisfactorily to windward, he did not return to America for two and half years. But there were other important factors in explaining this, the third most difficult period in Gau's astonishing life. And again he was puzzled by the failure of his countrymen to vigorously acknowledge his worth and achievements.

Stopping at Horta, the Azores, Jean wrote to his parents. The letter, dated August 1, begins with information about his reception and participation in a major fiesta on the adjacent island of Pico. He then addresses his aunt, Claire Gau, who appears to have enthusiastically shared his interest in ocean voyaging. Their correspondence discusses such boat matters as the number of coats of paint "below the float line."

But in a puzzling and cryptic statement, he says, ". . . you must not count on our meeting in Genoa. . . . I won't sail in the Mediterranean. . . but will make for Madeira, where I'll spend the winter before returning to the States. I don't think you'll succeed in getting me that special permit to enter France without getting into trouble."

This last reference may be related to the question of his nonmilitary leanings during the 1939-40 period; as World War II loomed in Europe Jean had booked passage for America in 1938 aboard the SS *Roosevelt.* The reference could also relate to the difficulties he anticipated in crossing the closed border after berthing *Atom* in Spain—private boats apparently weren't allowed to enter postwar France by water.

A navigational mistake follows: "It would be hard [to sail to Genoa] because during the next month [September] the easterlies will blow and I would have headwinds the entire trip." According to the Mediterranean Sailing Directions, the winds during this period are usually northerlies, not easterlies. He would have made a fast passage to Genoa.

Finally, the letter reveals a brief view of Gau's deeply held, simple, fatalistic outlook on life: "It is with great regret that I won't be able to see you again this year. God must want it so." But again the one constant thread in his life, his love of the sea, is evident. "I urge you all not to worry about me," he wrote, for "I am the world's happiest man because I am now realizing my childhood dream."

He departed four days later, as indicated in a letter to Claire Gau from the American consul, C. R. Wharton. But despite the letter to his parents and his aunt, Gau quixotically laid a course for the Mediterranean, not for Madeira. Why is not known.

"*Atom*, all sails set, in a light breeze steered towards Port Jefferson in narrow Long Island Sound to begin her first long voyage. The date is May 26, 1947." So begins Jean's account, subsequently printed in the October 2 issue of the newspaper *Nuit et Jour.*

The crew were my three best friends. *Atom,* loaded with supplies sufficient for a year at sea, rode above her float line, but under full sail she moved with an extraordinary suppleness. On Wednesday, May 28, at four o'clock I weighed anchor from Port Jefferson, bound for Montauk, where my friends, more deeply moved than I, left to return to their land jobs. On May 31 I departed Montauk for the Azores, sailing happily alone, towards the high seas and Great Adventure.

On the fourth day out strong southwesterlies pummeled us and for eighteen days I hove to as enormous seas broke over the deck, flooding it completely. It wasn't possible to remain topside but, because of chafe, I often had to change the sheet which held the stormsail to the foot of the mast. In the cabin it was very difficult to move about without being slammed against the bulkheads. It was impossible at times to light the stove because of the heeling. Fortunately, *Atom* hove to nicely, but now and then when she came into the troughs a waterfall collapsed on deck, completely burying it.

At first I was afraid of this but little by little I got accustomed and in time it was but a habit. Once the waves struck the hull with such force that I was hurled to the cabin floor. Another time the coffee pot was thrown against the opposite cupboard, leaving a mark to this day. *Atom* leaked badly around the hatch and I had to cover the berths with oilskins.

At night big ships, attracted by my powerful light, would wake me to ask if "all was well!" The weather was nice, the winds light and our progress slow. This meant I would be more than a month reaching the Azores, which I didn't mind because I was in my element. I spent the time taking sights, which, with the new navigation tables (which I found perfect), allowed me to get my bearings quickly. I speared many fish, which I gorged upon to the extent of nearly having indigestion at sea. Flying fish fell on deck at night; hearing them, I wanted to get up and fix breakfast—flying fish and chips!

The winds changed and I tacked for six days, but the southwesterly started up again and I fell into my easterly course. The glass fell visibly and by nightfall it was a real hurricane. I hove to under a jib but at four o'clock it was blown out. I bent on another and worked for an hour at the far end of the bowsprit, no small job 'cause I had to do it naked (this dried me more quickly).

On July 12, after a star sight, I was twenty-five miles off cloud-obscured Flores. Under jib and main *Atom* steered herself. At daybreak I went topside and there stood Flores dead ahead! It was an adequate navigation.

All morning I sailed along the island's picturesque coast, close-to, admiring the huge cracks and ravines into which the seas slammed to noisy deaths. From Flores to Horta was 150 miles, and the next day at nightfall Comprida lighthouse was sighted a mile off. I drifted slowly along the southeast coastline, passing in daylight the Castel Branco, a curiously head-shaped rock. Fertile slopes and cultivated fields got my admiring attention but the wind suddenly gave way to a thick fog, which obliged me to sail dangerously close along the Caia peninsula and the Hell's Cauldron, an extinct crater which the sea enters vigorously.

With the American ensign at the mainmast and the quarantine flag aloft, forty-six days out of Montauk, I entered harbor and was sighted immediately by the harbor master. *Atom* was soon moored to a huge buoy and I was given a great welcome by the authorities, who recalled my 1937 visit. Work aboard *Atom* took second place to the invitations that poured in.

In the harbor there was a yacht seventy-two meters in length, *Maybe*, belonging to a Dutch shipbuilder then cruising to the Azores. One of the yacht's launches came alongside with an invitation for lunch. The owner, his son, and friends, speaking Dutch, English, and French, greeted me at the gangway. They all seemed to know about *Onda* and her loss at Cadiz . . . from a Dutch newspaper. The next day these gentlemen paid a visit to the little *Atom*, complimenting me on her shipshape condition. They also enjoyed my drawings.

That evening the harbor master entertained *Atom*'s fo'c'sle gang at a dinner complemented by an island wine, his wife having prepared a strawberry cake which later found its way aboard. . . . In the street I was hailed as *El Solitario* by an old pilot who had piloted *Onda* on my first call here; it was the nickname the islanders gave me in 1937. During the daytime visitors interrupted my work, but on Sunday, July 20, the Horta Sporting Club gave a fiesta in my honor. I had to give a speech in Portuguese, which a girl friend wrote for me.* But I managed to slip through this delicate evening not too badly.

On August 5, at one o'clock, I weighed anchors after twenty-one days ashore. Frankly, I wanted to remain longer. Several friends came to see me off, seemingly more deeply moved at the departure than I. That evening I rounded the Ribeinha lighthouse and Fayal became part of the ocean mists.

For the first two weeks the weather was magnificent. Day and night my boat sailed herself, gently curtseying across a ballroom sea, making sixty-five to seventy miles a day. At sea there is always novelty, always

---

*"Johnny had the morals of a French tomcat," a prominent American sailor informed us. But a Frenchman, sailor, and a close friend of Gau said, "His love affairs were just typical sailor's romances, nothing more."

something unforeseen. And the clearness of the huge sky enabled me to make many observations and to prick my chart with great accuracy.

During the night of August 15 a blow shook *Atom,* throwing her skipper to the floor. Thinking we'd been struck by a boat, I jumped topside, but could see nothing. An examination of the hull revealed no damage or other evidence for the bump. This was puzzling until near evening the next day when I met a flock of six whales lying across my path. By tacking I avoided the brutes. I'm now certain *Atom* slammed into a sleeping whale.

On August 23 I sailed into an area of very strong winds, which created rough seas. All I could do was to let *Atom* drift under reduced canvas to the southeast. Five days later my reckonings indicated . . . land. By four o'clock I had discovered Portugal, close by the place where I made my first landfall with *Onda,* Cape Espichel.

That night I sailed near the Cape St. Vincent lighthouse, which reminded me of the terrible gales that had beaten the beautiful *Onda.* The next day the land had disappeared and I was sailing in the Bay of Cadiz. For two days I headed towards Gibraltar's Strait and at daybreak on August 31 I weathered the cape, passing into the rough waters of the Strait. About six that evening I reached the harbor, having crossed the Atlantic for the second time alone.

A westerly prevented my going ashore, and on September 5 I left in a high northwesterly breeze, riding a three-knot current which carried me in twenty-four hours to Alboran Island, 150 miles distant. But the next day a Levante blew in and for fifteen days I struggled to windward against a damned short and choppy sea until I reached Cartagena's harbor, where I anchored off the Royal Yacht Club landing. A toast greeted me at the clubhouse and that afternoon I attended a Snipes regatta and a bullfight, and much later a handsome dinner.*

On September 23, after a cannon salute and the hoisting of the Spanish ensign, ten members of the club sailed in company with *Atom* as far as the Escombrera Island, where they saluted me with, "*Adios!* If you can't make it, Jean, come back and be with friends!" Their friendly farewell carried the seeds of prophesy.

At two in the afternoon Cape Palos was rounded . . . several days later I reached the Balearics, to be welcomed by a tremendous

---

*Although Generalissimo Franco never visited Gau aboard *Atom* on any of the numerous times she stopped at Cartagena, his wife and daughter did on one occasion, spending thirty minutes admiring Jean's seascapes. It is surmised that the visit occurred on this layover.

northeasterly which prevented my landing at St. Anthony's harbor. I had expected bad weather but I hadn't anticipated that it would blow at hurricane force. That evening waves, arriving from everywhere, met on *Atom*'s deck, where they broke angrily. I had to lash myself to the mainmast. All hatches were tightly closed and all that moved firmly secured. The situation was now quite different from that of my first Atlantic storm, for here, in the Mediterranean, I had a coast under the wind. Consequently I couldn't heave to or I would drift towards the rocky, wave-washed coastline. And if I couldn't tack soon *Atom* would be smashed against the island's black rocks.

The best thing to do was to carry some sail to keep way on the boat, which now handled with difficulty. The tall sails resembled metallic curtains; had they not been new they would have exploded in that storm. Under a jib, reefed mainsail, and mizzen, *Atom* heeled until the waters reached mid-deck. Her rounded hull received the blows nicely although it seemed that each wave would do her in. At times I couldn't see the deck for the foaming waters washing across its surface. Spray, torn from the seas by the inclined shrouds, flew past. And then, slowly, the cabin top emerged from the roiling waters like a submarine. As I closed the coastline I prepared to tack, only to find that I couldn't spill the wind—it would have taken ten men to handle that mainsheet! Suddenly a blast of wind burst the sail, enabling me to come about. Exhausted, I hove to and went below to rest.

The next day I bent on a new mainsail, and under her stormsail *Atom* drifted slowly towards the African coast as far as Oran and the Lion Mountains. It was still blowing like a hurricane. Three swallows, blown off course, tried vainly to land on *Atom*'s rigging. They did succeed in getting into the cabin, where they sheltered until the next day. That night I left the light on so as not to disturb them. At daybreak my friends flew around the cabin and then away.

I resumed my northwest course and eventually reached Cartagena's harbor, hale and hearty, to the joy of my friends, who'd presumed me lost because of the bad weather. I was determined to push on for Valras but they strongly advised that I stay put because of the unfair challenge of headwinds all the way. Under these circumstances (they'd also offered to watch *Atom* while I was away), and unable to communicate with my parents because of the wartime restrictions . . . I nonetheless obtained a special permit from the Madrid government to travel through Spain, and in time reached border by taxi.

On October 15 near midnight I arrived in Serignan (by train) and without warning went to my parents' house. But next morning my incognito ended as journalists began their relentless pursuit (who told them of my arrival, I don't know) from Serignan to Beziers and return. They caught up with me at Serignan, catching me "in my lair," and I gave them a brief interview. For their part, they took a truly antediluvian photograph of me that will be the funniest souvenir of the voyage!

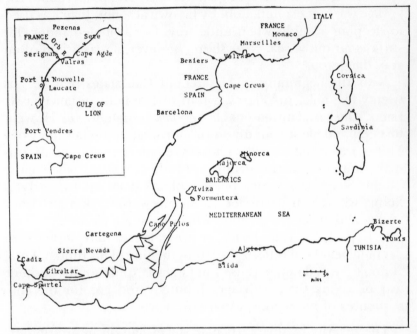

Figure 1. Generalized track of the 1947 failure to reach Valras

Valras' plans to celebrate Jean's arrival by sea, the climax of the ceremonies to be his triumphant passage up the River Orb, soured quickly as the news spread of his coming by train. Jean's only comment was, "I regretted not being able to reach Valras by boat because many of my fellow countrymen felt they'd been deceived.* After this breezy understatement he concluded: "But

---

*Close friends have said that "Johnny changed after his first voyage around the world." But researchers detect a change in him after this second crossing. The evidence is tenuous, however, consisting mostly of subtle nuances in his writings, correspondence, and recorded actions.

next spring I'll return to Cartagena, refit *Atom*, and cross the old Atlantic for the third time." This time, however, he remained longer than the two months following his 1937 failure to reach Valras by sail.

Before describing the arrangements made to greet his arrival and the excitement his feat generated, several points about the voyage warrant examination. By his own account, Jean was used to sleeping at night when underway. For a single-hander this suffices far out at sea. Near shore, however, it's risky and often very dangerous.

Near the beginning of his account Gau states that he was twenty-five miles off Flores, a four or five-hour distance at six knots, which isn't unreasonable for *Atom* in a fair breeze. He went to sleep and slept soundly until morning, and when he woke Flores was dead ahead. There are other examples of this marvelous but disconcerting aptitude for sleep when close ashore. Sleep is necessary, but the solitary sailor can't afford this luxury without an alarm clock at his side warning him each hour to rise and check his position when making a landfall.

It is probable that Jean's growing laissez-faire attitude to sleeping near land reflects the strengthening of his fundamental "I don't give a damn because I'm fatalistic" philosophy, another way of saying that, with age, Johnny cared less for the consequences of his actions, ashore or at sea.

The severity of this particular storm had an interesting aftereffect on Gau's seamanship. Never again would he take a reef in the mainsail (if he did, it's not in his writings), preferring to lower it completely. Interestingly, Jean referred to the late September storm as blowing at "hurricane" strength. But unlike his previous and later accounts, this one does not report actual wind and gust speeds.

Gau's commitment to the sea had deepened. Now, unlike most Mediterranean sailors—and indeed most sailors, irrespective of geography—he refused to make short jaunts during long passages, preferring to carry on regardless of conditions. In *Cap Horn à la Voile* Bernard Moitessier states that in analyzing the difficulties and dangers of sailing from Marseilles to Gibraltar in winter (Jean sailed in October), he travelled from one port to the next to avoid taking undue and unnecessary risks. This Gau seems not to have done, and he did so even less thereafter.

Finally, there is the point that in this corner of the Mediterranean, even in October, determined sailors are not prevented from putting to sea by the weather. Even though sailing can be very rough and treacherous at this time of year, conditions seldom *prohibit* it; many people cruise from southern France to the Balearics during this season. Yet in this same general region, a quarter of a century later, Gau again put to sea from Cartagena on two occasions and met with awesome and tragic consequences.

It is puzzling that Gau seemed not to display any sense of urgency in making Valras, knowing that this sympathetic community was planning to publicly celebrate his arrival. The local citizenry and even the national media were ready to hail him as "Gerbault's successor," thereby giving Jean the public attention and approbation he felt necessary to redeem his past. Why then this excuse that he would have headwinds to challenge? A possible explanation is that at this point in his career Jean lacked confidence that he *could* reach Valras by sail. After all, nine years before he had failed in this enterprise with *Onda*.

Valras wanted badly to celebrate Jean's arrival. As soon as he was sighted, the Port Vendres lighthouse was to signal Valras so that its people, the media, a band, and even the local rugby team could assemble in time to hail "the new Alain Gerbault!" The skippers of the town's small fishing fleet had planned to stop work to meet *Atom* and her dauntless skipper in the Gulf of Lion and to escort them in with horns, flags, and bottled levity. Near the harbor a band noisily tootled melodies, practicing for the time when local officials would greet the man who one day would represent southern France in the nation's pantheon of nautical heroes. The stage for redemption had been set; it lacked only a hero. But nautical heroes do not arrive on the platform of a train—and Johnny did.

A contemporary article in *Midi Libre* is of considerable interest, for it provides a sense of the excitement and general interest the middle-aged sailor held for the public.

The arrival of Gau has brought to Valras Parisian press and news cinema representatives. . . . Two boats, chartered by the town of Valras, cruised as far as Port La Nouvelle to intercept Gau's sailboat. One boat was to return immediately to Valras to alert the town officials, the other to keep *Atom* company until the entire Valras fishing fleet could escort them to the harbor. . . . Jean's odyssey has created many rumors. It was said, for example, that at night his boat had struck a sleeping whale and almost became a submarine! Others relate how that he navigates only by stars, carrying no compass aboard. . . . There is talk of *Atom*'s engine having been sealed off and that the skipper would use it only to enter a port or to avoid striking a shore during a storm. . . . There is rumor that he married a Serignan girl, who divorced him in America and married a doctor. . . . Others said that during the 1939-40 war his nonmilitary status was owed to the intervention of a provincial politician. . . . We only listened, and kept silent.

But if *Midi Libre* kept silent, its hero-hungry competitors did not.

Echo du Midi, on October 17, reported that in the previous October (1946) the Valras town hall had been alerted that a small sailboat similar to *Atom* had been sighted off Cape Bearn on the Spanish-French border. The next day the village's entire fishing fleet had prepared to put to sea to welcome Jean, but no sail had appeared on the horizon.

The article alluded also to the "shy sailor's" disinterest in publicity. "Yesterday morning Jean Gau was the guest of his aunt, Claire Gau, in Beziers. Journalists who had first gone to Serignan now went to Beziers (about 15 miles away) to interview him but were met with a closed door."

Le Republicain reported that "at eight o'clock we knocked at the Gau household in Serignan. Madame Gau greeted us. 'My son,' she said, 'left with his father at seven o'clock.' She added, 'I have only seen Jean twice in twenty years!* And I didn't recognize him when, near midnight, I opened the door.' Later, at his aunt's house at 2 Old Fortress Street, Beziers, we heard the same story. We noted the table was laid but were told, 'My nephew is running

---

*Three years later his mother angrily told an old friend of Johnny's, "I wish I'd had an idiot for a child. He'd stay home and not sail the seas!"

errands. You can see him tomorrow.' We wondered if he were shopping or trying to sell his sea journal to one of the major Parisian newspapers? Yet this American (he became a citizen in 1945) was seen having a drink at La Coupole pub around noon. . . . This mention of Jean's naturalization was, of course, a veiled innuendo, a dig at his World War II nonmilitary status.

Ce Soir, a day later, printed an interview that was bannered ATLANTIC SOLO SAILOR JEAN GAU RETURNS BY TRAIN! Its reporter had asked if Gau had been afraid during the storms.

"Afraid?" Jean removed a Gauloise cigarette from the corner of his mouth. "If I were afraid I would not sail alone on the ocean."

"But why do you sail alone? Isn't that only for misanthropes, or is it a longing for solitude?"

"Neither," replied Gau. "Between the sky and water I am not alone, because I live with the sea and the gale." That response nearly thirty years ago was not bravado, as his career subsequently showed. But the points raised about misanthropy and solitude were not entirely immaterial, as comments a decade later by Claire Gau revealed.

Jean had made a successful crossing of the Atlantic, and had he desired public attention he could easily have attracted a good press. Whether he now felt that his past debts to the community had been repaid is not clear. At any rate, a contemporary article from *La Voix de la Patrie* shows how uninterested in attention he had become! "Foreseeing new difficulties between Cartagena and Valras, Jean asked his parents to be very patient because of the strong headwinds he expected to meet." This doesn't agree with Jean's statement that the Spanish Civil War precluded communication with his parents.

The article continues: "But suddenly we learned yesterday that Gau had arrived at eleven o'clock Wednesday evening at his parent's home, having crossed from Spain by train and car. Early in the morning we went to Serignan to the small house on Pasteur Street, where we found his happy parents relieved of anxiety at not hearing from their son. . . . But the lone sailor had left already by train for Beziers to be with relatives."
This is interesting not only because it illustrates Jean's

deepened sensitivities to publicity and an uncommon desire for privacy,* but because it reveals a startling attitude toward his parents. Marie-Louise Gau had seen her son "twice in twenty years," yet he almost immediately quit the house to visit his aunt!

"At the age of 21 he exhibited his paintings in the Beziers theatre . . ." Again the article errs; Jean was overseas at the time. "When queried about his voyage, Gau replied, 'I left my boat in Cartagena and last Sunday decided to go to France by train. I stopped in Valencia and Barcelona and reached the border by taxi, where, in company with ten others, Canadians, Americans and French, I crossed clandestinely the mountain pass at the border." This is perhaps an exaggeration, for although the border was still closed because of the Spanish Civil War, to have crossed it clandestinely while his boat remained behind would have been foolish.

"I tried to avoid this interview," said Gau, dressed in a blue serge blazer, "because a friend has sold my sea log to a Parisian paper. I can't answer your questions satisfactorily." If his journal or log was sold and printed, we have not been able to verify it. At any rate, Jean mentioned that he "hoped to take back to the States many colored photographs and drawings, which the Americans really like. This way I'll save enough money to pay for my voyages. I also write for a newspaper, *Yachting Reader,* and *Motor Boating.* And I'll write several articles about the voyage, which, frankly, was exhausting." Yet he would subsequently write that he arrived in Cartagena "hale and hearty."

Sadly, his plans to write, draw, and photograph, as well as later stated artistic proposals, never materialized. Johnny was *never* to make money in this fashion. Only through spending grueling hours before the Hotel Taft's hot stoves did he achieve the means to live his dream.

The *Nuit et Jour* reporter asked Gau the questions most asked

---

*The following incident can be verified only to a point, but it illustrates the difficult and almost impossible task of understanding Jean's interpersonal relationships, behavior, and motivational basis. He accepted $300 from a prominent French newspaper before departing from America; for the money he was to provide the newspaper an exclusive interview upon arrival in Europe. But upon reaching Spain he generously and *gratuitously* gave interviews to both Spanish and French newspapers! The money was not repaid.

of single-handers. His replies afford some insight into his sailing expertise and simple sea-oriented philosophy. How did he sleep at night? "At sunset I drop the mainsail, haul the jib sheet taut, and slack the mizzen sheet.* *Atom* just steers herself and I sleep comfortably, trusting in my boat's progress."

Why did he prefer sailing alone? "Well, to be at sea for weeks or even months doesn't bother me. On the contrary, far from the strains of everyday living I feel I'm another person. Besides, I'm not alone." Lean-faced, deeply tanned, sitting in his parents' old-fashioned living room, Gau's button eyes unnerved the reporter by their lucidity and depth. "Frankly, I consider *Atom* as a live being, intelligent, sensitive. When the wind blows, this assembly of wood, metal, and canvas becomes a living thing to me. With all her whims, defects, and qualities, *Atom* does her job and I do mine. I love her as a—a good servant, as a man loves an animal, or his car. Let's just say that we're friends. OK?" Gau was smiling.

The reporter lowered his eyes and asked how the boat handled in a gale. "She's built of oak and cedar. She can bear the pressure of the waters. Her full lines give her a big margin of buoyancy." Jean smiled. "When she's hove to, she's indestructible. She's a cork . . . . a real cork!" Laughing, he pulled the cork from a long-necked bottle of *vin ordinaire* and refilled the reporter's glass. "We've already seen great difficulties together. We probably haven't seen them all yet!" This was Johnny in 1947: confident, cocksure, and—unknowingly—prescient.

Johnny remained in Valras and Serignan until the spring of 1948. In March the Colonial Maritime League gave him a party and a medal. A local newspaper stated that in Cartagena *Atom*, still silently awaiting her master, "carried supplies for more than two years, dried soups, etc." Could Gau have been intending as early as 1948 to make his first voyage around the world? The paper mentioned also a past incident: the "shy adventurer"

Atom's self-steering system included a large coaming-mounted coiled spring (in lieu of a shock cord) that returned the tiller to its correct position after a puff or gust had passed. A thin Dacron line, knotted to the bitter end of the coiled spring and wrapped four times around the tiller, was secured to the mainsheet.

recalled that in 1937 he had been hailed at sea by Gunter Prion, commander of the German submarine U-34, who checked the sailor's log before letting him proceed. Many years later the two sailors met again. Prion, one of Germany's most decorated skippers (he sank the British battleship *Royal Oak*), congratulated the "fearless Frenchman."

Still piqued by Jean's "horror of journalists," *Le Republicain*'s reporter described Jean as "a great and remarkable artist. This we discovered while looking over his album of colored drawings, masterpieces which Gau has reproduced with an amazing reality and truth which is seldom done, of the fears and pleasures of the great waters. . . . Near the end of the album we see *Onda* . . . a victim of the Civil War because of the extinguished Cadiz lighthouse." The album also contained "a scene of *Onda* stopped and visited by the German submarine." To date, this drawing, like most of the Gau collection, is missing. "Jean," the article concludes, "hopes to edit his album of drawings in the United States. 'I will finish it in two years.'" That would have been 1950. But as with all his artistic efforts, this too failed. That same month Jean returned by train to Cartagena, reclaimed *Atom*, and cleared for New York.

As though a personal fate were involved, westerlies and strong currents in the Strait of Gibraltar prevented him from leaving the Mediterranean. Abashed at his failure, Gau returned to Valras, and to a puzzled citizenry. This ignominious and silent return, following so shortly the fiasco of the preceding year, Jean glossed over later. But it became, in a way, a sort of triumph, inasmuch as it permitted him for the first time to see and describe the coastline and sea of his native country from the deck of his own vessel.

Jean's description of the failure, which he generously permitted *Midi Libre* to quote directly from his ship's journal, appeared on August 11, 1948.

After a short stay in Barcelona and Valencia I reached Cartagena on March 15 at ten o'clock. I went immediately to the yacht club and asked for the keys to *Atom*. I found her, riding to her anchors, in front of the club where I'd left her five months before. Sitting on my suitcase, thinking I was alone, I gazed with . . . pleasure and joy at my sturdy little boat . . . feeling . . . tenderness towards her. Our rapport was noisily interrupted by bursts of laughter from inside the clubhouse, where I'd been observed. The President, the Commodore, and several members, all friends, after their laughter subsided, welcomed me with an enthusiastic toast.

Aboard *Atom* all was clean and in perfect condition. I was glad to see that nothing was missing. From March 21 to March 27 I attended Holy Week festivities and was much impressed by the liturgical splendor and outdoor displays that mark the Spanish ceremonies.

After the feasts I started working, setting *Atom* ready for the long crossing. Spanish officials were very kind and provided me with a young lad from Cartagena to help me fit out the boat. As I worked topside I looked off towards the sea, cheered by the thought that I'd be leaving soon.

Often after work I would stroll Cartagena's old streets, stopping off at pubs where dancers and music charged the nighttime air. But during these days in Cartagena my best relationships were among the Spanish naval officers who were interested in my voyages and navigation methods. I especially enjoyed the friendship of Don Luis Verdugo, commander of the Destroyer *Lepanto*, a gentleman and sailor. Several days before I departed for America he invited me to lunch and presented me with a handsome ebony sextant engraved in ivory.

On April 26 *Atom* was ready, but the westerlies, which dominate from May to October, weren't yet settled. Despite my impatience I had to postpone the departure. On May 6, however, I was ready to break my long stay ashore, and after watering and provisioning ship, dropped the lines which held me from Great Adventure.

And now Jean, whose brush was more facile than his pen, wrote one of the most beautiful and sensous descriptions of a sailing departure in nautical literature.

At six o'clock I weighed anchor, my feverish efforts augmenting the jarring sensations of departure, that indescribable joy of moving into newness, the melancholy produced by the fast-receding present, and the growing anxiety for the impending but uncertain future. Fifteen minutes later I passed the jetties and at that point resumed my life.

Rounding Cape Tinoso, I came upon a fishing fleet far offshore, their lateen sails slatting as the boats rolled, their crews hailing as we passed. Before long brown sails and white cliffs were gone and I stood once more between wind and wave.

The sea stretched far away like a plain, a limitless desert; my eyes slowly searched for some impression of man but found nothing. As *Atom*, under a weak breeze, paced across this desert plain she left a wake that symbolically diverged towards the horizon. By sunset the breezes had freshened and I rigged *Atom* with fewer sails. The tiller lashed properly, I went below to prepare a dish of rice. After a pipe, I rigged her lamps and then slept, tired by the demands of departure.

The sounds of a large ship's horn tore me out of my bunk at two o'clock. On deck I was startled by the bright light of a Spanish warship slowly maneuvering around my ketch. "*L'Atomo, el yate del solitario!*" I heard a voice cry. Three blasts and the gray ship became part of the darkness.

May 7, up at dawn and all sails set and sheets trimmed under a gray sky and on a rough sea. I stayed at the helm until five o'clock. At sunset the wind suddenly veered, a gale blowing from the northeast with chunks of wind and rain. I got the sails off and set the stormsail. Typical notes for a typical day at sea. That night, as darkness arrived, so did heavy rains. Somewhere in that screen of rain a freighter blew its nose. A last look around the boat topside and I went below to rest. Of course, I couldn't sleep because the boat shook arrhythmically all night, its movements accompanied by piercing and sinister notes from the shrouds and masts as they sliced the winds. The hull, shouldering the waves to starboard, gave forth bass notes. Combined, the sounds and rhythms made a sort of symphony of the sea.

The next morning I popped my head out of the hatch at five o'clock. Everything looked—wow! A cold, icy spray and rain shower woke me up, but it vexed me too. Back down in the cabin a bowl of hot coffee provided a slow sipping pleasure. The weather was cold, rainy, awful. Wearing oilies over my woolies I climbed back on deck, where I took in the stormsail and hoisted *Atom*'s working rags. A strong easterly or Levante was moving *Atom* nicely at six knots as the Sierra Nevada summits and slopes appeared off to northward.

That evening a huge bonito was a special guest, his place of honor the pressure cooker, as the seas ran hard under a strong northeasterly. Under a stormsail *Atom* footed nicely, although slammed constantly by the cross waves. I rested without concern, for I trusted my robust little boat.

At three o'clock I was startled by the sound of a gunshot! Topside I found that the sail's sheet had burst under the strain. Over its objections I got it down, but *Atom*, without its steadying effect, rolled furiously. An hour later, the sheet changed and the sail set and drawing, I climbed wearily into my cold bunk and slept until daybreak.

The wind the next day danced in from the north and finally settled in the southeast. At noon it was blowing at gale force but about four in the afternoon it suddenly quit. Three hours later Gibraltar's brooding hulk of honeycombed rock loomed twenty miles off. Thoughts of making port that night were beginning to stir me when a high westerly suddenly sprang up, forcing me to tack. That night we sailed on a northerly course.

On May 10 I cast the hook in the small fishing harbor of Fuengirola, forty-one miles from Gibraltar, where I waited impatiently for a fair wind. Two days later a heavy swell forced me to abandon the dangers of that anchorage. I put to sea in spite of the bad weather and contrary winds. For nearly twenty days I fought foul currents, high winds, and nasty seas, an endless series of tacks first towards Africa, then Spain. Finally, I acknowledged that I could not reach America before the hurricane season.

On May 28 I wore ship and sailed back towards France.

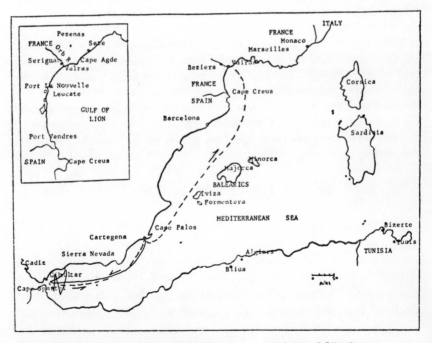

Figure 2. Generalized track of the 1948 failure to exit Strait of Gibraltar

The wind astern, the next day I entered Cartagena, where I sent a cable to my family. Once more I put to sea, my course France. The westerlies gave way as I rounded Cape St. Antonio and I had nothing but variable moderate breezes and calms. *Atom* glided slowly past the Balearics at a pace that allowed me to enjoy their beauty almost as much as had I been ashore.

After sixteen days of light airs a fair southwesterly carried me in three days to Cape Cruis, where I was becalmed for the night, only forty-five miles from home. At dawn the next day I got underway for Valras and soon weathered Cape Leucate and Port La Nouvelle, the coastal landscape becoming familiar. North of Gruissan, at the foot of the La Clape Hills, which overlook the coast between the Gruissan Marshes and the River Aude and on which stands the monastery of Notre Dame de la Clape, I caught sight of the old square Montolieu tower, and the St. Pierre tower, which is separated from the sea by a narrow beach. Then I sighted the small reef of St. Pierre, atop of which there are the ruins of a battery.

To the east of the last hills of La Clape I spied the square cathedral of St. Nazaire in Beziers, and finally the Valras water tower, the casino, the Lauge chalet, and the small lighthouse on the west jetty at the mouth of the River Orb.

Meeting with the Valras fishing fleet I was hailed by Antoine Sautier, who left his fishing to show me the entrance, passable only by small craft, into the river's mouth. At noon, without fuss, I sailed into the small basin of my youth.

I plan now to winter in Valras, and in April of 1949 to weigh anchor for the States. I will call at Cartagena, of course, before challenging that terrible west wind, the stiff currents of the Strait, and the Atlantic's vastness.

So ended the *Midi Libre* article, and Jean's plans to be in America that year.

Fortunately, as there had been minimal press coverage when he departed,* now minimal attention was given his dismal return. Gau casually revealed that he intended to make "his next cruise" a year later, that is, in 1949, that he would return to Valras, and that from there he would "sail for Panama and the Pacific." Jean was now publicly announcing his intention to sail

---

*By train to Cartagena.

alone around the world—in view of his recent inability to sail out
of the Strait of Gibraltar, perhaps a rather quixotic announcement. Could Johnny have been trying to smooth over his fail-
ures? His remarks seemingly created little interest at the time.
Perhaps little Valras was beginning to doubt.

Two days after his return, *Midi Libre* complained that it was
difficult for reporters to interview Gau. From now on, El Solitario would avidly seek obscurity. But his reclusive habits, like a
flint rock, would continue to give off sparks of notoriety.

In Valras, Jean occasionally accompanied fishermen friends
on their stout, and stumpy, colorful craft in the Gulf of Lion. It
was during this period that a minor and humorous incident
occurred. Jean had never been other than a social drinker, but
was an accomplished swimmer. One evening, returning from a
party on a bicycle to where *Atom* was moored in the basin off the
River Orb, Jean decided to take a shortcut. He plunged the
bicycle into the basin's waters!

His activities during this period ashore included such ship's
work as splicing lines, tying fancy and complicated sailors' knots,
and a considerable amount of sewing sails with palm and needle.
He visited sporadically with his parents but showed no interest in
his father's vineyard. He did not participate, even as an observer,
in local yachting activities. Equally as odd, *Atom* never left the
harbor except to test repairs to her engine. *Atom* was Jean's
home. That she was also a sailboat seemed almost incidental.

On May 10, 1949, the forty-seven-year-old sailor set sail and
cleared Valras, bound for the States. His going was in the finest
Gau tradition. No one, or at best only a handful, knew of his
departure. This time he would succeed in passing the Strait of
Gibraltar to reach New York, where a small but enthusiastic
group of well-wishers would remove some of the stings and
bitterness of his almost three-year absence. But now Jean's mind
was made up. He would sail alone around the world. Of that, he
had absolutely no doubt.

His third Atlantic crossing, from Europe to America, was
relatively uneventful. But *Midi Libre* hailed the event with a
banner: BEATING ALAIN GERBAULT'S FIRST CROSSING RECORD, GAU
SAILS 9,000 KILOMETERS IN 65 DAYS.

Once she reached the northeast trade winds area, *Atom* made a good ninety to 100 miles daily, "which wasn't bad. Happier than Gerbault, I wasn't obliged to keep the tiller for twelve hours, nor to stay up at night. With the winds on the quarter it was an easy and pleasant navigation." Stripped to "Adam's clothes," he sat in the mainsail's shade entertaining himself with his favorite books, particularly Columbus's journal. Jean's rapport with "his element, the sea" was clearly evident when he wrote, "I often thought I was on another planet."

He entered "a hurricane area" only 780 miles from New York, and on September 1 was sighted by an American Task Force fleet; it dispatched a ship to inquire if he needed assistance. Jean asked that his position be relayed to the *New York Times.* He was informed that a hurricane northwest of Bermuda carrying 115-knot winds, was moving northeast. "I was in the way," he dryly noted.

When he was ninety miles off Montauk he crammed on sail, including "the staysail, and the flying jib." *Atom* soon reached her speed limit—according to Jean, eight knots. On September 6 he sighted Block Island and the next day he entered Montauk, sixty-five days out of Gibraltar.

"On September 11, 1949, I cast anchor in New York harbor at College Point in the very place where, on May 24 two years before, I had departed for a big cruise which had lasted more than two years, 248 days of which were spent at sea. I was glad to think that my arrival would go unnoticed," he wrote, "but God Damn It! the Navy had signaled my arrival far out to sea. The next day *Atom* was invaded by reporters and cameramen. . . . Many offers were made by radio and television but they didn't interest me."* In a final and somewhat revealing note, he said, "I was very happy to have achieved what I wanted to do."

---

*He did appear, reluctantly, on one radio show. It was a fiasco; Johnny froze, unable to respond to the interviewer's questions. Many years later, after his great voyages, although his hermitlike habits had increased in depth and possibly in variety, Johnny mellowed. His public talks, including radio interviews, were funny, effervescent, his offbeat adventures delivered in a rich, sonorous voice. He did not hesitate to use salty words or gangway gestures. "Gau could have made a million bucks on the lecture circuit!" commented a retired Annapolis business executive—a hard-nosed tribute to his talents for telling a good story in the grand manner.

Gau's concern for avoiding the 1949 hurricane is notable in light of his actions in subsequent situations. When in sight of land on this voyage he had reduced sail so as not to arrive at night; this excellent practice was not always followed so keenly in future. Lastly, the "shy mariner's" oft-stated dislike of publicity is difficult to accept in view of his request to relay his position to the *New York Times;* he could have asked that a message be relayed only to his New York friends.

Midi Libre reported on September 15, 1949, that "Gau had reached his goal after more than 100 days of fascinating adventure." The brief article is notable only in that it states that he sailed from Valras to Cartagena in five days, a feat that he would never duplicate.

5

Challenging a Distant Sea

A small, happy crowd greeted Jean as he and *Atom* neared the New York pier, and among them was the ebullient Eli Agnel, who called to the grinning mariner, "*Sies lou roi de la mer!* (You are king of the sea!)" Lines were tossed and eager hands warped the salt-grimed ketch alongside the pier. Shaking his gray head for emphasis, her skipper rasped out replies to the good-natured queries and jibes. The date was September 11, 1949.

Also in the noisy and exuberant gathering was Jean's good friend and confidant Margot Panisse, whose loud voice he later said he never forgot. That evening, over dinner and drinks, Margot read a poem she had written to commemorate the successful voyage:

This atom, infinitesimal atom!
Has *within* a colossal power
For it marries the fecund sea
And a particle of earth . . .

69

Gau quickly resumed both his old job at the hotel and his Spartan existence, commuting from *Atom*'s slip at Lampe's Boatyard in Flushing to the Hotel Taft. And life in New York went on.

One year later Pierre Gau, aged 75, died in Serignan of a heart attack. His son learned of the death at the Long Island home of his close friend, Joe Cordonat. In a letter written eight days later Jean said, "My sorrow is great. . . . And only my hard job lessens it." He then mentioned that he was now grateful for not being able to exit the Strait of Gibraltar in 1948 because "it let us be together for a longer time." In the letter we catch also a brief glimpse into the quiet years before his first great circumnavigation: "For me it is always the same, *Atom* to Taft and back again. How happy I was on the high seas. How I long for weighing anchor and sailing around the world under a warm tropic sun, and most of all, in the open air. . . . If only I could sleep!"

He did not return to France, however, to see his mother, and in view of her grief it is unlikely that he mentioned to her any plans he had for a world voyage. Then, on September 15, 1952, Marie-Louise Gau died, and Jean, now fifty years old, flew to Serignan.

Of Johnny's remaining relatives only one, his aunt Claire Gau, was particularly close. A former schoolteacher, now retired and living in the older part of Beziers, Claire's stern questioning and breadth of interests had created over the years a rapport with the headstrong Jean, only ten years her junior. At times it was a rapport fraught with conflict.* Nonetheless, by her steadfast insistence on principle, and by her careful arguments, Claire Gau gained the admiration and respect of her nephew, and became one of the few important women in his life. It is likely that he had confided to her his plans to sail alone around the world before telling anyone else. A year later he spent the month before his departure in her Beziers home.

In April of 1953 the Gau house on Moliere Street was placed on the market. Johnny reportedly pocketed several thousand

---

*They differed strongly on religious matters.

dollars from the sale, which he immediately banked to help pay the expenses of his impending departure. For the voyage he had decided to replace *Atom*'s old ten-hp. engine and to install stainless steel rigging.

On the evening of April 28, 1953, over a bowl of pungent bouillabaisse at Le Provençal Inn in Valras, Jean announced his intention to sail around the world. He would leave Valras, he said emphatically, at the end of May. One of his fishermen friends got slowly to his feet and leaned forward, his large red-boned knuckles pressed against the heavy oak table. "You will return to Valras, no?" His concern expressed the pleasure these lean-bodied, sun-darkened fishermen felt at Jean's decision to leave little Valras on a voyage around the world.

Prodded by the smiling figures at his side, Jean rose to answer, thick eyebrows arched and eyes sparkling in the firelight. His heavy, rough voice revealed his feelings as he replied, "Yes, and in two and a half years—I will return to Valras, to my friends!" Several in the crowd, knowing that this would be a new world record, greeted the announcement with renewed Gallic levity and vigor. Rough hands reached for the glinting half-emptied bottles of wine that, like ramparts, protected a huge wheel of cheese, plates of pears, and great loaves of bread on the long table.

But Jean's words were toasted by more than these weathered toilers of the sea. Chef Chabert, one of his most ardent local supporters, announced that he would welcome the intrepid voyager on his return with a *fete grande*! This culinary gesture was an appropriate flourish; it recognized the uncommon spirit and achievements of one Valras now accepted as an old tarback, a true deep-water man. Basking in the warmth of camaraderie, blazing logs, and his own musings of what lay ahead, Jean smiled his rich, serene smile.

But if Jean talked frankly with these admirers before flying back to America, he was even more candid with the two women who, in different ways, had figured so largely in his life, Margot Panisse and Claire Gau. Margot, speaking to a reporter in June 1953 just before Gau's departure, emphasized that he was "an extremely shy person, who disliked attention and publicity." She added that "he had always preferred quiet departures."

Two months earlier Jean had visited his aunt, Claire Gau. Now, talking with reporters, Claire recalled that her nephew had been reluctant to go out for fear of being recognized and interviewed. The confident, direct schoolteacher stated that her nephew was simply "afraid of being viewed as some kind of curious animal." His distaste for questions was such, she said, that Jean "had rather face gales at sea." Jean had often confessed to her, she said, "People frighten me, Claire. I prefer the sea." Nowhere have we encountered a more revealing note—the voice of the true hermit crying in the wilderness for the impersonal and tolerant sea.

While Jean was quietly stowing last-minute items aboard the heavily laden *Atom* in America, Claire Gau was reading to reporters excerpts from a recent letter her nephew had written. "I'll write the story of the voyage, and wherever I call, paint pictures that I'll try to sell." In time he did write the story. A hint of bold enterprise was evident: "I'll take pictures and color films and, if possible, make a film about the giant dragons on Komodo Island. I'll be busy, believe me." Only a real adventurer would dare to cross the poorly charted waters off the old Netherlands Indies by sail!*

To the reporter's question, whether Jean Gau would settle in America or in France after his return, the honest old disciplinarian looked directly at him. "It depends on the success of the voyage," she replied, "and the value of the materials that he brings back." Few of these plans or prospects for a golden future materialized. But *Midi Libre* quoted Jean that in Bora Bora he would visit the grave of his "tutor, Alain Gerbault." This he did achieve.

---

*Johnny subsequently (and on many occasions) told of witnessing the shooting of a giant Komodo dragon. A goat, tied to a bush, was used for bait. Jean vividly described the way the crawling giant lizard, when shot, immediately collapsed "like a deflated bladder." We have no evidence of his ever landing on Komodo Island, yet the credible vividness and fine detail of his story is puzzling. Did Jean Gau make an unreported layover on Komodo Island?

Jean Gau's Account of His First Circumnavigation

On the morning of June 30, 1953, *Atom*'s lines were cast off, her mission a voyage around the world. In spite of a thick fog—which at seven o'clock had not lifted—my patience at an end, I weighed anchor. With the help of her engine I left Montauk harbor, guided only by the sounds of the bell buoy at the channel's entrance and by the somber tones of the unseen Montauk lighthouse horn.

Sea breezes arrived several hours later, clearing up the mists. I stopped the engine, set *Atom*'s sails, and on a course of 162° headed for the distant Bermudas. In time the American coast was lost to sight.

Now I was at last free of the problems of catching a subway train and punching time cards, the din of dishes being washed, the vulgar noises of airplanes. I now heard only the wind laughing in the rigging and the happy *shush* of *Atom*'s bow wave. What a wonderful joy to be underway in a small boat, moved only by the winds that blow!

Before me on a table lay a chart of the vast Atlantic into which I now sailed. On its clean surface I drew a line from Montauk to Puerto Rico via Bermuda, a distance of 1,320 nautical miles. Sailing close to the wind, the tiller lashed a few degrees under it to compensate for old *Atom*'s tendency to gripe, I enthusiastically resumed my old sea ways. Up at dawn, a breakfast of pancakes, flying fish, and coffee! At eight o'clock the sun obliged with a sighting which, crossed at noon with a meridian sight, gave me what I needed to know. At four o'clock, on deck to obtain the day's final sighting, I was happy to find that I'd not lost my hand at using the sextant.

In spite of the weak breezes *Atom*'s average speeds were from sixty to one hundred miles daily—not much, but I didn't ask for more. After twelve days of idyllic sailing, despite having to sail close to the wind, Bermuda lay only forty-two miles off. *Atom*, responding to my suggestion, tacked. We now headed southeast to avoid the coral reefs that lace the islands Juan Bermudez happily sighted. At twilight David Head light was sighted, *Atom* having made a good 120 miles in twenty-four hours. Not bad!

Now Sargasso weeds playfully grabbed the log line, causing *Atom*'s crew endless work hoisting it on deck every thirty minutes. Finally the line broke and I had the job of replacing it with a spare. *Atom*'s sails during this time seemed to attract hordes of flying fish, something I didn't mind—having a hot skillet usually nearby.

The Doldrums were entered on July 16 and I consulted the Sailing Directions; they warned that sailboats can expect to find nothing but dead calms, variable winds, and downpours. Well, everything was just the opposite. Instead of calms I had air, lots of it! In just five days we crossed this area, dreaded by sailors of yesteryear.

Having entered the trade winds, *Atom* steered southeast, still close to the wind. But now the waves, rushing vigorously against *Atom*'s port bow, caused my boat to rear often, pushing her nose into them. I didn't like it because she then fell flat like a tunny. Sometimes I worried that she would open herself, the way she jerked and plunged. The spray now reached midway up the masts and pricked, like thousands of needles, at my face. Every quarter of an hour a huge wave, which seemed to roll over the other waves, hissed as it broke over my boat, determined to crush her with its weight. Every time this happened *Atom* was submerged and covered with roiling waters. And then, like a lady getting to her feet after a nasty fall, she'd emerge in a few seconds, determined to carry on. For my part, I couldn't sleep, but having no tiller to bother about I managed to rest a bit. *Atom* could take care of herself. Of that I was certain.

After five days of this rough sledding a noon reckoning placed me seventy-five miles off Puerto Rico. But, not wanting to enter San Juan's harbor at night, I reduced sail. It was nighttime so every half-hour I obtained a star sight. I was pleased to note that my observations fitted nicely with the distance recorded by the log.

I reset the mainsail at midnight. Near three o'clock the visibility was good, the moon full. Well protected by my oilies and a Thermos of boiling black coffee, I spent most of the night in the cockpit smoking countless pipes.

At three o'clock, having not yet caught sight of the San Juan light, I lowered the main to get some rest. A last look towards the southwest and I saw the blinking dot on the horizon. It was twenty miles off.

Aware of the distance to the light, I slept with one eye open. For safety I set my alarm clock for 0530 and placed it in my bunk. Better its tinny sound than that of surf pounding on rock!

A few hours later the alarm clock banged away. Jumping on deck, I saw in the dim light the northeast tip of the island. The tiller was put hard over and I breathed deeply. Now, for the first time since leaving Montauk, I sailed with a quartering wind. By eight o'clock I was off the lighthouse, perched above Morro Castle and the harbor's entrance. Twenty days after departing the States I dropped *Atom*'s anchor in Caribbean waters.

A boat soon approached. Aboard stood a giant Negro, who welcomed me in Spanish. But pointing to my quarantine flag, he refused to board. So I handed him the ship's papers. Soon a young immigration officer arrived and then the customs official. I was impressed by the hugeness of his briefcase, but all he asked was for details of my voyage.

After a short call in Puerto Rico I dropped *Atom*'s mooring lines at noon. Waiting outside the channel were the glorious trade winds, blowing high from the northeast. With all working rags drawing, *Atom* sped cleanly along the north coast of the island. At nine o'clock I rounded the northwest headland, having made a good sixty-three miles in nine hours, at an average speed of seven knots. The next day we sailed through the Mona Pass and into the Caribbean.

If the trades were high, so were the swells. *Atom* was tightly buttoned down because every minute a wave would climb aboard and generously soak me. But *Atom* happily, even eagerly, carried on, making between 92 and 142 miles daily.

On July 18 we left the area of hurricane weather. We were now 135 miles from Panama, which it seemed possible to reach within two days. But then the unexpected happened!

The trade winds suddenly stopped blowing, but the swells continued and even became worse. No longer steadied by her sails, *Atom* began rolling horribly. Eight times a minute she shipped a green one! Frankly, it was painful sailing. In the cabin I was constantly slammed about. For the first time I sensed that my boat was in distress, that she was actually drifting towards a coast that I knew to be close. Because of the high waters obscuring the horizon I couldn't shoot the sun. I tried several times but without success.

On the nineteenth land was within sight. According to my calculations it was the Mulattos Archipelago. But to my great surprise I saw that the coast trended northwest! This meant that *Atom* was drifting southeast, almost *against* the swells.

The next day, after some coarse acrobatics in the morning, I shot a series of observations. My plot indicated that a strong current was carrying *Atom* towards the Gulf of Darien. This meant, I hoped, that there was no immediate danger. I needed rest so I climbed into my tossing bunk and closed my eyes. But not my ears.

I spent a bad night. At daybreak the roaring of breakers brought me on deck in an instant. Horrified, I saw that I was close to several islets scattered along a line of sea-bashed reefs! I sprang to the engine switch, flipped it on while holding my breath. It coughed and then started immediately. Nervously, I steered northeast, looking for a passage through the reefs. All around me and only yards away from *Atom*'s bow the waters clamored and thundered. Christ! I didn't know what to do, what decision to make.

Suddenly I saw a small beach. I quickly stopped the engine, letting *Atom* drift until I could let go her anchor. Hot, sweaty, breathing roughly, I then noticed several canoes drawn up on the beach. Just beyond I saw many small huts at the fringe of a dark forest. I was facing, I tensely realized, a small Indian village somewhere in Central America.

Before long about thirty persons had gathered on the sandy beach, eyeing me as I stood eyeing them. They, however, were moving and pointing. I stood waiting. Then two canoes, manned by four Indians, put off from the beach. I was puzzled and wasn't certain what to make of it. I turned, went below, and loaded my rifle. Returning to the cockpit, I placed it in full view of the approaching canoes. Then I hoisted the American flag.

I heard someone say, *"Americano!"* Then one of the Indians, who seemed to be their chief and who spoke Spanish rather well, seeing me nod, jumped on board. I gave him some cigarettes, which he immediately tossed to his followers.

The Indian soon reassured me that all was well. He proudly stressed that he'd been a sailor and had sailed on schooners in Central America. To prove it, without asking my permission, he ordered his followers to cast my second anchor. That done, I put away my rifle and went ashore with him in his *cayuca.* *

On the beach I met the entire village, one by one. Everybody talked at the same time, but in a foreign language. But my guide put an end to my embarrassment by dragging me off to his hut. There an Indian woman served us, in a huge and unique wooden dish, breadfruit balls, plantains, artichokes, green boiled bananas, and a type of very spicy smoked fish. Noticing my hesitation, the chief began eating, inviting me to do so. I hadn't eaten for twelve hours so I relented. I could hardly move afterwards!

My inner hunger satisfied, I began to notice the hut's furniture. Suddenly I spied on a narrow shelf a series of reduced human heads, as

---

*To ward off any unpleasantries, Gau explained that he was an American naval officer "on official business, and was expected in Panama!" Always the adventurer, he then placed a large sailor's knife in his belt before going ashore. The Indians subsequently showed him how they made poisoned arrow snares, using lianas, to kill prey. Gau was shown concealed pits in which embedded blackened arrows and bamboo spears awaited unwary prey. He admitted "keeping *both* eyes opened that night." In later years he enjoyed imitating the cries and sounds of jungle beasts.

big as a fist, and stuck on tiny poles! I couldn't conceal my emotions. On seeing me start the chief told me that the heads belonged to the former members of a neighboring enemy tribe, the Chocos. But, he said, I had nothing to worry about with his people. He strongly urged me not to venture out of their territory, however.

Having calmed myself a bit, I asked him how they preserved the heads. He seemed eager to explain the process: After the head is detached from the body an incision is made from the top of the forehead to the nape of the neck. Starting from this incision, the skin is delicately separated from the skull, which is tossed away. The eyelids and lips are tightly sewn. Then the incision is sewn, except for a small slit. This pouch is then filled with very hot sand and placed over a fire onto which certain herbs are thrown. The pouch is both reduced and mummified.

Satisfied with the explanation, I then learned that the entire village wanted to visit my boat. So we paddled back to *Atom* and climbed aboard, and I gave each one some tins and cigarettes. Every man, woman, child, and old person in that tribe smoked—little *Atom* was a smoke-filled room afloat!

Later I was invited to visit each hut; Ourari, as the chief was called, acted as interpreter. From him I learned that they were of the Cuna tribe. Small in size and short-necked, they have powerful arms and chests, a result of spending much time paddling their heavy log canoes. Paddling, for them, is easier than walking; their legs are short and thin, their feet very small. The women, with gold rings through their noses, are picturesque. [They wear] enormous silver earrings and bright clothes, which are covered by necklaces made of silver coins of all sorts: dimes, quarters, shillings, escudos. . . . Some of them, I noted, had as much as $300 in change around their necks.

That evening I ate again in Ourari's hut, mindful of the blackened and sightless eyes that looked on. Afterwards the villagers gathered in front to ask hundreds of questions. I even had to tell my adventures in Spanish, Ourari translating word by word. That night I slept restlessly, the breakers incessantly reminding me of my boat, alone and pulling at her anchors, only a few yards from the beach. At daybreak the sea was calmer, and after a short breakfast Ourari gave a signal for my departure. The villagers began gathering on the beach.

Saying goodbye to these kind Indians, accompanied by Ourari, I boarded *Atom*. As we got underway several canoes formed a line on either side of us. We were so close to the reefs that the canoe Indians could almost reach out and touch their black, coarse surfaces. They pointed out one of the passes to me but it seemed *very* narrow. I nervously mentioned it to Ourari. He answered that it was the widest!

Standing forward, Ourari acted as a pilot. "*Adelante despacio!*" he cried. "*Poco izquierdo!*" and I steered slightly to the left. I immediately put the engine in neutral when he barked, "*Alto! Alto!*" It was necessary to wait for the right moment, right after the passage of a big wave, and to maintain *Atom*'s bow between the lines of canoes.

A deep wave passed, then a second and a third. But no signal from Ourari. I became impatient. At last, as the sixth wave passed, he cried, "*Adelanto todo!*" It was *full steam ahead,* let me tell you! With *Atom*'s throttle wide open, I expected a catastrophe any second. My heart beat as if it would burst. But like an arrow *Atom* darted between the canoe convoy, brushing the boats closely. In front of her a great roaring wave approached, foaming and tumbling. Ourari was shouting, "*Todo! Todo! Hombrecito! Todo!*" But the throttle *was* wide open!

The shock from that wave was terrible. *Atom* reared vertically and then plunged deeply into the trough, her propeller roaring above the din of swirling waters as it lifted out of the sea. A second wave, approaching, broke, but *Atom* made it safely through the tumult and out of the tight pass. My God! She'd had a close one. I shook my head.

Shaking my hand, Ourari said, "*Amigo Americano, Buen Viaje!*" One of the canoes picked him up, and he waved. Back on the small beach the villagers yelled and waved as the little *Atom* gained the open sea.

But outside there was no wind, only a heavy swell and a contrary current. I had enough gasoline for perhaps 200 miles, but I wanted it kept for emergencies. This, I decided, was one. Still, I knew that the countercurrent of the Gulf Stream reaches a top speed of five or six knots twenty-four miles off Cristobal near the Manzanillo headland. I would need some gasoline to combat that, I knew. Nevertheless I had to use the engine to get out of the region. Lashing the tiller, I headed for the cabin.

Surprise! Fruits and vegetables of all sorts lay on the table, on the bunks, and over the cabin floor. Huge stalks of green bananas, papayas, breadfruit, mangoes, coconuts. I was immediately moved by the generosity of those kind Indians. I was now ashamed to have loaded my rifle.

About midnight, or ninety miles later, I killed the engine and lay below to rest. The heat was stifling! Having worked incessantly for sixteen hours, the engine had overheated *Atom*'s small cabin. And of course the boat was rolling badly. It was impossible to sleep.

At five o'clock I sighted the Manzanillo headland, and, about sunset, was closing its lighthouse, when I noticed in the southeast an ugly band of anvil-topped black clouds. The horizon was suddenly struck by flashes of lightning. Oh boy! "A *chocosan!*" I cried aloud. These violent storms occur in the Gulf of Darien, their winds often with the strength of hurricanes. There was nothing I could do but secure the boat and wait for something to happen. I stopped the engine.

In minutes a terrific blast of wind arrived and slapped *Atom* over onto her port side. The sea was as bright as day as the lightning flashed without ceasing. In the distance I heard rain approaching. In seconds the skies burst open and I was inundated. Simultaneously the wind veered and *Atom* was thrown onto her starboard side. I was worried for fear the mainmast had been struck by the lightning, but in that torrent I could see nothing.

The rain fell faster than it could drain from the cockpit—I sat with water swirling about my calves. But I was worried about the masts, to hell with the rain! Sick with worry, numb with the cold, I spent most of the night in *Atom*'s cockpit. In time the storm lessened, but slowly.

Down in the cabin later I found an awful mess. Books, charts, clothes, pans, coconuts everywhere! Some were rolling like bowling balls from side to side of the cabin. Hastily I made coffee and ate some of the fruit that I had managed to avoid stepping on. I went back on deck.

It was nearly daybreak, and as soon as I looked I knew what had happened. The port shroud, a half-inch-diameter stainless steel cable, had ruptured near the fitting. Only a few strands now held it in place. It had to be repaired at once or the mast would go overboard. Grabbing an extra cable, I managed, after some fancy gymnastics, to jury-rig a temporary stay. Finished, I slipped down the mast shaking and exhausted, and fell into my bunk. But rest I could not! I knew that a countercurrent, moving at four knots, was carrying *Atom* away from her course.

The storm had cost me many miles, but at seven o'clock I was again steering southwest. By noon we'd reached the lighthouse, where the current flows at six knots. Even though my speed was about seven and a half knots, I was worried by the swiftness of the roiling waters. But by twilight Toro Point was reached and several hours later I sailed into Cristobal's harbor, where I hastily anchored. I hoisted the yellow flag and threw myself into my bunk, more dead than alive. For eighteen hours I'd helmed the boat and for more than fifty-two hours I hadn't shut an eye.

Harbor officials woke me at eight o'clock. Seeing my state, they were considerate and soon admitted me to pratique.

At sunrise on December 11, 1953, after nearly four months ashore, I left the mooring lines at the Cristobal Yacht Club. A pilot boarded at six o'clock with two Dutch sailors, who helped with the hawsers as we passed through the different locks. After the first three locks the passage was easy and interesting, especially on Lake Gatun, whose waters inundate twenty miles of jungle, the drowned trees emerging like dead men's fingers above the waters, the whole a strange and surrealistic landscape.

I spent ten days in Balboa, in which time I visited the ruins of old Panama City, plundered and destroyed by that rapacious buccaneer, Henry Morgan, and the infamous Golden Path, built by slaves for the transport of Conquistador treasure in Peru. I departed on December 23.

After the last buoy I set the sails and lashed the helm, letting *Atom* get down to the business of crossing to the Galapagos. *Atom* now scudded towards great adventure, for ahead lay the sea of my youthful dreams, the biggest ocean on the globe! Perusing the chart, I discovered that from the North to the South Poles, from the eastern to the western shore, the Pacific is larger than all the countries of the world thrown together. My study showed that it contains more than one-third of the land surface, is nearly twice the size of the Atlantic, and is three times wider than the Indian Ocean, itself larger than Asia. For the first time I felt a tingle in my spine as I realized the scope of what I was doing.

While *Atom* loped along I thought about the first sailors who had dared to sail their primitive craft on this unknown sea, about crews decimated by hunger and scurvy, about fearsome sea monsters. And I thought about *Atom*'s ketch rig and her self-steering ability, which made my voyage possible, and about the latest American methods of celestial navigation. Having taken my own moral bearings, so to speak, with a light heart I laid a course for the enchanted isles of ancient mariners, the Galapagos.

The passage began well, but that evening the northwesterly freshened. Hours later, shaken by heavy seas, *Atom* headed under a jib only. The next day I rounded Malpelo Rock, having sailed ninety-five miles under that small rag. Frankly, I was pleased for I'd often heard sailors lament having to do the leg in eight to ten days. On the twenty-eighth the fair breezes gave way before a cruel calm and *Atom* took up her old habit of wallowing madly in the heavy swells. I was then in 5° North Latitude or the Doldrums, a term I now think means The

Tosspot!* From every corner came rain and nervous puffs. Sometimes breathing was difficult because of the rain. Hanging lifeless, the sails noisily slapped the masts and shrouds at every lurch of the boat. Just to get out of that overwhelming area I changed sails or trimmed constantly.

Eight days later, at nighttime, a violent squall banged my boat, throwing her on her side. But *that* wasn't the time to reduce sail. To take advantage of this godsend I sat at the helm all night, a giant sponge, and the next day we cleared this grim region.

On February 27 I crossed the Equator at 89°30′ West Longitude and, thirty-five days out of Panama, reached the outlying islands of the Galapagos. Sixty miles off stood the high meadow of San Cristobal Island, which was my destination. But the breeze was too gentle, the current too strong. Here a branch of the Peru Current runs among the islands and forms fast-moving rivers that surge from one island to the other. This mighty stream carried me northward and at daybreak I was dangerously near Tower Island, the smallest and most deserted, and bleakest, of the islands.

On Tower's southwest side is a narrow entrance, thirty yards wide, that leads to placid Darwin Bay. Generally regarded as an impossible anchorage, except for skippers with knowledge of a small ledge nine fathoms deep, it is rarely visited. But unable to check my curiosity, I entered the entrance under power. Soon *Atom*'s wake was like a crack crossing the face of a mirror. I motored several times around the silent bay, often so close to its vertical walls that I could have touched them, searching vainly for the shallow ledge.

The abundance of life in that small bay is fantastic. Atop the cliffs seabirds hopped, shrieking. The smell of their droppings was awful. Pelicans soared and wheeled over *Atom*'s masts only to fall missile-like onto their prey, while along *Atom*'s planking svelte seals, deer-eyed, broke the waters to bark softly and then disappear. Fish swarmed everywhere, their shapes and colors strange to my eyes. I noticed some with odd flowerlike bodies and others that, had they not been so small, would have scared hell out of me. The blurred outlines of dorado, sea turtles, the ghostly shadows of skate and of nature's marauder, the shark, these make Darwin Bay a natural aquarium.

I came to anchor in ten fathoms, but *Atom*'s stern was within reach of the crater's black walls. I couldn't trust the anchor to hold in the bay's

---

*The drunkard, the sot.

sandy bottom. Convinced that I wouldn't spend a quiet night, I got up the hook and sadly reentered the open sea. On February 28 I crossed the Equator for the third time.

Two days later I was hove to and San Cristobal could no longer be seen. The next morning I sighted Española Island several miles off, which meant that the currents had swept me 15 miles southward. Regaining my original course, I weathered a dreary cape separated by high cliffs and rounded the island, whose jagged ridge lines suggested castles and temples from seaward. The breezes quit so I started the engine; I had to reach San Cristobal *before* nightfall to avoid problems with its tricky and dangerous entrance.

I began a mad race with the setting sun.

I still had four hours of daylight. Averaging seven knots, I felt that I could make it, but I also faced the strong current that had swept me toward Espanola. Glancing constantly at my wristwatch and at the sun, which by six o'clock had dropped out of sight, I took bearings on oddly shaped Dalrymple Island, about four miles off. Three hours later I was off the entrance, and by the light of a pale new moon made out the darkened outlines of dangerous Lido headland to port. To starboard the sea pounded and thundered on the Schianoni Reefs. With God's mercy, and the engine, I followed the compass in. Within thirty minutes I was anchored off the beach at Porto Chico, fifty days out of Panama.

I lay over for one week. With new friends I visited the island's craters and volcanoes. For their pleasure I shot a wild goat, which I carved, salted, and gave to them.

With sleepy seagulls my well-wishers, I sailed from the harbor at dawn on March 1, standing for Floreana Island about fifty miles away. That evening at five o'clock I reached it, having made the leg in nine hours. Shortly afterward the wind dropped. I noticed that the Humboldt Current was moving me westward, away from the island. As I watched, the enchanted isles mysteriously subsided beneath the gentle surface of a perfectly calm sea.

Ahead now lay the Gambiers in 23° South Latitude, a jog of 3,000 miles across belts of calms, trade winds, and variable breezes. After twelve days of indifferent sailing, on March 4 I entered the trade winds and *Atom* kicked up her pretty heels. With a quartering wind she made for the South Seas while I set up the self-steering system. Pretty simple, this! A storm jib was set above the mizzen sail, which lay sleeping on its boom. The jib now resembled a giant weather vane, which, moved by the winds, worked the tiller by a series of ropes and blocks. By this means *Atom* kept her course like a steamer on the high seas.

In these parts of the ocean the southeast trades blow the entire year. Now they raised big hillocks and lacy swells that made *Atom* pitch slightly. A herd of clowning porpoises soon joined in the fun, pitching and rolling around her stern while *Atom* poked her nose among the white circus horses, fancifully laced with foam. Several days later she was surrounded by a score of dolphin or dorado. These fish, which the ancient Spaniards named for their grace, like to gambol around sailboats. Their other interest is providing excitement for flying fish and small octopi. The best way to catch dorado, incidentally, is to bait the hook with a piece of nylon cloth. If the dorados aren't given enough time to study the oddity, one of them, more curious than the herd or more hungry, will take it. For such simple labors I often had half a dozen pounds of fresh seafood.*

On March 29, at 17° South Latitude, I entered an area where one can encounter either southeast trades or the high west winds of the Southern Seas. This then was an area of sudden wind storms varying in force and direction. The barometer needle bounced around and gave me no useful information. Gradually the sky grew mean-looking and the air became cold and sharp. And then the whimsical wind jumped all over the compass! I didn't particularly want to lose my sticks, so the sails were dropped and *Atom* hove to under a storm jib. *Crack!*

The port backstay had snapped near the turnbuckles. I was more angered than worried because this was the fourth stainless steel cable to break since I'd left New York. Oh boy!

The wind then started to blow in earnest. Its face rubbed wrongly by the rough wind, the sea began punishing *Atom*. She'd seen worse times, however. Shouldering the rude seas aside on her starboard bow, she rode wonderfully while her skipper commenced working to repair the snapped shroud. By means of tackles I jury-rigged [the backstay] . . . and with nothing left to do, went below. Several days later

---

*Many sailors have complained about the difficulty of catching fish at sea. Gau's method: "Dorados commonly sought shelter beside *Atom*'s hull at night and in the morning would chase flying fish. Now, you cannot catch a single dorado; there have to be several present. To get their attention I stirred the water with a stick. They're very nosy, you know, and one would investigate the disturbance. Before he arrived I removed the stick and tossed my baited line (a cloth on a hook) at him. But I'd pull it back so that he couldn't study it. Soon other nosy fellows would arrive. *Then* I'd toss the line over and, sure enough, I'd catch one!"

the weather cleared and, catching a nice southeasterly, we blithely resumed our course.

On May 2, a Sunday, my plot located me thirty-five miles from Mangareva and about five miles from Timoe Atoll in the east. I became anxious because by evening the atoll, a ring of coral surrounding an islet and coconut trees, would be hard to see. I didn't want to be too near it at night so I tacked. Then I saw it, perhaps three miles off on the port side. As the sun skipped behind the horizon I rounded Timoe's sea-lapped northwest headland. That night I hove to, drifting slowly towards the Gambier Islands.

The next day it was all sail and a fair wind, and at eight o'clock that evening I was in the fairway of the islands where the reef lies five fathoms deep. Suddenly the water under *Atom*'s keel was a shining green where it had been a deep cobalt blue, and I saw my first coral. I stood for Akamarov Island and soon after weathered Makapov rock, which placed me in line with Mount Duff. *Now the entire archipelago opened!* It was the most tense moment of my voyage, because it was my first meeting with the islands of the South Seas. Frankly, I can't describe my feelings as before me a magical and charmed scene unfolded. As we made way the thrill increased, erasing the miseries of the voyage. It made me appreciate the slow pace of what I was doing.

The Sailing Directions indicated where to expect an entrance buoy to Rikitea harbor, but not finding any, I entered the complicated labyrinth of submarine shoals using a hand compass. Seeing some fishermen in outrigger canoes, I hailed them in Tahitian—they replied in French!

"American, no?" Seeing me nod, they asked, "You have the cigarette?"

Again I nodded, stating that I needed help getting in. A tall tea-colored Mangarevan jumped aboard after tying his canoe to *Atom*'s fat stern.

"Mamatoui," he said, "pearl diver and pilot, at your service!"

My feelings of enchantment were rapidly diminishing, and I exploded, "Where the hell are those damned buoys?"

Grinning broadly, he answered, "The buoys? Oh, you see that stump standing on the reef over there?" He pointed. "That is it! You are surprised, no?" (I was stunned.) "We call it beaconing the French way!"

Helped by this superb pilot, I anchored at midnight off the small commercial wharf, not far from the residence mole where a tiny French flag flew bravely. I had been at sea seventy-four days and I was happy to come out of it, for a while.

On May 17, at eight o'clock, the "pilot" came aboard, bringing in his canoe bananas, taros, mangoes, oranges. After shaking his hand I steered a "proper course, the French way," using the famous channel buoy, a stump on the reefs.

As I left the barometer was falling and the sky clouding. Abeam of Kena Island a squall struck, but I got bearings on the nearby islands just in time. I couldn't leave the tiller nor take my eyes off the compass as rain, like a cat-o'-nine-tails, lashed my face, falling so hard that I couldn't hear the engine. Through the rain screen I saw the dim outline of another island to starboard, and at ten o'clock I sailed out of the stony ring.

At sea I began to worry about *Atom*'s rigging. It seemed wise to cancel my intended visit to the Marquesas. . . . Let's face it, I was aching to reach Tahiti! About 900 miles west of the Gambiers lay this magnet of the seven seas, but between them was the ugly Tuamotu archipelago, a group of nearly a hundred low atolls. Feared by sailors, many of these corals lie just below the surface, their presence undetected until a poor sailor's keel gets the word. Most of the Tuamotu are deserted, the water surrounding them considered the most dangerous and difficult passage in the world.

Since leaving Mangareva, *Atom*, close-hauled on a starboard tack, had fought day and night against a stiff westerly. A midday sight on April 17 showed that the wind and the current had shifted me considerably off course, to 31°05′ South Latitude. I was now in the austral winter, and because I was on the edge of the great Southern Ocean the weather conditions were unusual. The South Pole gales rage incessantly in these parts, having no land mass to interfere. Often these gales do not allow the barometer to fall nor the poor sailor to reduce his sails in time. Almost instantly, therefore, the winds can veer and the seas become quickly populated with wild white horses. In thirty minutes this cold breath from Antarctica caused the temperature to drop from 35° to 15° Centigrade—I thought about winter in New York.

6

A Crowbar at Five Fathoms

On April 20 the wind settled south-southeast, and *Atom*, under a storm jib hauled taut, flew before the gale on a northwest course. She would rise from an abyss between liquid cliffs only to begin sliding down rolling crests. I anxiously watched the speed of the various waves, trying to determine which was the faster. Suddenly there was an apparent silence—almost a perfect calm in the midst of the tumult. Looking around, I saw a wall of water rise majestically, becoming higher and higher as it approached. Instinctively I grabbed the mizzenmast. I held my breath. The huge green barrier began bending forward, and at the same moment *Atom*'s stern seemed motionless. With the thundering noise of a watery avalanche the huge green toppling wall broke, smashing down onto *Atom*'s deck, sweeping before it everything not fastened securely—everything! Only a stalk of bananas tied to the backstay remained. Still holding tight, resisting the force of the swirling waters, I watched with keen sadness as fresh vegetables and fruits bobbed and rolled to leeward. Albatrosses, drawn by the anticipation of a shipwreck, descended often to examine this strange apron of fruit spreading over the sea's cold surface.

On May 29 a noon sight located me 104 miles southeast of the Duke of Gloucester Islands. My log showed an average speed of five knots, and the current I estimated at two knots. All was well. The next morning a stray beam of sunlight through the half-opened hatch woke me up. With one eye I glanced at my alarm clock—0715—and at a mirror set at a forty-five degree angle above the cabin compass (a poor man's version of a telltale compass). Closing the eye, I then listened carefully to the purring drone of *Atom*'s revolving propeller—the silent engine was in neutral—and to the sounds of seawater rubbing old *Atom*'s sides. Calculating rapidly, I estimated our speed at five knots. Lulled by the motion, I slipped into a half-sleep, mumbling, "It's nice weather. *Atom*'s on course. It's only seven or so in the morning. Grab another thirty minutes or so . . . " But at every lurch that annoying little sunbeam flashed across my eyelids. Unable to sleep and hungry, I got up. After putting the coffeepot on I looked out the hatch to see that all was well with my ocean.

I checked the self-steering system first, for I've always enjoyed watching the motions of the mizzen boom as it slowly swings every few seconds working the distant tiller. I admired the rig's simplicity and efficiency. Satisfied, I turned and looked forward—*oh God!* Straight ahead, thirty yards from *Atom*'s bow, was a beach with sand and trees. An island!

Tacking was impossible. I grabbed and freed the jib sheet and the mainsheet. Quickly I cut the self-steering ropes and pushed the helm hard over. *Atom* now moved slowly as her sails, breathless, began slatting. I was close to panic, because her bow was then only yards from the vertically-faced beach. Suddenly with a *Boom!* *Atom*'s sails filled and we fell away from this menace.

I hurriedly made up the sheets, and with the wind ahead *Atom* regained her speed and we began filling away. Dumbfounded, still shaken, I stared at the nearby island. I could not figure what had gone wrong. Later I sat on my bunk, a cup of cold coffee in hand, and began to laugh. There was nothing to laugh at but I laughed like a madman, a demonic laughter that thrilled me before I had finished.

Relieved, I checked my previous day's reckonings, but I found no error. The only answer was that the currents were stronger than I'd reckoned. For these parts of the ocean I grimly concluded that the Sailing Directions were less than accurate in their description of the currents.

Later I took bearings to identify the island. It was Nukuntipipi, the southernmost atoll of the Gloucesters, which old Quiros had discovered in 1606 while looking for a continent. I sailed around this silent, deserted, jewellike atoll at a safe league's distance. Nukuntipipi is truly an emerald isle in a sapphire sea! I was fascinated by its contrasting colors, the olive green of the palms against a backcloth of lustrous blue, a creamy beach whose trees concealed a mirrored lagoon with waters of luminous jade green. Near its southeast foreland a purplish blue sea contrasted vividly with the dazzling white of the ephemeral breakers.

For five weeks my voyage had been especially hard, and I needed shore leave. But Nukuntipipi, unfortunately, has no entrance. The currents soon carried me to westward, and this small paradise became a mere vapory haze on the ocean's face. To the north, in time, another haze materialized. It was the atoll Ann Annunga.

The sunset was depressing. About eight o'clock squalls arrived and the fun began. But below, in the dry coziness of my little sitting room, I ate well, and later lay in my bunk to enjoy the melody of the shrouds singing and whistling to the beat of a pattering rain. I was immersed in the sounds of the sea. . . .

On June 7 the sun found a hole in the baggy clouds and, despite heavy seas, I obtained two sights which placed me in the neighborhood of Mehetia, an isolated ocean bump sixty miles east of Tahiti. But as I neared the islet the weather changed its face, stirring up rough seas, which caused me to miss seeing Mehetia. Two days later the weather cleared completely and I saw in the southwest, seventy miles off, the summits of Mounts Aorai and majestic Arohea. Favored by a fair breeze, *Atom* perked up as though she knew where lay that pearl of the seven seas—Tahiti!

The next day we sailed along Tahiti's north coast, and the sight overcame any fatigue or anxieties I'd had. I soon tasted the sweet-smelling welcome of Tahiti. I was deeply stirred, for I'd nearly forgotten the smells and odors of earth. Having tired of open spaces, my excited eyes swept the distant mountains and valleys, noting every detail. But I felt a tinge of sadness; I'd arrived fifty years too late. Progress was everywhere.

But the timeless sky, the land and the seas, they hadn't changed. From *Atom*'s small deck I saw mountains dressed in forest green and vertical rock walls, still unclimbed, and I sailed over unsounded deeps—there remains something for the jaded eye. And protecting this ocean gem is a belt of coral that inhibits wanton destruction from waves spawned by the eternal swells. I soon sighted Point Venus, where Captain Cook conducted his famous celestial study of that body's passage in the sky. And my glass aided me in recognizing the enormous tamarind tree he planted. Villages came into focus, and through a screen of lush vegetation in the bottomlands between the great mountains, Aorai and Maran, I saw the meadows of the famed Diadem.

But it was time to think about my boat. The batteries, I discovered, were too low to start the engine. About four o'clock Fare Ute headland was abeam, and a mile later Papeete's harbor blinked its lashes behind a fan of breaking surf. After getting bearings on the towers marking the entrance I suddenly sighted a narrow cut in the 180-foot-wide reef belt. With the towers in line and the compass bearing 137° *magnetic*, I entered the cut under full sail.

I estimated that a three-knot current ran in the boiling rock cauldron of the cut . . . the seas thrashed about noisily. Suddenly I was sailing on a silken sea, but at the same moment the wind jumped ahead. *Atom* lost way immediately, hardly steaming the current, and I grew worried as I sensed her drifting toward the reefs. No doubt about it, she was the prey of that awful current. But the sudden arrival of the pilot boat with a towline saved us when we were only yards from the hard coralline face of the reef.

Towed to the commerce pier, I moored my boat among several romantic Gambiers Island schooners. After receiving pratique I relaxed with that peaceful feeling that comes *only* after a hard voyage is over.

While cleaning ship I admired the girls passing by, black hair floating in the scented air, *tiare* flowers behind their ears. I stepped to the post office, where a large packet of mail was handed to me. Stuffing it into my pockets, I sauntered about Papeete's colorful harbor. I returned to *Atom* tired, but remained topside to witness my first Tahitian sunset. Surely these are the most magnificent sunsets in the world. Awed, I stood on deck witnessing a miracle in color.

Earlier, I'd seen many stern-looking, enigmatic-faced Chinese. This naturally suggested a Chinese dinner, which, washed down with a decent Beaujolais, refreshed the inner man. That night I was lost in the forests of sleep.

Across the harbor was the sloop of a retired major, who began to invite *Atom*'s crew over for sundowners. To reach the sloop I simply swam the distance both ways. It was good exercise and I'd done it many times when one day, as I neared my boat, I saw a wahine standing on the deck. She was signaling to get my attention, which she had, for sure! Actually she was trying to warn me. "Don't look around!" she shouted. "Don't stop! Don't change your speed!" After I'd climbed aboard she pointed to the long black shadow of a shark.

The local boatyard couldn't accommodate *Atom* for three months. But when told that her bottom hadn't been cleaned since leaving Cristobal, eight months before, the harbor master said, "Gau, you're in for a surprise! A *bad* surprise." He then removed his boat from its slip and *Atom* went in for a cleaning. Once the painting was done he went over every square inch of her hull. To his astonishment, he found only one wormhole. "Don't touch it," he said. "Leave it alone. It'll come out by itself in a few days."

Three days later I found hanging from the hole a long white worm resembling a long soft piece of macaroni. Its head was slightly larger than its body. The head had a circular horny disc, which enabled the little beast to mouth its way by digging galleries in *Atom*'s belly.

One Sunday, enjoying myself, I attended a *tamarara,* a kind of cookout, where chicken, fish, lobster, pork, breadfruit, taros, yams, and other delicacies, wrapped in leaves, were placed on embers in a hole in the ground. As the foods were braising we danced or jumped, according to one's condition, to the fast rhythms of drums and guitars. Flowers behind my ear, heavily garlanded, I ate with my fingers. Then, the dancing resuming, the jerking and swaying figures sensuously highlighted the evening. With the sounds of drums and guitars in my ears, the vision of bodies interpreting the joy of living in my brain, I somehow made it back to *Atom*, where I slept as a sailor ought.

Finally the day came. Helped by my Tahitian friend, Tetua, on March 21, 1955,* I raised *Atom*'s anchor from the harbor mud where it had lain quietly for nine months. A firm handshake and Tetua dove into the waters. As *Atom* motored quietly across the harbor a nearby schooner sounded her horn. Outside, I set a course for the Leeward Islands and their most famous member, Bora Bora, one hundred miles away. As we cleared Tahiti my heart sank, for I was leaving an island men dream of finding, an island where there is peace, where life is absolutely infused with charm. But Tahiti soon gathered her flowered skirts and stole quietly away in a blue haze. I now faced the other half of the Pacific.

That afternoon I sailed off the neighboring island of Moorea, but the sight saddened me because the sea was so beautiful, the sky so blue, the winds so gentle. I mused for some time, asking myself, *Why* was I

---

*This date is highly suspect. Gau's passport, examined twenty years later, showed an American Consulate stamp for Noumea, New Caledonia, dated *28* March 1955. The pages remaining in the passport do not show a French Entree stamp for Noumea. Whether Gau called there—he was off New Hebrides in mid-June—is unknown.

leaving? The only answer was the attraction of adventure and a peculiar passion for struggle, with its loneliness, its privations and fears, to say nothing of the long spells of despondency that must occur on small boats making long passages. I couldn't explain it then; I can't now, especially to one who is not attracted to the deep sea. But since I'd committed myself to the long voyage, I would—Goddamn it!—do it. To clear away my misgivings, all I needed was a good strong north-easterly.

Three days of pleasant sailing off the Leeward Islands, and at five o'clock on March 24 I entered beautiful Bora Bora. White-sailed catamarans, like royal swans, animated the lagoon. In Fanui Bay I found Bob Grant's boat laid up, her compass busted by a fallen spar. Bob, whom I'd met in Papeete, had been roaming the South Seas aboard American boats looking for adventure. His frank, tough face, bronzed by spray and sun and framed by a thick black windjammer's beard, conceals a nasal oath-laced Boston accent. And in this colorful language he informed me that he, too, was planning a crossing to the New Hebrides.*

---

*Jean's lifelong fight against established order was exacerbated when he'd visited Tahiti earlier. There, the enforced attitudes of the missionaries toward clothing had, so he believed, introduced pneumonia. Tahiti is subject to numerous sudden showers, and the native's wet clothing contributed to lowered resistance to pulmonary infection, a situation Jean deplored in conversations with friends. But if his sense of injustice was ineffectual, his friend, Bob Grant, vented his antagonism at the church in a devastating manner: he made fun of its hold on the public.

One day Grant said, "C'mon, Johnny, we're gonna play a dirty trick on the priest." Uneasy at his new friend's offbeat conduct Gau agreed reluctantly to accompany Grant to church. There the preacher (or priest) "dirty, and holding a big cigar," stentoriously cried, "Now everybody sing!"

Later as the collection plate was passed the priest, waving his thick cigar, croaked, "Now, we collect the money!" A plate was passed among the sullen gathering. A dour-faced deacon eventually reached Bob Grant. The plate was thrust at him, the deacon determined no one escape.

Grant began by searching a trouser pocket to its depths. Then he methodically searched the other pocket, his huge frame bobbing and twisting with obvious sincere effort. He stood up abruptly to search even deeper in his trouser pockets, first one, then the other, tugging, his shirttail awry, his arms pumping with New England vigor. Electrified by the sight of the bearded man struggling frantically to find a coin on his person, the small gathering began twisting in their seats. Gau, making himself smaller in the pew, whispered loudly, "Bob, please let me give him a coin . . . *please!*"

"No!" Grant's great voice raced through the sultry room.

He abruptly sat down, bent over and removed one shoe which he promptly placed in the collection plate! As the deacon started Grant deftly removed the other shoe and dropped *it* into the plate! The deacon grabbed the plate with both hands as Bob shouted, "I've got it!"

The sound of a single coin, an American penny, falling in the plate was lost in the howling din of the faithful. Jean guffawed so hard he slid out of the tiny church pew.

Next day in the village of Vaitipe I had the ship's papers stamped after tramping for two miles over a green path beside the lagoon. The vegetation I passed was lush and, even though all green, variegated. In the shade, women sat weaving mats while their men split sea-warmed coconuts to be dried for copra. In front of the French administrator's office, beside the lagoon, I found a small monument to Alain Gerbault. That grand seaman's profile stood in relief on a bronze plate, and stamped in the marble, in French, were the words: "First Frenchman to Circumnavigate the World Alone, Alain Gerbault, 1893-1941, in Firecrest, 1923-1929."

Eight days later I had to leave Bora Bora, or I couldn't have ever! It is that beautiful and magical. But ahead of me lay a tricky and dangerous passage: Samoa, New Hebrides, Coral Sea, New Guinea, and the nasty Torres Strait. On April 2 *Atom*, in company with Grant's boat, *Korrigan*, cleared Tevanui pass for Samoa, some 1,200 miles westward.

Korrigan's brown sails standing proudly against the sky, she soon overtook the much smaller *Atom*. In Bora Bora I'd exchanged the mainsail for a smaller marconi sail, which would make handling easier at night and in gales. Since *Atom* and crew are never in a hurry and sail only for their pleasure, that she had a smaller sail area didn't matter. But at five o'clock that evening I chanced to look aft and was startled to see that *Korrigan* had changed course and was headed northwest. I wondered why.

Because the trade winds were feeble and astern *Atom* made little progress, her self-steering barely working. Twenty days after leaving Bora Bora my sun sight placed me in the vicinity of Rose Island. At dawn on April 23 this mysterious island was only a few miles away.

A deserted atoll of square shape, Rose Island lies in 14°32' South Latitude and 168°08' West Longitude. Actually the atoll has two islands—Rose, which is about 500 meters in diameter, and Sand, 200 meters long and 100 wide—and a sandy part of the reef. A thick stand of trees, sixty feet high, identifies it, as do the thousands of seabirds that inhabit the trees and surface.

I was stopping because of a personal reason, one that began seventeen years ago. In 1938 my first boat, . . . *Onda*, was moored in a New York shipyard undergoing refitting. I slept aboard to save costly rent in town. The elderly night watchman had been a master mariner, and he often came and spent the evenings with me in the warmth of my cabin. We had in common a love of boats, and the old man . . . had himself roamed the South Seas, and gave me much free advice. One evening he said, "Listen, son, you still want to sail around the world?"

I looked at him evenly. "But of course."

"Well, you'll probably pass through or near Samoa?"

"Yes." I shook my head. "I wouldn't miss seeing those islands."

"You'll have lots to choose from, lad. There are dozens of 'em." He bent forward. "But I want to tell you a secret. My course is done, so I may as well tell you."

He waited for me to relight my pipe. We studied each other closely as he said, matter-of-factly, "In 1923 I was shipwrecked on Rose Island"—he pointed without hesitating to a small island on the chart before us—"Here! You see it? I was bound for 'Frisco out of Melbourne on a small 200-ton tub. Never-ending weather, including the threat of a hurricane, made us stop at Rose Island. We was moored to the rocks and riding to two anchors. We felt pretty safe."

He sat on both hands while I relit my pipe. "No sir! That hurricane hit us and turned that lagoon into a boiling pot in minutes! The anchors broke, or the chains did. Anyway, we was on the beach at the time, and saw our boat smash on that coral and sink in six fathoms."

He was getting ready to tell me something, so I studied him closely. "Now, Jean, I want to tell you—and don't ask too many questions—that there was on board that tub *two hundred bars of silver.*" This time I didn't relight my pipe.

The old man bent forward suddenly. "They're still there!" he whispered. "Only I knew they was aboard. I been planning to go back since to get 'em. Anyway, we fixed up the two small boats and eventually we reached Manua Island. But before we left Rose, since the masts was popping out of the water, I had 'em cut so nothing could be seen of the wreck. I took accurate bearings." He leaned forward and tapped the chart with a thick finger. "Now you take the bearing of this rock cape by the tip of this clump of high trees. . . . "

Still talking, without hesitating, the old seaman began to draw a plan. From the tone of his voice and his excited manner I knew that the yarn was not invented. Finished, his eyes glittering, he handed it to me. Since that day my mind has been focused on Rose Island.

While in Papeete I bought from a Chinese storekeeper an underwater helmet, a primitive model where the air intake was regulated by the tongue. I couldn't afford a better one than this, which I'd found behind a counter on a dusty shelf. I paid ten bucks for it, and a friend who worked in a hospital filled four bottles with compressed air. I'd previously read that old wrecks are often covered with a thick gangue of coral that requires explosives to remove. So my friend had also given me a small box of dynamite, which I stowed under *Atom*'s cabin table.

I'd been told that dynamite in that form wasn't dangerous, but getting up or sitting down, I stubbed my toes on the box, and each time I had a *queer* feeling. So, convinced that I wouldn't need it, I gave it away. My Rose Island wreck, I figured, wasn't too old, and surely coral doesn't grow so fast. This, remember, was my first encounter with the Pacific. I had a lot to learn.

About eight o'clock I arrived off the island and, with the sails down, motored to the northeast side of the reef, a flat impassable barrier strewn with huge blocks and lashed by vicious waves. At the entrance waves were breaking on both sides in an inextricable tangle of teeth, points, shoals, reef, and foaming breakers. A strong current was flowing, roaring like a cataract, through the pass. It was a daytime nightmare.

Frankly, to go ashore at Rose Island had been almost the chief reason for making the voyage. And now that I stood off its entrance I was afraid. What if I didn't make it through the pass?

Reason warning me of the danger, I started to tack. Suddenly, impulsively, I gave *Atom*'s accelerator full throttle. She threw herself into the narrow opening . . . the waters boiled and the din of the breaking and rushing waters was deafening. The tiller was hard to handle and I was really worried. I couldn't afford any error. At full throttle *Atom* seemed to gain slowly but in the middle of the cut I sensed that we'd stopped—oh Christ! Should I tack? No, that would only bring us onto the reef quicker. Then calm of a sort returned and I began to perceive that we were making some progress. Seconds later my anxiety diminished as *Atom* entered a quiet lagoon, which I crossed until I felt safe from the barbarous din of the cut. Rounding up, I anchored in twelve fathoms a few yards off a small white beach.

I had reached a seventeen-year-old goal. Small in the eyes of the world, as an achievement, it may well be. To me, however, it was exciting, and such is the nature of the soul that I cast a conqueror's glance over the lagoon, its awesome pass, noisy breakers, and distant reefs. But a great weariness overcame me and I lay down on the warm deck and fell asleep.

I slept until noon the next day. Then, like a startled rabbit, I got up and loaded the dinghy with the diving helmet, the rifle, and some food. The most important gear placed aboard was my hand compass. Rowing, I soon was above the wreck—and at the first dive I found it, in five fathoms! The old man hadn't lied.

My excitement was curbed, however, by the sight of coral wrapping every inch of the wreck. I tried to attack the sharp rough surface with a large screwdriver but the gangue, fifteen inches thick, couldn't be broken. It barely broke under my feeble efforts.

The first bottle of air nearly exhausted, I rose to the surface, fervently cursing myself for getting rid of that dynamite. I climbed into the dinghy to sit and to think. With the setting sun, I noticed, the light on the bottom was diminishing. Discouraged, overwhelmed with regret, almost sick with the magnitude of my stupidity, I acknowledged that there was nothing I could do.

I returned to *Atom*. My stomach, twisting with hunger, reminded me that I hadn't eaten since before arriving at Rose Island. But hunger of that sort is easily remedied. Before long the day's emotions overwhelmed me, my head grew heavy, my worries faded, and I fell into a restless half-sleep.

At dawn, rummaging around in *Atom*'s engine room, I found a crowbar. To reduce the diving effort I moored *Atom* nearly above the wreck site. I dove and vigorously attacked the coralled wreck, but underwater I had little strength. The need to constantly regulate my air flow by tongue made the problem worse. Fifteen minutes later I had made a hole about the size of a fist, at the bottom of which the crowbar could tap the hull. Frustrated, worried, I jammed the bar into the hole. Using it as a lever, I actually twisted that crowbar a bit! That damned coral would not give. I returned to *Atom* and to the two remaining bottles of compressed air.

After a good meal I calmed down, reasoning that without the right materials my efforts to recover the silver were foolish. Thinking no more about the wreckage and its silver bars I went exploring, landing the dinghy elsewhere on the beach. As I landed clouds of birds arose, and within seconds they had become aggressive.

To avoid a sudden shower I ran to a stand of trees, and stepping into the shade, I was immediately bathed by a dampness and a heavy smell. The density of that vegetation was so great that the rain couldn't penetrate it. The shower over, I emerged from the stand on the other side of the island, where I faced a great expanse of white breakers beyond which lay an enormous blue tablecloth of sea. Breathing deeply the good salt air, I sat in the shade eating papaws and drinking coconut juice.

While I sat I watched several dazzling-white birds sitting quietly on the branches of a nearby pandanus tree. Suddenly I raised my gun and fired at the middle of the covey. With a thundering noise thousands of birds rose at the sound. Oddly, in the midst of this great booming, rushing noise I heard the cackling of startled booby birds. As the noise died I picked up the poor bird I had shot. I felt ashamed and remorseful as I examined its torn body, ruined by my bullet. Poor white bird! Encounter with man, I thought, was seldom worth the effort. Having gotten used to solitude over the years, I no longer felt its weight as do most people. Still, holding that small warm bloodied body I was overwhelmed with feeling. When I viewed the poetry that is this white-belted virginal island, where only birds of the sea live, I felt I had intruded on a small planet.

Much of the afternoon I spent exploring the island. I found—let the record show!—*no* footprints. Nor was Sand Island any more productive, except that to windward I found in the surf all sorts of debris: tree trunks, pieces of cork, glass fishnet balls. I also found the half-buried and worm-eaten stub of a ship's bow, and nearby, small sand mounds that contained turtle eggs.

Laden with papaws, coconuts, turtle eggs, and shells, I boarded *Atom*, where I spent hours stowing things properly. Then oysters seemed a fitting dish to celebrate my long-awaited presence on Rose Island. From a bar not far away I collected several the size of soup plates. Aboard my boat I started to prepare them Tahitian style: brown the meat for a while, add coconut milk, and wash with lemon juice.

By the light of a setting sun I opened the first oyster. *Gling!* Rolling in the dishpan was a pearl the size of a small marble! The second oyster was opened in half the time, and *again*, a pearl as big as the first. The third was just an oyster. But two out of three isn't bad. Rose Island, I gloated, had many thrills.

The next day at daybreak, outfitted with my diving device and a bag, I emerged on deck—Jean Gau, Pearl Diver! Some time later, the bag full of shells, I rowed back to *Atom* and emptied the bag of gray-lipped mollusks on the deck. Though my hands and fingers ached, I kept cutting the oysters open until I had eleven splendid pearls, which I placed in a small canvas bag. Two of the pearls were especially lovely: one a pastel blue, the other a delicate opaline yellow. Both were of a good size. With these gems under my belt I felt not too bad about my inability to reach the wreck and pry open its encrusted secrets.

That afternoon I decided to explore elsewhere in the lagoon. I dove deep and entered a coralline forest, where, in huge blocks of multicolored polyps, I saw plants with waving leaves and hosts of start fish, fast of fin and extremely wary. I found giant tridacnas, those wolftraps of the South Seas. And where the lagoon bottom descended rapidly, its shadowy deeps becoming purplish, I saw the outlines of luminous shrubby trees, with animated flowers and black-finned sharks nervously circling the area. What a sight! What a riot of colors that, with distance, faded delicately, almost imperceptibly. I was strangely moved at the sight of this watery fairyland, this strange surreal seascape beneath the surface of Rose Island's lagoon.

Three days and I made ready to leave my island. Satisfied now with my lot, I broke anchor on April 26. As we neared the awful pass the boat picked up speed, but the helm seemed lifeless in the rushing currents. Ahead seemed nothing but boiling, crashing waters. But there is a god who watches over the lone sailor: *Atom* was thrown out of that tight entrance like a cork from a wine bottle! Some time afterwards I looked back at Rose Island, but she had disappeared, even the tall trees, behind a lip of foaming surf that curled and broke and will forever.

April 28 I passed the Manua Islands, and one day later the high peaks of Tuitila Island loomed in the twilight. The next day *Atom* sailed between Aunuo and the main island, and against a stiff tidal current. About four o'clock a strong gale of wind blew and I got the main down and a gasket passed around as a blinding rainstorm obscured everything. But I had picked a good compass direction from my chart, the line between the entrance to Pago Pago and the end of Aunuo Island. Suddenly in the dark and rain a strange thin figure emerged, shaking to the motion of the swells, a figure that at first seemed to bar my way. Puzzled, I then discerned a green light flickering at one end, and the sound of a sad bell was heard. As we neared the faintly obscene figure I recognized, here in the Pacific, a big black buoy of the American type used to mark channel entrances. Despite its ugliness I was happy to see it! And then the clouds evaporated, the wind fell off, and Pago Pago opened her green arms, rimmed with high mountains that plunged quickly into the sea.

The magic of this island was revealed as I sailed past a headland. The harbor, completely obscured from seaward, stepped out to meet me. As we closed I anxiously searched the forests of masts. Then I spied *Korrigan* moored at the American naval station. As we neared, the black-bearded friendly face of Bob Grant, like a jack-in-the-box, popped out of the hatch. Beside him I saw the head of a handsome Samoan girl.

"C'mon, Johnny! Give us a line from that damned tub of yours."

From Bob only would I allow such talk of *Atom*!

Later, formalities of entering port over, we went aboard *Korrigan* for dinner and tall ones. Bob introduced me to Nanai, whose sarong needed no alterations. Nanai was large velvet eyes in a coffee complexion, a smile that revealed pearls, black glossy hair, and a red flower behind a perfect ear. And she spoke English with a delicious island accent, which contrasted amusingly with Bob's twang.

While Nanai prepared dinner I recalled with pleasure the inevitable menu: fried potatoes, beefsteak, onions, vegetables, butter, and breadfruit, all washed down with a sprightly Beaujolais from *Atom*'s private cellar. What a pleasure to contemplate a dinner like that after having been deprived for so long! What a hunger awaited Nanai's efforts!

While we attacked the dishes Bob told me more of his adventures. Part of his ability to tell a great tale lies in making the listener part of the adventure. That night it was merry in *Korrigan*'s cabin, merry with a gaiety that only a small band of happy souls can make. And it washed away or pleasantly mocked the unlucky days at sea.

The meal over, I asked Bob to explain his sudden change of course upon leaving Bora Bora. "Ah, Johnny,"—his teeth gleaming and his laugh tinged with mischievousness—"I deviated from my course only to, you know, *enjoy* the scenery. You know, the landscape of Suvarov Atoll (about 300 miles east-northeast of Rose Island)?" I bit my lip to avoid asking the big question—did Bob find *his* rare pearl. I didn't ask, thinking, "You keep your secret, Bob. I'll keep mine." We parted the best of pals and remain so now.*

Five days later Bob left for Port Vila in New Hebrides. But I was in no hurry, for there was plenty to do and to see. Bob advised Nanai to settle on board *Atom* for the length of my stay (I didn't object). Minutes before his departure Nanai gave him a basket she'd plaited of bamboo, filled with fresh foods. I gave him my costly diving apparatus, saying, "It will be very useful, my friend, if you ever feel like seeing more of *your* island." This strong and vigorous man was moved more than he cared to show. When he left, *Atom* accompanied *Korrigan* as far as the entrance, where I tacked while Bob Grant, alone, headed out to sea.

Busy at the helm, I watched the lovely Nanai. Tears the size of pearls welled in her lively eyes, unable to detach themselves from the brown sails of the distant *Korrigan*. A little later *Atom* returned to her mooring.

Later that evening, when I returned to my boat laden with vegetables and fruits, Nanai welcomed me with her delicious smile and served me

---

*But did Jean keep his secret from Bob? Not recorded by Jean is the fact that Grant asked him about Rose Island. Gau proudly showed his eleven pearls, "the size of a fingertip." Bob Grant, clearing his throat, asked, "Is that all, Johnny?" As Jean watched, his dark-bearded friend opened a bag *full* of pearls, which he'd presumably found at Suvarov Island.

an appetizer. Humming a folk song, she then prepared the evening meal. A clever cook and expert in preparing raw fish à la Polynesia, she cut the fish into small cubes, soaked them in the juice of lemon, and washed them in coconut milk. A chicken simmered in the stew pot, luxuriating in a bath of tantalizing odors. Later, with yams, taro, and toasted breadfruit, we ate what a sailor might call a feast.

Sixteen days in paradise lapsed quickly. But despite the tranquility there and the hardships ahead, I felt the need to carry on with my original plan. But this particular leavetaking was very difficult. Yet I felt an even greater lure, the lure of the unknown of tomorrow, and for this inexplicable reason I put to sea on May 17. In the cool of the morning *Atom* motored slowly out of the quiet harbor. A lone figure at the end of the wharf waved and called, "*Aaloa uma tofua manuiri. . . .*" I cannot translate, for its poignancy is still with me.

7

En Route to Adventure

Tutuila Island dissolved behind a curtain of rain and *Atom* once more was in the passionate embrace of a mighty sea. It was two days before I recovered my sense of sea routine. Then my heart swelled with the mixture of sadness and joy which the sea has always provided. Her sails bellying, *Atom* self-steered toward New Hebrides and Port Vila on Egate Island, about 1,200 miles distant and fifteen days' sailing time. But the trade winds "wore out," or something, and a calm slipped in, assuming command of a sea whose look was that of youth—no wrinkles, absolutely none. Then warm puffs arrived to dally with *Atom*'s skirts, but these fickle weaklings soon left. The circle was flat and oily but every ten seconds the widespread undulations of a swell caused *Atom* to heave and fall in a motion long and gradual, an absolutely perfect rhythm. But she rolled also, and at each roll the racket of clicking blocks and slatting sails increased until water began slopping on deck. Then the oscillations diminished, whereupon the boat found her balance again, only to begin the cycle moments later with no obvious apparent reason for it.

Slowly, steadily, *Atom* and her patient crew performed this melancholy ocean ballet. Seabirds flew past, at times hovering to watch the

101

camel crossing the strangely moving desert.

One week after Samoa I stood off Fiji, and between May 24 and 26 crossed the 180° meridian. Consequently, the day of May 25 is not recorded in *Atom*'s log.

A group of New Hebrides islands hove into view ten miles eastward the morning of June 11. At nine o'clock I passed the eastern headland of Tongariki, steering for Egate thirty miles away. As we neared, the weather looked bad, by sunset it *was* bad. The barometer fell quickly and the high breeze which had blown for an hour gave way to a stiff gale from the south. The heavens turned black. A tremendous swell lifted the boat several meters high in seconds, the winds gusting enough to put her beam-to. *Atom*'s skipper has never feared (too much) the conditions of wind and wave, but when there's a coral reef in the vicinity, he admits to worrying. I couldn't leave her to herself so I took the helm to try to minimize the harsh lurchings of the boat. It was hard going because *Atom* actually dove, nose first, into the waters, and the shock made her shudder like a drunkard. I was worried for fear her sticks would be tossed overboard. By midnight the storm was at its climax. The clouds dumped their vast reservoirs and the din was almost overwhelming. Sea after sea came out of the starboard quarter to climb quickly aboard *Atom*'s bow and run aft to threaten the crew. The sky was streaked with red and glimmered dazzlingly while, like a rain of fire, lightning fell into the sea; it was a nightmare in color! I had to stay at the tiller twenty-four hours, each of which seemed a leaden eternity.

At dawn it was still pitch-black. Thirty minutes later it was blacker than ever. But any sailor knows that daylight has to come in time. And it did, under a gloomy sky, while the frenzied Pacific, lashed by the winds, tore and plucked at its own body. In the midst of this natural orgy I sighted to leeward, about ten miles off, the island of Matasso, and to the southeast, about fifteen miles away, Egate's tall peaks. With the main down I tacked and ran under reduced rags for Matasso to find shelter from the storm.

Sailing close to the wind, hours later I was under the lee of the island, whose wild beauty picked up my tired spirits. Although I looked for a good anchorage, I sensed that the depths close to the beach were excessive. Egate was fifteen miles away, and to reach Port Vila I would have to sail seventy-five miles in a straight course. But, under sail, this means sailing perhaps three times that distance. To try meant also fighting the southeast trade winds and the Equatorial Current. The only thing to do was to stay put. This upset me, for I had expected mail at Port Vila and I was anxious to see Bob Grant. So I hauled *Atom*'s mainsail and laid a course for New Guinea, 1,300 miles away. It was the only thing to do.*

Atom could tend to herself under the winds then blowing. I went below to rest, but the bunk seemed to keep slipping away, a sensation I'd not experienced before. But my eyes finally closed, and as the strains and worries yielded I slept.

On June 12 I sailed into the great Coral Sea. I now question the wisdom of giving such an attractive term to this dangerous region: shores, islands at sea level, coral barriers, and everywhere a swell, an unrelenting, never-ending undulation from the Pacific. That body, swollen by the permanent blowing of the trades—blowing always in the same direction over boundless sea spaces—creates waves that sometimes attain the heights of winter storm waves in more temperate areas.

On June 26, Taguea Island, in the Louisiade Archipelago southeast of New Guinea, marched over the horizon. A reef which begins northwest of Port Moresby runs along New Guinea's southern coast to the archipelago, a distance of 500 miles. In many places the submerged reef extends one to ten miles from the land. . . . the reef slopes gently on its interior side, but to seaward it plunges vertically two or three hundred feet.

The weather was thick, the seas heavy, the land hidden by a dense mist. But the sun sneaked through and allowed four shots, despite the boat's violent jerks and the heights of the waves. Once plotted, my data showed me to be within half a mile of error.

During the southeast monsoon season the weather here is usually misty, especially in the period of strong winds. A ship, under those conditions, will near the reef barrier before it sees the land. My best solution was to tack landward in daylight, following the reef edge, and at night to stand carefully out to sea.

After twenty-five days of this exhausting navigation the sky cleared and my sun sights located me about thirty miles southeast of the entrance I sought, Basilisk Pass. Soon the mountains of New Guinea† stood outlined in the mists—I recognized Mount Astrolabe at once. To

---

* Years later Gau, asked if he'd ever seen the harrowing ceremony in which young men dive headfirst from great heights, their feet bound by a vine, replied, "Oh, you mean in New Hebrides? I stopped just to see the ceremony." Pressed for details, he said, "You mentioned it. You saw it?" His interviewer shook his head. "Then," rasped Gau, "I can't tell you more." Although he commented on the ceremony's now lost religious meaning, he would not provide more details. Knowing that he did not anchor at Egate, we are puzzled. Did Gau go ashore, contrary to his account?

† The second largest island in the world.

the west, waves pounded angrily against the remains of a steamer, creating spray and a strange halo above the wreck. As the roiling swell poured through a wide gap in the reef a column of atomized water sprang up, roaring, from the cut. The sight pained me, for it reminded me of my first Atlantic crossing and shipwreck.

But my somber spirits lifted as I sighted, two miles westward of the hulk, a tiny figure looming vaguely through the vapors: a buoy, looking petrified in the mists and spray, pointed like a thin finger at the entrance. Under sail I entered the winding channel. Inside the lagoon the swell gradually diminished, and on its lake-green surface naked Papuans sailed strange spritsail catamarans. Forty-five days after finding no anchorage at Matasso Island, I anchored in Port Moresby Bay.

Three days later three men standing on the pier cheerily asked permission to come aboard. Down below, we talked until one asked if I liked to shoot. "No. I don't like to kill animals." But I was told that they had in mind hunting in the jungle. The chance to see the famous New Guinea jungle was too great. I accepted their invitation, for the moment overcoming my distaste for shooting.

By jeep we drove at dawn to the edge of the dense jungle. Minutes later we walked into the depths of an equatorial forest. One of the men, a botanist, named many of the plants, giving them long names. For my part, I saw the indestructible teak, giant rubber, banana, mango, and sago trees. The latter, incidentally, holds inside its trunk a marrowlike substance which is eaten over much of Polynesia. I recognized ebony, mahogany, red pepper, prodigious lianas, and palm trees of every sort. On a winding, narrow path, between thickets of bamboo and cactus, the vegetation thickened until daylight failed and it became hot and moist. A large iguana flashed across the path, to be lost immediately in the brush. An hour later we emerged from the brush into a glade where several huts squatted on stilts.

The mushroom-shaped houses were raised to afford protection from headhunters. As we approached, native women, stark naked, ran off, gesticulating and cackling like parrots gone amok. Sitting alone in front of one hut was an old Papuan, who, seeing us approach, smiled. Soot-black, squat of body, thick-headed, with a low forehead, large flat nose, and thick lips . . . the *perfect* cannibal of my youth! Dressed in a cloth of fiber, his tatooed body was covered by cabalistic figures executed with an extreme delicacy and design. Big copper bracelets adorned his fleshy wrists and forearms. A pig's tooth rested in one ear.

He eyed me closely while puffing an enormous pipe.

Someone spoke to him in Pidgin English. When he'd finished the old cannibal turned, spat with disgust, and said in perfect English, "Gentlemen, I want to help you, but *please* speak English." Flabbergasted, I asked, "But where did you learn to speak English . . . ?" He had learned, he said, both language and table manners in a mission school.*

Resuming our trek, accompanied by a new guide named Nakouzi, we crossed under countless liana arches, stepped over thousands of fallen trees, and tore our hands on giant brambles and thorny bushes, always walking on a carpet of moss and dead matter which gave under our uneasy gait. I enjoyed seeing the great variety of trees. Some, barren and skeletonlike and supported by thousands of flowery vines, appeared mummified. Others had strangely colored branches. Extraordinary to my eyes but commonplace to those of Nakouzi was this combination of beauty and menace.

"What's that?" he suddenly screamed. Poor Nakouzi had mistaken a snake for a vine. Told they were harmless, he picked it up by its neck.

---

*On another occasion in Port Moresby, an octogenarian Papuan visited *Atom* daily to "bum a cigarette." When Gau prepared to weigh anchor, he discovered that *Atom*'s hooks were caught in coral. He asked his "old, wrinkled friend" where he could find a diver. "Me dive, Cap'n." The black stumps of broken teeth appeared behind the elderly man's bluish lips.

"You!" Gau thought, "you old thief! I'll probably never see my anchors again."

"Gimme cigarette first, Cap'n."

After the men had smoked, the old man dove into the water, "down, down deep," Gau recalled. As he loosened the flukes Gau hoisted the anchor. Another smoke and the Papuan dove to recover the second anchor. He failed, so the two men manually broke it out. To show his appreciation, Gau gave his friend twenty-five pounds Australian, a bottle of whiskey, and a carton of cigarettes.

Grinning happily the old Papuan said, "Thankee, Cap'n! Tonight I gonna get drunk."

"But why?"

"Because tonight I gonna beat my wife."

"Beat your wife! But why?"

"Because when I'm *not* drunk she beat be!"

Earlier Jean's insatiable curiosity led to the following dialogue aboard *Atom* between the skipper and the old Papuan.

". . . Have you ever eaten, you know, man's flesh?"

"Sure."

"Does it taste good?"

"Very good."

"Does it taste like lamb?"

"No. Good."

"Like wallaby?"

"No! Very good."

"Like beef?"

"No, no! Tastes *very* good!"

Someone suggested a smoke—a good idea, for we were all shaken by his yelping.

Thirty minutes later we were off, Nakouzi leading at a good clip. Suddenly he signaled us to fall into step with him. As we did we heard bushes bending and the cracking of twigs. Nakouzi suddenly stopped in front of a bush. He bent over and pushed aside a branch, his grinning face showing clove-black teeth. Before us, a couple of wallabies capered in the middle of a small dale beyond the bush. One of the men fired four rounds, the sounds dull and leaden in the thick moistness. The smoke, like a miniature cloud, lingered two feet above the ground.

Our guide dodged into the brush and reappeared, drawing by the legs two superb four-footed animals with silky-gray mouse fur. A strange animal, the wallaby, for its hind legs are five times the size of its forelegs, its tail flat, and the head that of a gazelle. One of the Papuans suggested we eat.

I kindled a fire while Nakouzi skinned the beasts, which we roasted on bamboo spits. As other men disappeared into the jungle to gather fruit, the smell of grilled meat, like a natural incense, rose in the dense air. It actually made me tipsy.

I noticed that when Nakouzi said lunch was ready his eyes were glazed and his nostrils actually dilated. In time, as our small party gallantly devoured filet of wallaby, washed by juices of wild lemon, the formidable appetite of Nakouzi gave me a high idea of the stomach capacity of Papuans.

Sated with food and exercise, we reached Port Moresby late at night.

I began a difficult and dangerous leg of my voyage on July 21, 1955, when I left for Torres Strait,* the passage of which is barred by the Great Barrier Reef, which reaches to New Guinea in the Gulf of Papona. This phenomenal barrier consists of a 1,600-kilometer-long shoal or bank and a dangerous archipelago 2,500 kilometers long. Nearly five thousand kilometers of submerged rocky coral, and only one pass (Bligh Passage), with a sandy islet called Bramble Cay to mark the entrance.

Beyond the Basilisk Pass an enormous swell and strong wind met us. But with her small sail area *Atom* crossed the gulf in two days, and on

---

*Discovered by Luis Vaez de Torres in 1606. By sailing it, Torres proved that New Guinea is not part of the Southern Continent. James Cook named it Endeavour Strait in about 1770, but the historian Dalrymple, using one of Torres's ancient letters, proposed the name it now carries.

July 24, at two in the afternoon, we stood off the channel's entrance, a few miles northwest of Bramble Cay. It was then too late to reach one of the islands before nightfall. To moor leeward of the cay wasn't conceivable—I didn't want to anchor in thirty or forty meters on a coral bottom. And I couldn't heave to because the currents here run four to five knots. The only maneuver was to remain in the middle of the channel by jogging on and off until daybreak.

I spent a restless night, tacking often, my eyes trying to pierce the tarry black, my ears straining for the sounds of waves crashing on unseen reefs. But I heard nothing except the monotonous whistling and moaning of the winds nervously thrumming in the rigging. At five o'clock the winds, which had blown steadily through the night, abated.

I knew that in the strait during the southeast monsoon season the trades let up for two or three hours, about five in the morning, and as the sun rises they pick up. As the dawn glimmered feebly in the east, though the western sky remained pitch-black, I tacked. Close to the wind, *Atom* made for either Dalrymple or Rennel Island, her navigator insisting she'd find a safe leeward mooring after several hours' sailing.

I ached with fatigue. Suddenly I saw to westward a white line against a black sky! I rushed up the ratline to the spreaders. As far as I could see a fringe of foam stretched in an arc across the horizon. Slipping down the ratline, I quickly tacked northeast. Down in the cabin, I examined the chart and concluded that what I'd seen were the Warrior Reefs, which lay from northeast to southwest a distance of thirty-eight miles.

The sun was rising, but the absence of wind made me worry that we were being pulled by an unseen current. I was soon convinced of it, that we were being sucked and pulled towards the reef, whose dark bulk loomed through clouds of spray. Christ! What could I do? In minutes we'd be aground. I jumped down into the cabin and hastily gathered money and ship's papers and placed them in a waterproof bag, my ears filled with the smashing din of breaking surf. Through a porthole I saw the ugly reef mass, only yards off, waiting for what seemed inevitable. I could *feel* the sharp, coarse, poisonous surface as I stared. A dampness began spreading at the roots of my hair. My heart was beating wildly. I couldn't bring myself to act, to think. And in that state I began to roll a cigarette. The paper tore and the lighter failed to light because it lacked gas-my God! The engine! In my excitement I'd forgotten *Atom*'s engine.

Stumbling, falling, I managed to jump into the cockpit and hit the button in a panic. The engine started immediately and *Atom* moved rapidly away from the white spray and heavy breakers, away from the yellowish green skin of the stony reef.*

When the reef was but a thin line, almost a memory against the horizon, I breathed deeply. I soon grew angry with myself for having forgotten that I had an engine aboard. But as my anger cooled I felt that indescribable feeling that follows great emotions. I even began to smile thinking about the dangers I'd faced, for if it had happened at night . . . well! All's well, you know, that ends well. *Atom*'s star hadn't been eclipsed yet. I sensed, however, that before we arrived back in France we would see more. To recover completely I ate an excellent snack and drank an old Sauterne, which soon warmed my spirits.

The trees of Dalrymple Island were soon spied and by eleven o'clock I had doubled the island. I proceeded to Rennel Island, and four hours later I anchored to leeward in green clear water in front of a small hamlet of ten cabins.

After two sleepless nights I was tired. But as I started below a small boat paddled by two natives ventured near *Atom*. A giant Negro, speaking English, welcomed me from the boat. His partner, a slim person of a clear brown color but with strange coppery-looking hair, asked me politely for permission to visit "ship." I gave full honors to my guests and at their invitation joined them ashore for a visit. And this is how I met the island's owner, Tom Savage, and his family. After dinner with them I met the island's entire English-speaking population, about thirty persons.

Like other islands in the strait, Rennel is an atom of ground emerging from the sea, the work of countless corals. On its thin layer of sand and humus a vigorous vegetation grows that supports several species of coconut.† Theirs is an ideal climate and the landscape is really very satisfying. At low tide coral gardens come out of the sea to provide entertainment.

Less than fifty years before, however, the Torres Strait natives were fearful cannibals and headhunters, with a preference for the saltier

---

*Later Jean related the incident to his sense of superstition and to fate: "In Torres Strait I'd spent the night steering. Tired, I went below to make coffee and to rest. But my mind warned me to have a look around. I climbed the mast and saw a line of reefs! The boat had spoken to me. Later, below, it happened again—*flap! flap! flap!* The boom squeaked also. Well, I went topside, saw nothing, but I was worried. I climbed the mast. Oh hell! Reefs were barring my way! I just had time to tack. . . . Believe me, there's something behind it. . . . *Atom* was talking to me."

†One of the few Pacific areas where early European settlers never introduced pigs, dogs, rats or other domestic animals, Rennel Island is rich in bird life, including many species found nowhere else.

white man's head. But their descendants today live a happy, contented life, peaceful and without care. They are not Australian aborigines but have in them the characteristics of the Papuan and Melanesian stocks. Born divers and fishermen, they live chiefly on profits from nacre, pearl, troca, trepang, and turtle shells. Every three months island schooners carry their products to Thursday Island, where the Japanese and Chinese traders ship it all over the world for the making of jewelry.

Their diving and fishing, incidentally, is nearly always done in ten to fifteen fathoms of water along the pulsing reef, where they risk the sea snake and the shark. During the daytime I sat aboard a small sloop, where, through a wooden box with a glass bottom, I watched the work of these extraordinary people in their submarine playground. As the copper-skinned divers snuck in among blue, yellow, green, and ivory coralline bushes I thought of *my* efforts back at Rose Island. At times their labors were interrupted by huge fish and on the surface by lazily moving snakes, but the divers seemed to ignore them. Several hours later, loaded to her Plimsoll marks with nacre, troca, and shells, the sloop headed in, but near the reef in shallow water they stopped to fish. Using a five-pronged spear, they seldom missed their prey at twenty to thirty yards. Finally, with the fish tossed in among the troca and shell, we headed in.

At the village we offloaded the treasures as the women began cooking in large ovens built of coral blocks. Later, in the open air, sitting on mats in the shade, I ate grilled oysters, fish, wild pigeon, and poached turtle egg. For dessert there were papaws, bananas, and pomegranates. After the huge meal—one that would be big even for serious gourmets—I rested until July 28, when I felt an almost forgotten urge.

I lay a course for Coconut Island, twenty-one miles away in the southwest. While I tidied up the deck, now inundated with fruits of all sorts, *Atom* settled down to her job and Rennel Island slowly slipped into memory astern, as substantive as morning mists.

About noon, as the bell of a small chapel rang out the Angelus in the clear ocean air, I moored to leeward of Coconut Island. That afternoon in the company of a man called The Teacher I visited the island, returning late to *Atom*. It was a quiet and calm night, the sky pregnant with prodigal stars, fair signs of good weather. . . . I was up and had the anchor on deck at sunrise, taking departure for Thursday Island sixty-eight miles away.

Even though it is small and surrounded by seven other islands, Thursday is an important outpost for shipping because it overlooks the narrow passage which opens on Torres Strait. It also is the home port for a fleet of ketches which work the nacre-troca-trepang-pearl circuit.

With the winds abeam, I soon reached the islands Bet, Sue, Poll, and off-lying Harvey Rock. Everything went well as far as Twins Island, where I altered course between Tuesday and Wednesday Islands, the narrowest part of the strait, where the currents are strong and strongly felt. Night approaching, I kicked the engine on to compensate for the current. The sun slid down the backside of the mountains and in the growing dark, as I cautiously approached, watching the beach's dim outline—the sailor's greatest curse is apparent distance at nighttime—I came on a tangle of silhouettes of ships riding to their anchors, their shadowy hulls merging with the thick darkness beyond. I managed to slip in between two ketches, anchoring in six fathoms.

Later I sat on deck, happy with having crossed the Pacific Ocean alone and safely. The thought of having guided *Atom* through the vastness of the Coral Sea, with its islets, rocks, visible and invisible shoals, foul currents, huge swells, and great winds—when I recalled these I admitted it was no small thing, the making of that passage. The biggest requirement had been an exceptional amount of patience and the ability to endure, to suffer without consequences, the whims of the globe's largest sea. And I thought, too, that old Magellan had to have been a damned joker to have called this troubled sea the Pacific!

I needed gasoline and food badly. To buy these I had expected to find a postal order awaiting me in Thursday Island. When I found it hadn't arrived I was shocked. I really was very short of cash. I didn't panic because I knew that I could always sell one of my Rose Island pearls.

To get the loot I went to a Chinese trader whose address a friend* had provided. In the back of his shop the Chinaman examined the two pearls I placed on a thick black velvet cloth.

"How much," I asked, "you give for these?"

Behind the slitted eyes I saw a careful checking of emotion. He was, I felt, rightly surprised by the quality of the large pearls that lay before him. He did not look me straight in the eyes but asked, "Is that all you sell?"

"Yes." I breathed deeply. "The others I keep."

"Please to show them all, do." He continued to look at the white pearls on the black cloth. Stupidly I emptied the small canvas bag. His eyes, no longer slitted, rounded and he lost his composure. With a

---

*The "friend" was a crocodile hunter named Jeff, who, unable to stand the stench of crocodiles that pervaded his boat, visited *Atom* daily for a drink.

magnifying glass and a pearl gauge he deftly measured their dimensions, candling them before a small light before looking at me. "Where you find these?" he asked. "Where you from?"

"That's my secret," I said. "I only want to sell those two pearls." I began collecting the others.

"No!" His eyes now were slits as he said, "I buy all or none!"

I needed money. I had to have food and gas. To wait for the postal order in that outpost might take months. In fact, I had no way of estimating when, if ever, it might arrive. *I had to have money.*

"How many dollars you give?" Neither of us was smiling.

"Four hundred thirty-five."

I took the money and left behind the small canvas bag.

Seven days later I was ready to leave, and in early May weighed anchor. But before I would enter the huge Indian Ocean I had to cross the Arafura and Timor Seas. The Arafura crossing, fortunately, was uneventful, with only feeble variables and an oily sea distinguishing it. Beyond Australia's bony northern finger, Cape Van Dieman, a heavy swell made the sea choppy. The humidity was terrible. A month later my sightings placed me off Christmas Island, where I called for a week, the guest of its governor. Attracting man's interest only because of its rich deposits of bird droppings, Christmas Island is a lonely pellet of an island in the vast Indian Ocean, its sole inhabitants birds and quarry workers.

I then headed for the Cocos Islands lying at 15° South Latitude and 100° East Longitude. The southeast monsoon was blowing fifteen to twenty knots under a sky so overcast that I was upset, fearing my positions were in error. Fifteen days later I determined my position to be fifteen miles *west* of Cocos. To reach them I would have to beat against the monsoon winds and the swells in which *Atom* had been pitching tremendously for some time. While I pondered my quandary the bobstay suddenly parted flush at the bow. The masts, no longer supported by the stay, threatened to go overboard any minute. I tacked immediately and thereby forwent calling at Cocos. After roadside repairs we continued our heading, which was for Durban, South Africa.

As we sailed we met with herds of whales heading south. Despite their enormous size and volume they moved with a surprising agility, like fat men ashore. Watching their graceful motions, I was sobered by the thought that these grand creatures might one day be extinct and man would survive.

I then was not far from Madagascar and in those parts of the ocean where hurricanes originate. I couldn't dally because I knew the season of powerful atmospheric depressions was approaching. Already violent storms were breaking at the rate of three or four a day in the southwest. I actually ached and was miserable at not sighting land.

A few days later, Land Ho!

By nightfall, however, a stiff gale caused me to lie to under bare poles. The next day in late afternoon, after 103 days at sea, I stood off the entrance to Durban and waited until a small launch led me to a pier.

The next morning, coming on deck, I was startled to find before the hatch a box with cabbage, eggs, bread, and a note: *Well done, Jean. Congratulations! I'll see you at five.* It was signed, *Bernard Moitessier.* I was puzzled. Who is he? I wondered. But in the following three months Moitessier would prove to be the most sympathetic and pleasant person I'd ever known. As I started below with the goods a dinghy rowed by a young lady and a small girl came alongside.

"*Atom!*" the lady shouted. "Are you Jean Gau?"

"Why," I cried, "you speak French!"

"But, of course," she replied, "I *am* French!" She introduced herself as Madeleine Merlot, who, with her husband, Joseph, sailed freely wherever their fancy dictated. Now she had come to invite *Atom's* First Officer to dine that evening in the company of my new friend, Bernard Moitessier. It was to be a happy evening, for we talked not of islands in the sun but of the sea, of boats and their handling.

Days later the famed Marcel Bardiaux arrived in his boat, *Four Winds,* to make a loquacious foursome of French boats in the harbor. Often we got together for evening meals aboard the Merlots' yacht and each person shared the best of his adventures.*

One evening Jean casually asked Moitessier, "And how do you heave to in a storm, Bernard?"

"As usual. A mizzen sail and the tiller lashed to windward. But, unfortunately, the last time I did not have a sea anchor aboard."

Crossing his legs and pursing his lips, Gau, nearly a quarter of

---

*The presence of the peripatetic Frenchmen in Durban's harbor prompted the press to joke about the instability of the French government, its citizens fleeing to the corners of the earth. But in the bright interior of their yachts the happy sailors, pushing aside empty soup plates, raised full glasses as they swapped experiences under sail. While in Durban, reportedly, Jean learned from Moitessier how to use outdated nautical almanacs in lieu of buying later editions. Another time both men, hungry and broke, caught a seagull, which they roasted over an open fire.

a century older than the handsome French sailing vagabond, replied, "One of these days, kid, you'll get into trouble that way. You see, Bernard, to heave to is to lie abeam of the waves. By drifting sideways your boat creates a windward slick that dampens any wave that approaches." In the quiet of the cozy cabin, only the whisper of a glass being refilled or of a dish being stowed in the distant galley disturbed the silence.

"Sea anchors," Jean continued, "don't create a slick. And if you're under bare poles your boat's drift isn't sufficient to create a slick either."

The fifty-three year old mariner told the small gathering how he preferred to bend on a fore topmast sail and lash the tiller completely to leeward. If, however, the winds slacked somewhat, he might set the mizzen sail (usually an old jib), thereby permitting *Atom* to point a bit.

"But," asked Moitessier, "what if a wave *did* cross the whirlpool created by your drifting? I mean, Jean, what if the wave slammed into your foresail?" The group knew that *Atom*'s jib was held to the mainmast by a single bowsprit stay.

Vexed by the question, Gau answered that no wave had as yet crossed the slick when either *Onda* or *Atom* was hove to. Moitessier's question would prove relevant eleven years later, however.

"And as for sea anchors, the last time I used one was aboard *Onda*. I thought the Atlantic would take my bones!" Because there was no whirlpool created by the sea anchor, he had thought that the waves would do him in. So he cut the sea anchor line. *Onda* then assumed her proper position creating a slick that, Gau explained, dampened the waves.

But neither Gau nor Moitessier could agree with Bardiaux about the need to make way while hove to. "You'll get it one of these days, Marcel!" muttered Jean, shaking his head. It was then that Bardiaux mentioned having been capsized while hove to.

Finishing their drinks and still friends, these highly individualistic sailors parted, each convinced of the rightness of his method of handling a boat under storm conditions.

Besides heaving to (or slowly drifting to leeward over

thousands of miles of ocean in her lifetime), *Atom,* then gaff-rigged, her main and mizzen protected by baggywrinkle, spent thousands of hours self-steering. To self-steer his ketch Gau used the simple and reliable sheet-to-tiller arrangement: when his boat wandered off course the balance of forces on her sails changed, the change producing varying tensions in her sheet and running rigging. If the sea or the weather indicated some degree of heavy going ahead, he often bent on a staysail to the mainmast, using it in lieu of the furled mainsail. He then flattened the jib amidship. Next, four turns of a Dacron lashing, fastened at one end to the mainsheet and at the other to a long coiled spring secured to a cockpit bulwark, were taken around the tiller. By experimenting with the angle of *Atom's* heading and the wind, Gau found the right arrangement and lashed the tiller securely. *Atom* sailed on. Thus when the breezes freshened she responded with more weather helm, and when they lightened with less.

Jean also spent many evenings ashore with other friends.

One day a teenage boy, nicely dressed in his school uniform, asked permission to visit *Atom.* He accepted my invitation and we stepped down to the cabin, where he asked me many questions about my travels. His curiosity satisfied, he asked if I would like to meet his parents and to have dinner with them. He insisted, and after I had agreed he said, "I'm sorry, Captain Gau, but when you meet them *please* do not mention that you are sailing *around* the world."

"But," I responded with surprise, "why not?"

"I'm ashamed to admit it," he replied in a level voice, "but my parents are strong believers in a Bible that has been handed down from generation to generation in our family. On the front page is an engraving that shows the world as *flat.* My parents would be scandalized if you or anyone made remarks that varied with this portrayal of the world in Holy Scriptures."

Puzzled, I asked, "But what am I to do . . . ?"

"You might say you are traveling for pleasure *on* the seas of the earth, but please, sir, don't refer to the *globe!* This slight difference won't disturb you, will it, sir?"

"Ahhh . . . no . . . if that is all."

"Good! Let's go, sir."

We were greeted heartily by his parents. But before I could attack the huge dinner, I had, instead of an appetizer, to listen *while standing* to a chapter from the Holy Bible, which remained lying on the table during the entire dinner. Later, the dinner over and my hosts for the moment distracted with other matters, my young friend caught my attention. He lifted the cover of the Bible and showed the endpapers to me. I saw an old etching of the earth portrayed as a quadrilateral held by four strings!

I was relieved when the time came to go, because during the meal I feared I would unintentionally break my word, saying quite naturally *sphere, round, globe,* etc. But all went well and that night the lad thanked me heartily.

I carefully checked *Atom*'s rigging to ensure that it would be adequate for the stresses of the heavy seas I expected to find off the Cape of Good Hope. The boat was in sound condition, and at eight o'clock on February 9, 1955, I weighed anchor. Moved by the sight of Bardiaux's French ensign and the salute of his foghorn, I motored out of the harbor. Outside a fair northeasterly was blowing at fifteen knots. Soon the skyscrapers of Durban retired from sight, no doubt having business on the other side of the horizon. A day later the log showed that *Atom* had made 135 miles in twenty-four hours. This was just too good. It simply could not continue.

Within forty-eight hours of departure the winds hauled ahead; they now blew at gale strength. Under reduced canvas *Atom* tacked night and day, now to the empty south, then towards Africa's coast some sixty miles away. Influenced by the swift Agulhas Current, she drifted an estimated fifteen to twenty miles westward, which helped. But once on the Agulhas Bank the going was very heavy because of huge seas, which were terrifying to look at. At 36° South Latitude the wind was icy, and in spite of thick woolies I was cold and had to keep the Primus stove going. At midnight on February 28 I spied the Cape of Good Hope lighthouse, and weathered it next day.

This now placed me in the South Atlantic, where I sighted several ships, but at times the swells were so great these huge vessels dropped out of sight. In the afternoon a cross swell arrived from the south as the westerly lessened progressively. I became anxious—would this be the Black Southeaster, the wind feared by sailors in these parts? The winds then veered southeast and the seas began breaking in a curious manner. I was then only a few miles from harbor, so I dropped the main and motored toward Table Bay at Cape Town, South Africa.

Under a sunny sky I tied up at the Royal Yacht Club, twenty-one days out from Durban. Still in my sea clothes, I accepted an offer to belly up to the bar, only to be honored later with an honorary membership for the duration of my stay. That evening with friends I ate heartily. Back aboard much later, I fell onto my bunk and slept like a dead man. Dead, yes, but happy!

Next day voices crying, "*Atom*! C'mon, we're waiting for you for breakfast!" brought me to my feet all standing. With my new friends I went off later to visit the cape's famous lighthouse, which I had watched so ardently from seaward days before. From its observation deck I saw the sea spread like a giant cloak over the horizon. Far out an awful weather was raging from a southeasterly. As far as I could see waves broke at great heights. A man, I thought, had to be *mad* to risk his life on such seas in a small boat. As we watched, hundreds of seabirds, like scraps of paper, swept the air. Below us waves relentlessly assaulted the stern rocks. Finally, leaving that breezy, forlorn point we drove to Hout Bay, where we purchased lobsters at a ridiculously low price.

That evening I knew we'd made a toothsome investment.

8

Hurricane!

The inevitable day of leave-taking arrived and on March 21, 1956, *Atom* departed for the long haul under Africa's belly, South Africa to the Azores via St. Helena and Ascension islands. Like many others, this crossing began nicely. Several days later the southeast trade winds, however, blew out two jibs, and the strains of the sea broke the tiller. I shipped a spare one and on April 18 arrived off the entrance to Jamestown, St. Helena, at twilight, only to discover that *Atom*'s iron lung wouldn't start.

I hove to for the night but discovered the next day that the trades had blown us almost fifteen miles leeward of the island. I didn't relish the hard beat to windward against the current so I altered course, and with the trade winds astern *Atom* sought Ascension Island, 700 miles away.

After eleven soporific days of navigation I dropped *Atom*'s worn hook in Georgetown's harbor, fifty-two days out of Capetown. Even had I wanted to stay longer it was necessary to depart to reach France before winter. By May 12 *Atom* had crossed the Equator at 20°19′ West Longitude. Now the same southeast trade wind that had accommodated me on the other side of the world gave me a lift, so to speak, as far as 2°50′ North Latitude. But three days later I stumbled into these

117

damned Doldrums, to be greeted by a host of evils—lightning, strong gales, storms, and rain.

The transition from that belt of evil was effected two days later as I entered the northeast trade wind area. The winds, however, were blowing from the north only. So *Atom* sailed close-hauled on a starboard tack for thirty-six days in a race with rising breezes and a lively sea. All openings closed tightly, *Atom* pitched so strongly that I was certain she was trying to toss her sticks away. On June 17 I cut the wake of my 1949 Gibraltar-New York trek at 23° North Latitude, 40°04' West Longitude. I had looped the loop but the trip was far from over; I so advised the crew! As proof of that the trades grew erratic and the equatorial current caused me to drift nearly to the middle of the Atlantic, to the eastern edge of the Sargasso Sea, where I meditated for seventeen days.

Puffs, dancing from every quarter, with long intervals of flat calms, entertained *Atom* and me until July 21. Our progress northward had been so slow that I began to worry about the water supply. But finally a storm hit and hit hard. After the first blasts of air the rains came with the intensity of a cow pissing on a flat stone! That night I happily filled the water tanks. Six days later a good wind arrived and it made me happy to see *Atom* come alive. I reckoned that with luck we'd make the crossing in two or three days, such was our speed. But next day the wind quit in favor of an easterly and I began to tack. Day after day, for more than a week, *Atom* slugged it out for every mile she gained. Finally, on August 5, we stood off the Azores, and two days later rounded, close-to, the Cape Comprida lighthouse.

Since this was my third time in these parts, this particular landfall was familiar. Under motor I entered Horta's picturesque harbor in the early afternoon. As soon as the hook was down the pilot boat came alongside and Joao Silveria, the harbor's well-known, gregarious pilot, stepped aboard and handed me a pack of mail.

The Equinox was then somewhere between the Azores and Iberia. I felt it time to put to sea. In good spirits and health I weighed *Atom*'s hook, and for one month had fair weather but slow passage. On September 9 I fetched the Portuguese coastline off Cape St. Vincent, where *Atom* was promptly becalmed for more than a week. I knew, of course, that the relative safety of the high seas was over. I was now on the famed Iron Line, the name given the procession of ships making the Gibraltar-Cape St. Vincent passage. To avoid being boarded at night by these mastodons of the sea I kept my eyes opened. Helped by the occasional weak breezes, I arrived off Cape Spartel on September 17.

The entrance to the Strait of Gibraltar dead ahead, I started the engine, and at seven o'clock that evening began my approach to the strait. One hour later the malevolent Levante, or easterly of the Mediterranean, blew in gale force. Under all sail and engine *Atom*, terribly shaken, stayed nicely on course in the seething wastes of the Strait, her skipper at the helm all night. The next day, off Gibraltar, we were signalled by the Lloyd's station and soon a pilot boat with boarding officials approached. In short time—the British are beautifully efficient!—I was granted pratique.

Eight days later it was time to head for the Mediterranean, or Latin Lake, as some authors call it. On October 3, after weathering the headland, I trimmed *Atom*'s rags and laid a course due east. Helped by a friendly westerly, we made about four knots. The next day an unfriendly easterly chased off the west wind and I now fought to gain distance. My logbook at that time reads: *Drizzle, cold, nasty weather. Over my woolies I wear rubber foul-weather clothes. But now I can face without fear the green waters of the Mediterranean, having survived the savage seas outside!* And so we tacked towards Spain in the morning and towards Africa in the afternoon. Near evening I speared a bonito, which provided a tasty court bouillon, fish in wine sauce.

That night, in heavy seas from a northeasterly, I let *Atom* fend for herself under a stormsail as big waves trammeled her decks with a thundering and deafening noise. At three o'clock in the morning a noise like a cannonade woke me up!

On deck in seconds all standing, I discovered that the stormsail's sheet had parted. I didn't want to lose the sail but I knew it would be damned hard and wet to get it down in the dark. But I managed to do it and *Atom*, no longer protected by the small sail, rolled tremendously. One hour later, after exchanging sheets, I got the sail up and went below to a light, uneasy sleep.

At daybreak, aware that I'd lost time tacking, I decided to enter the small harbor at Fuengirola, Spain, and there came to anchor at five o'clock. The next day the heavy seas obliged me to leave this endangered anchorage. Despite the foul weather I got underway, and for seven days I hammered at and was hammered by wind, sea, and current. But I managed finally to reach Cartagena, Spain, where I put in.

The boat really demanded my attention; knowing a bit about the Mediterranean's wrath, I put something extra into my labors. But at night I strolled the old city's streets, often stopping off in pubs, where the wild fandangos, guitars, and castanets excited my soul. Among my many friends there were the naval officers, especially the commander of the *Lepanto,* Don Luis Verdugo. We were both men of the sea and it showed in our relationship.

One day a red-haired man, one arm in a sling (he'd fallen from a mast on his boat) and rather paunchy, approached my yacht and hailed, "Hello, the *Atom!* Are you the skipper?"

I nodded.

"I'm Errol Flynn," he said. "How do you do?" He offered his hand and I jumped onto the pier. Astonished, I asked, "The actor?"

Assured that he was, I accepted his offer to join a party that evening aboard his schooner, *Zaca.* Before he left he patted my shoulder in a friendly manner. I liked him.

That evening I was in a large group aboard his beautiful boat, where Flynn, whose face was heavily lined, introduced me to his young bride and to his guests. After the meal he talked about his past. As a bachelor Flynn had left his native Melbourne with two pals on a small yacht for Port Moresby. His partners left for other parts but he stayed to run a plantation. But anxious to return to Melbourne he set out on foot, penniless, en route shearing sheep in the Australian desert.* At the end of the evening, as his guests were leaving, Flynn grabbed my arm and led me to a corner of the large cabin. He mentioned having read something I'd written about New Guinea and we discovered a mutual interest in that strange country. As I got up to leave he asked, "Jean, do you need some money?"

"Not at all," I replied. "I am a cook. I work to make a living."

"But," he said, "it's been four years that you've been away. No matter how hard you worked, your savings must be finished?"

I thought for a moment and said, "It is enough."

"Then you won't accept anything?" His face showed a sincere interest.

"No. But thank you anyway."

---

*Flynn, like Gau, disliked the killing of game without cause. He told Jean that as a boy, he once threw a long string, to which bits of food were tied, to his father's ducks. The hungry fowl gobbled the bait. When his father, seeing the ducks all cackling and jostling together, cried, "How cruel!" Flynn responded, "What about your collection of stuffed animals!"

However, Jean wasn't certain if Flynn was pulling his leg when he related how, as a young sheep herder, he had to castrate the sheep by "using his teeth." After a stage pause, Gau added drolly "That tale was kind of hard to swallow. . . ."

"Jean, you are wrong not to accept something!" I was touched by the way he said that. "I have money I don't know what to do with and I often spend it on people whom I really don't know." He did not pause as he said, "Doctors have given me two years to live. . . . " Moments later as I took my leave he said, "I'm sorry, Jean. I would like to help you."

I never saw him again, but two years later I learned of his death in Canada.

On October 17, the tanks full of water and gasoline, the galley fully provisioned, I set out for the last leg of my journey. It was a moving farewell. By seven o'clock, my mind confused by feelings and urgings, a melancholy mixture of anxiety and excitement, I reached the piers at the harbor entrance. Shortly afterwards I was at sea and ready, indeed eager, to pick up the threads of adventure.

A light southwesterly helping out, we soon rounded Cape Palos, where I met a fleet of fishermen, their lateen sails flapping as the boats pitched. Having recognized *Atom*, their crews ceased hauling their heavy nets to hail us.

Under a feeble breeze *Atom* barely slid across a billiard table of a sea, but at sunset the breeze picked up and the going got rough. Having tended to the self-steering system, I lay below to my "digs" to fix a tasty dish of rice, Valencia style. Dinner over, I set up the running lights and rigged a powerful masthead light before returning to the comforts of my cabin, where the demands and exertions of departure overcame me.

The next day, with all sails drawing, I doubled San Antonio Cape, but was chagrined to find the northeasterlies dying as variable winds and breezes took over. *Atom* slipped slowly past the breathtaking Balearic Islands.

A few days later a southwesterly pushed me to Cape de Creus, where I was becalmed for a night, only 45 miles from my goal. At daybreak I was underway, soon rounding Cape Leucate and Port Nouvelle, whose coastal landscapes I quickly recognized. East of the last hills of Cape Clape I saw with excitement the square tower of St. Nazaire, the Beziers cathedral, and finally the water tower of Valras and the small light-house on the west pier at the mouth of the River Orb. As I steered *Atom* "home," to the small basin where I passed much of my boyhood, brief flashes of youthful antics and longings merged with my other thoughts.

But even at Valras the inevitable day of departure arrived. On May 26, 1957, numerous friends, some coming from afar, came to see a middle-aged *Atom* and her even older spray-thatched skipper make last-minute preparations for sea. I wanted the stay to be longer, particularly in Valras, for there the thoughts of my boyhood had germinated, dreams that I have now fulfilled. But, still wanting the emotions and pleasures of adventure, even its risks, I left.

It was a perfect day, with a clear sky and a sea sparkling with life and motion. At nine-thirty, escorted by many friends on fishing boats and yachts, I put to sea again. At the pier a small crowd had gathered to give me a send-off as only the French know how!

Where before my departure had been joyful, I now felt sadness and regret. A last look at the land, the boats, the beach, and Valras receded, like a pleasant dream, in a misty haze. How many times from that now barely visible beach had I gazed at the Mediterranean and dreamed of sailing bluer seas!

Her sails drawing and the tiller lashed, *Atom* carried on while, to relieve my feelings, I busily stowed the gifts and packages of friends.

That evening the sky darkened, filling with thick clouds. That night the light slapping of the bow wave was the only sound heard. At nightfall the next day I was not far from Cape Sebastian when gales and squalls dropped in. At three o'clock in the morning a furious northeast blast suddenly rose, and increased as the sky cleared. By sunrise it was blowing strongly, but the sea was not heavy, merely short and choppy. Actually it was a weather moderate enough to continue my southerly course, but the Cape, not yet rounded, forced me to judge it best to stand out to sea. About noon a gust struck *Atom*, who was half laid by its force despite being under jib and mizzen only. The moment the bow was buried heavy seas broke over the jib, snapping the bowsprit like the sound of small gunfire. I waited until the swells had ceased a day later before tidying ship and repairing the damages of that storm.

Although the storm wasn't strong as before, it blew hard, and the morning of May 29 the waters were rough. Astraddle the stumpy bowsprit, I worked hard getting a jury-rig, but *Atom*'s nervous jerks gave me a sitz bath every few seconds. Eventually I got the job decently finished and resumed my southward journey.

The storm abated on May 30 and for the next sixteen days I had to helm incessantly to catch each puff of air. Slatting sails, banging booms, and rattling rigging—their doings annoyed me more than the rigors of a full gale! In the days of light breeze that followed I got familiar with the seas again. On June 3 I sighted the Balearics about noon, but was delayed in shooting the sun by the good-natured gestures of the crew of a Dutch cargo ship. This happy encounter could only mean one thing; I was entering the shipping lines.

About three o'clock in the morning of June 4 the noise of an engine got me up. On deck in two jumps (maybe it was only one!), I was dazzled by the lights of a liner, passing yards from *Atom*! I was paralyzed with fear as the blind, unthinking thing thrashed its way through the blackness. I stayed awake and watchful until dawn, unsettled by the sight of that obscene leviathan who had nearly caused the loss of my boat.

On June 10, just as I was starting to worry about the uncommon duration of the fine weather, the northwesterly freshened somewhere along the east coast of Ibiza, and when I rounded its northeast extremity the wind blew at gale force. At nightfall under reduced sails, shaken a bit by the beam seas, I made for the Formentera Island light.

In spite of the foul currents and light airs, on June 15 I had Cape Palos in sight, twenty-five miles to starboard. At nine the next morning I kicked over the engine and made for Cartagena's harbor forty miles away, leaving an oily sea and a scorching sun.

After mail and drinks at the Royal Yacht Club I found a shipyard, where I bought a beam of Oregon pine fifteen feet long and four inches in diameter. Sunday was spent planing and rasping and installing a new nose for *Atom* under a torrid Spanish sun and the quizzical looks of friends and onlookers. On June 19, provisioned and watered, I waved to my pierside friends as I put to sea.

Out beyond the jetties feeble southwesterlies played around, but twenty-four hours later the wind veered and drew ahead. It blew at gale strength the entire night and next day. I didn't want to lose an inch to the wind, sea, or foul currents so I slugged it out with reduced canvas. Until June 29 the days were sunny and the winds irregular northwesterlies, interrupted by the calms which had sprinkled my course since leaving Valras. At three o'clock Gibraltar's outline shouldered through the mist and I anchored not far from the naval base airfield. Three days later, resupplied, I left, a strong Levante helping to make the forty-mile race against the incoming current exciting.

Abeam of Tarifa headland the wind became a moderate gale. A tanker, heading against the sea and wind, shipped seas mightily, showing me how rough the waters really were. To reduce *Atom*'s tremendous divings I towed a hawser, which helped to hold her ahead of the waves. Shortly after noon I sailed into the Atlantic, having spent six hours at seven knots crossing the Strait.

About one o'clock the wind ceased, leaving an excessively rough sea in which *Atom* acted like a drunken middle-aged schoolmarm, wetting her nose and yawing several points on either side. This continued until twilight when it breezed up for a while.

After three days of Iron Line jitters, and calms, on July 6 the breeze progressively increased in strength, whereupon *Atom* put under her slim heels 90, 110, 112, and 115 miles daily. For my part, I was anxious to begin a true high-seas navigation.

On July 13 I anchored under a setting sun and under the guidance of a Funchal pilot in the Madeiras. But the next day I couldn't land because, as though it had been looking for me, a strong Levante blew in at gale force. From *Atom*'s deck the small port was nothing but spray. The heavy swell caused *Atom* to swing like a pendulum. To make the punishment complete, sacks of air burst and fell down the mountains around the anchorage and under their blows *Atom* walked around her hook, the chain stretched taut as an iron bar. I was concerned because if one link broke *Atom* would smash onto Funchal's slanting beach, where, tumbled about by the strength of the surf, the pebbles actually moaned. On deck I flaked out a strong line and a second anchor just in case.

Not far away a schooner rode to two anchors. During that restless night, both came home and did not take hold until she was almost ashore. That night I sat up as taut as the chain. About four o'clock I sensed that the wind was lighter. Day was barely breaking when the wind stopped. It had been a hell of a night, but happily there'd been no damage. The first sun rays bristled on the rough stubble of the mountain's face and clouds, entangled in the peaks, stormed down the steep rugged gorges, which resembled ancient wrinkles. Later the sun burned away the mists and red-roofed dots of color flashed into sight.

I sat contemplating this charmed sight until I saw my good friend, Jose Aquinos, his straw hat failing to hide a friendly face, approach in a whaleboat. My hand met his heartily when he stepped aboard—Jose is a lover of the sea, and as a ship's boy roamed around the world aboard square-riggers.

Later I went ashore to spend the evening with his happy family, their contentment gotten from that peace that common work provides. These happy islanders spend their lives cultivating gardens, hunting in the mountains, and breeding children.

Jose lent me a motorbike and I took off to see this island, which in some ways resembles Tahiti. I stopped along the cliffs of Cape Carajao on the island's south coast at a point about 500 feet above the sea. At that elevation there was no horizon, the blue and blue were one.

Looking like a seabird hovering lazily on updrafts, *Atom* swung to her mooring in the bay far below. *Atom* was the right name for my boat! This I now grasped for the first time, for she looked so insignificant in the huge panorama before me. The view impressed me also with the immensity of the universe and with man's role, if any, in it. I filled both mind and eye with the island's charms, stopping wherever I could harvest an impression.

One day, while roaming in the countryside, I saw a taxi parked next to the road, its driver reading a newspaper. Two steps away a man was painting a landscape. Because I draw I was interested and, thinking him to be an islander, hailed him. *"Boas tardes, Senhor!"*

Looking around, he answered, "Hello!"

That alone would have startled, me but when I recognized Winston Churchill my stupefaction was complete!

"What can I do for you?" He was smiling.

"Oh, nothing. But I am a painter myself and your painting interested me. I came over to look at it."

"But," said this thickset man, "do you know anything *about* painting?"

"Well, I paint portraits and landscapes, but my speciality is seascapes."

He shrugged and looked off to the sea. "Oh, that damned sea I never could reproduce," he said. "How do you catch the motion of a wave? Can we see what you've painted?"

I explained that they were aboard my boat.

"But which boat?" he asked.

"Well, there is in the harbor a small American yacht, *Atom.* . . . "

Until then our conversation had been in English, but he suddenly replied in French. "Ah! *You're* that crazy Frenchman who sails across the oceans?"

"Yes, sir," I smiled and nodded. "I am the one." He agreed to visit my boat the next afternoon.

Naturally I doubted that he would have the time or interest, but I spent the morning tidying up the permanent disorder of my cabin. At four o'clock a motorboat approached and Sir Winston was piped aboard the *Atom.* For more than two hours, over good cigars and tumblers of cognac, we looked at my paintings and talked art. Then, wishing me a good wind and fair sea, Sir Winston got up to leave. He wished me farewell in French. Then, in English, he said, *"Never, never give up your ship!"* He smiled broadly. As the motorboat moved off, the statesman, smiling, raised his arm and I saw the famous salute.

Getting the anchor aboard on July 16 was difficult; the gale two days before had caused it to bite deeply. I worked with the windlass for more than an hour to persuade the hook to change its mind. That chore over, accompanied by fishing boats I left Funchal, and off the jetty set and trimmed my sails. With a fair wind off the quarter I headed southwest on a port tack. From Madeira to New York is about 3,000 miles, but by sail, of course, it's much longer. This is because sailboats usually sail down as far as the Tropic of Cancer before turning westward to get south of Bermuda, where they then turn north for New York. By this route they have favorable trade winds, the Equatorial Current, and the Gulf Stream. But the price is 4,500 miles.

At nightfall *Atom* slept on a large, quiet lake. Noisy gulls, which had rummaged through her wake for the microorganisms we had disturbed, had flown back to their islands. Peace reigned over the quiet, still waters. At midnight a light breeze stroked the surface, filling *Atom*'s sails. She moved forward, tearing on either side of the placid surface a thin hem of foam. Beneath her bows the waters chattered and gossiped. Northward the dark outline of mountainous Madeira and the lights of Funchal reflected on the waters far out to sea.

The first week I had moderate trade winds, but they became unsteady, disappearing for long intervals, and in their passing hardly wrinkling the face of sea. I knew now I could not beat my 1949 crossing time but because of the niceness of the weather and the sea I didn't feel badly about it. But it was important not to hang around too long because of the scousy condition of *Atom*'s derriere.

Since leaving Madeira the dorados had been scarce, but on August 4 waves of flying fish, chased by voracious dorados, left silvery sprays off the bow. The dorados, which hung about for some time, filleted nicely, I might add.

On August 10 small islets of seaweed, remnants from the Sargasso Sea, drifted into view. An area between the North Equatorial Current and the Gulf Stream, the Sargasso Sea is located southeast of the Bermudas and has a surface area about the size of France. Everywhere it is covered with a bladdery kelp, whose shining colors transform the blue sea into mobile meadows. I had often wondered if these weeds were detached from some deep abyss of the ocean and dragged by currents to the surface to be continuously replaced, or if they were debris eternally suspended in the middle of ocean currents. Little was then known about them, because the Sargasso Sea isn't on the shipping lanes. Isolated in a desolate part of the Atlantic—why, I'd also wondered, is there no Pacific equivalent?—it has little interest for scientists.* But I was curious and wondered what surprises this corner of the seas, forgotten since windjammer days, might have for *Atom* and me.

I now had time to recall the stories of my youth. I remembered Columbus's caravels first encountered these weeds, which thwarted their passage and alarmed the crews. For three hellish weeks those early seamen were the victims of fear, heat, and privation before finding an exit from this carpeted sea. And I recalled that long after Columbus, navigators believed that no ship could enter and pass through these ocean meadows. So were my thoughts as I slowly sailed along the southern margins of the Sargasso Sea.

On August 20 I was at 23° North Latitude and 55° West Longitude, south of the center of the "sea." It would be, I calculated, but a day's journey northward to the actual center, a deserted spot without wind or current in which wreckage of all sorts was supposed to have gathered. Strange creatures, large and small, undoubtedly lived among the algal mass there. I *had* to pay a short visit to the heart of this mysterious meadow.

At five o'clock I tacked and proceeded northward. As I sailed into higher latitudes the trade winds weakened and the sea carpet became more apparent. At noon the breeze began to fail so I started the engine. That day we zigzagged across dense acres of weed and wreckage. At nightfall I stopped the engine. I now was not far from the very middle of the Sargasso Sea.

After a good meal I lay down and fell into an uneven and restless sleep. I had nightmares—until dawn my dreams were of merciless fights with grotesque creatures. I woke with a start! Through the portholes I saw a glimmering haze. Hurriedly I went on deck, but saw nothing abnormal. *What* could have caused that light, I wondered, uneasily.

A deadly silence was all about, and in its tenseness there was a thrill.

At dawn I was on deck: not a breath of air. In the absolute calm that prevailed, I could see for great distances all that floated. Aided by the engine, *Atom* picked her way amidst the algal islets, a path winding and eerily still except for the engine's throaty cough.

I leaned overboard, trying to pierce the algal cloth with a boat hook. In the seaweed mass I saw many pinkish fish, sea anemones with long venomous hairs, and sea-green medusa or jellyfish. I lifted a mass of

---

*Since then, scientist John Teal has made at least three research cruises there, including one to the Sargasso Sea floor in a research submarine. See *The Sargasso Sea,* John and Mildred Teal, Atlantic-Little, Brown, 1975.

seaweed on deck. Moments later I heard a crackling noise as hosts of tiny animals, hidden in the slimy, fleshy mass, rushed out onto the brightly lighted deck: crabs, sea horses, ringed worms, shrimp, and variously shaped crustaceans covered with transparent armor, all stirred by the unknown sensation of being removed from their environment. Curious, I watched these tiny inhabitants of another world panic. Were they not so small, I admitted, they would terrify and frighten man.*

Suddenly I was startled by a shock somewhere near the bow of my boat! *Atom* had hit an enormous tree trunk, so barnacled it hardly floated. Many large fish surrounded it, and they seemed to rush at *Atom*. I hit one of them with my fish spear but lost it. The next one I harpooned with more skill but it was so large I had difficulty getting it aboard. This huge nameless fish weighed about ten kilos, and it leaped mightily in the cockpit until it died.†

This exploration of the Sargasso Sea had upset my schedule, and concerned about the approaching Equinox, I started *Atom*'s engine to resume my course. But after making a few yards the engine quit! Knowing that there was almost no chance of finding a ship in the vicinity for months, if ever, I sweated blood. I immediately attacked the engine with muscle and words which, even today, cannot be printed. After thirty minutes the engine started. But the thought of having to spend time trying to sail from that windless desert had upset me greatly.

Near the end of the day the first breaths of the trade winds arrived and in time I gained the clean open spaces of the ocean.

By September 1, at 29° North Latitude and 65° West Longitude, I had reached an area of high pressures, calms, and variable winds that exists between the trade winds and the westerlies. The trades became more irregular, weakening and tiring by stages. For more than seven days it was nothing but calms, variable breezes, heavy storms, driving rains, and constant sail changes. Finally, I had to lie ahull. Gradually

---

*Not all life in the Sargasso Sea is small. Over the years Jean often saw fights between phosphorescently glowing giant squids and small whales ("The squid or octopus usually won") in various parts of the world. One of the more memorable death struggles between these awesome creatures occurred somewhere in the Sargasso Sea, but presumably not during this expedition.

The "glimmering haze" probably resulted from the bioluminescent properties of various organisms in the algal mass.

† Possibly *Histrio histrio*, a Sargassum fish that has evolved frilled appendages making it almost indistinguishable from the Sargassum weed.

the wind veered southward and settled southwest. *Atom*'s performance soared and for several days we made decent progress.

During this leg of my voyage I was to have an unforgettable lesson on the fragility of human existence. The morning of September 18 the stillness puzzled me. Without any evident reason a strong southeast swell raised and lowered an oily sea that was completely smooth. The barometer, which I checked constantly, fell slowly but consistently. Was it, I wondered, the symptoms of a hurricane? My doubts ceased at four o'clock when an American seaplane dropped a warning marker: *You are in the path of a hurricane.* As the plane departed a feeling of disaster rose. I wasn't certain that the *Atom* could weather a hurricane.

The textbook explanation of hurricanes is that as the storm moves westward, sweeping close to the West Indies and the southern United States, it then shifts northward before veering northeast and dying eventually between Newfoundland and England. Its slow speed of advance is not the same for every storm, but the whirlpool itself has terrible blasts, which can reach speeds of 150 to 200 miles an hour. In the northern hemisphere hurricanes invariably move anticlockwise around a central axis, where the winds are nil but where huge ocean waves clash furiously. The right arm of the hurricane is termed the dangerous semicircle and the left the moderate semicircle. The dangerous right semicircle centripetally and fatally draws a ship towards the storm's middle but the moderate semicircle centrifugally drives a ship away.

Heavy weather arrived in the guise of a sky strangely upset and a rising sea. *Atom*, crammed with sails, was trying to reach New York, 300 miles away, before the storm hit. Her sunburnt sails taut-bellied, *Atom* flew over the sea as short and nasty-tempered squalls came one after the other from the south, tearing away clouds heavy with rain. I sailed as fast as the sea conditions permitted, steering so as to reduce the harm from the powerful waves. At nighttime the blasts of air were so violent that I ran under jib only. In the cabin, conditions were moist, warm, and oppressive. I tried to cook something but the nervous strain was too much.* I lay on my bunk but couldn't sleep because of the boat's jerkings.

At daybreak the weather was dreadful. Through the portholes I saw a sky and sea which looked strange and gloomy. Clouds, torn by the

---

*During storms Gau used a paraffin oil stove. Thus, in heavy weather, *Atom*'s interior was bathed in a dim greenish glow, as the deck and port lights were constantly submerged. The air was close, and damp, the tiny paraffin flame signaling hope to the tired sailor as it befouled the cabin air.

winds, scudded rapidly northeast. Under a jib of iron plate *Atom* fled, chased by an angered and rapacious sea. Astern, frightening waves rose in a manner suggesting that they were falling on deck purposely to smash it. But the most fearful moments were when *Atom* plunged her nose beneath the waves in dives that resembled a death wish.

When the wind, increasing in intensity, veered a few degrees, the rigging howled. The low harsh notes made by the masts and the shriller tones of the shrouds combined in a sort of crazed symphony. Because *Atom* ran the risk of being pitchpoled by running under the jib, I lowered it. *Atom* then rode bare-poled.

To assuage the roiling waters I lashed a pierced two-gallon can of oil between *Atom*'s windward shrouds. The thin oil film spread slowly to windward, dampening the waves and reducing them to large swells. The wind hauled to the southwest, which, according to theory, meant *Atom* was to the right of the hurricane's trajectory, or in the dangerous semicircle! This meant that I had to change course immediately and try to reach as quickly as possible the moderate semicircle.

Such theories read well in books, and powerful liners benefit from the explanations. Aboard a small windship it's another matter. I could avoid neither the dangerous semicircle nor the center of the storm. I must face it.

At five o'clock the wind's clamor ceased suddenly, creating an immediate and strange sensation. *This meant that I was at the center of the storm!**

I opened the hatch and quickly glanced around. Not a breath of air. But the scene appalled me. Waves, shaped like pyramids, rushed from every corner of the ocean. Above the pointed masses thousands of frightened seabirds whirled off and away, crying. I quickly closed the hatch, frightened by the noise of tons of water tumbling on deck. The boat struggled like she had gone mad. I felt the worst was still ahead. I knew that I had to remain as calm as possible.

Thirty minutes later it was horrible. The winds—making an inde-scribable sound—suddenly came out of the north. This meant I was now on the lower side of the moderate semicircle. Under the weight of that mighty blast *Atom* immediately lay abeam to the seas. I expected to hear the jarring sounds of two tons of internal ballast shifting in the

---

*We accept this even after examining a hurricane chart that showed the eye of the storm (on the nineteenth) to be about 1,000 miles east-southeast of New York City. This is partly because Hurricane Carrie was essentially a seastorm, and data from which the chart was prepared were accordingly scarce and scattered, and also because we have yet to discover in Gau's writings any intentionally dishonest major error.

bilges. My mattress slid onto the sides of the boat and the cabin lamp went out. I crawled, stumbled, and groped in the womb-dark blackness of my small cabin. Every fifteen minutes I pointed my torch at the instrument dials. At one point, the glass read 730 millibars and the anemometer needle jerked between 115 and 120 miles an hour. For four hours *Atom* lay on her side, like a wounded thing.

Near nine o'clock in the morning I sensed a degree of hope as the weather began to improve. That afternoon Hurricane Carrie was but a memory etched acidly in my brain.

And I had the memory, too, of a gallant little boat that had survived a sea so savage it would have taken the life of a much larger ship. And I had also the lessons that I'd learned about the phenomenon of great storms at sea.

Later, despite the state of the sea, under jib and mizzen *Atom* scudded before the storm, which abated quickly. From a Puerto Rican radio station I learned of another storm off the Florida coast.* But then, fumbling with the receiver dials, I heard over the 14-megacycle band the call of a ship in distress: *German ship* Pamir/*86 men on board/in Hurricane Carrie/all sails blown away/cargo shifted/50 degrees list/lying 400 miles ESE of Azores/asking immediate assistance!* The call was repeated in German, English and Portuguese. An Azorean station replied: Pamir/ *give us your position!*

The silence was moving. I learned afterwards that only six men had survived.

On October 3, 1957, I dropped *Atom*'s anchor off the front of the Sheepshead Bay Yacht Club, and by this action ended my first round-the-world voyage. For four years I had had a perfect communion with my boat. And for four years I had had a voyage generous with deep emotions, adventure, and the freedom that a man needs.

Researchers mining the rich ore of Jean's life are often rewarded with shining nuggets. So it is with Tahiti.

Faced with a beat to windward to make a landfall at the romantic Marquesas, Gau instead wore ship and headed for Tahiti. There in Papeete's flower-scented harbor the fifty-two-year-old sailor met a black-eyed, black-haired wahine. Her name was Taime.

Certain elements in their meeting transcend the usual "sailor's romance." Theirs was an attraction that was mutual, instant,

---

*Hurricane Frieda, September 21.

and, for the duration of the visit, constant. Jean's chivalrous nature and lifelong desire for privacy precluded, except in the vaguest way, any mention of their meeting in his manuscript. But years later, on another continent, he revealed in public talks how he met this woman, who figured largely then and in a later period of his life.

Shortly after being granted free pratique in Papeete, tired and needing rest, Jean "locked himself in his cabin." In New York Gau had devised a means of impressing visitors (including girl friends) that he wasn't aboard. Although a large padlock was seen on the washboard hasp outside, Gau could remove certain screws from an inside fitting that held the cabin hatch. He then pushed the hatch cover back, the large locked padlock still tightly grasping the dummy hasp. But in Papeete the graying sea hermit had been observed.

On the second night, about four A.M., there came a light tapping on the hull. Gau awoke. He peered cautiously out the dark porthole—into a woman's face! He quickly undid the "closed" lock and pushed the hatch cover back.

A woman's voice called softly, "*Atomie* . . . you here?"

"What you want?" Gau tried to sound curt.

Silence. Then the voice, which Gau now noticed was musical, asked, "You normal?"

"I think so!" replied an incredulous Gau.

As he stared at the framed companionway, the outline of a wavy-haired head and strong shoulders emerged from the dimness. He smelled the thick scent of island flowers; as the figure moved, the scent spilled into the darkened cabin.

"Two days—and no woman . . . " The outline stood dark against the star-spangled sky. "What's the matter?

"I . . . ah, I . . . well, ah . . ."

"You *need* wahine to clean ship!" Jean was now aware that someone had climbed over the "locked" hatch, and stood facing him in the dark cabin—someone exuding the scent of *tiare* flowers, island smells, the odors and stirrings of almost forgotten desire. Someone had touched him!

Taime soon taught the happily domesticated sailor to pick coffee beans and to make coffee in a skillet, admonishing him, "Don't spend money. Use money only for liquor and tobacco." Her advice was followed: years later, asked how cheaply one can live on board a sailboat, Gau replied, "In Tahiti, maybe twenty francs a week, if one has no accidents and catches fish."

Lots of fish!

But if the above version of how he met Taime was told to close friends, Johnny had also a version for his audiences. And they loved it!

"One evening," so Jean related this timeless tale, "I was sitting on *Atom*'s cabin top, quietly smoking my pipe, when a sweet-eyed wahine, named Taime, tied her little canoe to my bowsprit, climbed aboard, and asked if she had permission to do so."

> "But you've already done it," I said.
> She laugh. She walk across the deck to shore and bought groceries. Then she say, "Good night!" The same thing the next night.
> So I asked her, "Where you go every night, eh?"
> She laugh. "Fishing."
> Next day she ask me if I want to go—fishing. I say, "Oh no. I'm fed up with fishing."
> She say, "Oh! But I'll bring my guitar. You bring cigarettes and whiskey."
> W-e-l-l, under those conditions I decide to go fishing. . . .
> Next evening we went to buy some food, took her canoe. We go together inside the reef. We cast a small anchor. She lit a sort of lamp, fixed it to the hull, and we started fishing. Every second she had a fish, while I . . . well, she laugh at me. "But you have not rebaited your hook!" she cried.
> At three o'clock we had enough fish in the little canoe. She say, "We stop to have a snack." Then she play a little tune on the guitar for me and told me stories. . . . At abour four o'clock she say, "That's it. We have enough fish." I tell you that canoe was full of fish!
> "What you going to do with all that fish?" I asked.
> "Sell it at the market."
> "You spent all night fishing! Now you will spend hours selling it in the market?"
> "No, no. It is already sold."
> "What? But . . . how can you sell fish before you catch it?"

"Oh, how stupid these Frenchmen are!" Then Taime say, "Will you help me to take the fish to market?"

"Have you got a wheelbarrow? A cart? *Anything* to carry them?"

"No. But this bamboo stick in the canoe, we can use it." It didn't make sense, but then she seized the fish by the gills and slipped them onto the pole. Then she said, "You go ahead with the pole on your shoulders. I'll walk behind. We'll have to make several trips."

Here I was, a fool, entering the big crowded market in Papeete at four o'clock in the morning, carrying dead fish over my shoulder and followed by a native girl! So I walked ahead, unaware that Tahitians are merry people and like to laugh at others. And they did.

They cried, "Hey, look! Taime has caught a *big* fish!"

So I told her, "Look! From now on, I'll help to carry the fish to the marketplace but then *you* enter it alone."

She say, "But it's just fun! The Frenchmen don't know how to laugh."

Well, one night she say, "Atomie (my nickname then), Atomie—I don't feel like fishing tonight."

I say, "Well, don't go."

She say, "May I sleep on the other bunk?"

"Sure. Why not?"

W-e-l-l, Taime stay for nine months!

Gau's telling of this story never failed to stir an audience. His voice pausing or falling to make a point, the fingers of his right hand snapping at the roll of his wrist as he placed a particularly Gallic point to the tale, the intensity of his thought-filled gaze, delighted both teller and audience. Once more a woman had lent a measure of direction and point to his sparse existence.*

But even in Tahiti Jean felt the challenge of distant waters. "Every wave that struck the reef," he wrote in a letter to *Midi Libre*, "seemed to me a challenge that was saying, 'What are you waiting for?'" The depth of this feeling was revealed twenty years later on the other side of the world, in Ocean City, Maryland, when the seventy-year-old mariner interrupted a friend, "Listen!" He was listening to the sibilant voice of the surf, a mile away.

---

*One day Taime bought a small motorbike. A novice, she fell on her first outing. Sitting up, she examined her cuts and bruises and began to laugh. "Why do you laugh?" asked a surprised Jean. "Well, I'm not going to cry!" replied the spirited Tahitian.

On October 3, 1957, "at three in the afternoon *Atom*'s hook dug into the familiar bottom off the Sheepshead Bay Yacht Club. With a splash I was ending a happy four-year cruise, one filled with emotion, pleasure and adventure. Now I would have to submit to the rubs of civilized life. But not for long, because one day I will again seek the spell of Polynesia and the *joie de vivre!*" This ending to his first voyage around the world, printed in *Midi Libre*, differs slightly from the ending of his manuscript. Researchers, intrigued by finding other examples of textual differences, conclude that Jean's courtly and basically conservative nature inhibited him from freely describing many of his personal adventures in writing. Yet in conversation he could be extremely frank and spontaneous; a good example is the story of Taime.

But if we have the skipper's slightly different versions of his arrival at Sheepshead Bay Yacht Club, we have also the version of his arrival by *New York Times* reporter and nautical writer Ira Freeman. Shortly after Gau's arrival, Freeman wrote, "This is the fourth long, lone cruise for the 55-year-old French-American chef." After referring to Jean's hometown as "Valras," the interview continues:

> "Well, how was it?
> "What, the world? Very enjoyable," Mr. Gau said. He is a slender, aquiline-nosed, vivacious fellow in rough sailor's clothes.
> "Oh, you mean the voyage? No troubles, no sickness, no accidents, only a few gales. The worst storm was Hurricane Carrie. . . . I closed myself in the cabin. . . . and drew pictures for twenty-four hours."
> Mr. Gau showed an album of his colored-pencil drawings, done in photographic realism and meticulous detail. Now he must work ashore for a few years to save money. Then he will sail back to Tahiti and end his days there.

That Jean had already succumbed to Tahiti's lures was, according to Bernard Moitessier, very evident in their encounter nearly two years before. But now Jean revealed his thoughts more fully.

> "Do not believe the cynics who tell you Tahiti is spoiled," Mr. Gau said. "The climate is perfect. You really do pick food off the trees

and out of the sea. The girls are not like Gauguin painted them, but beautiful; also undemanding, sympathetic, good housekeepers and sailors."

It is an interesting string of attributes, ranked in order and reflecting El Solitario's view of women.

Fifteen years later Jean remarked to reporters, "Tahitian women are the best to sail with because they know all about sailing. And they leave you alone when you want to be left alone. Chinese girls are like that, too." It is the voice of the aging but still vigorous village cock.

Shortly after the interview Gau was paged on the club's loudspeaker. At the clubhouse he met a naval officer, who, after ascertaining that Jean was "Cap'n Gau," shook his head and chuckled.

"Did you call me here to laugh at me?" asked Gau testily.

"I'm sorry, Cap'n Gau. Of course not, sir. You see, I'm the guy who tossed that hurricane buoy to warn you." The officer smiled. "I'm just glad to see that you made it, sir."

The two men later went to the local Weather Bureau office to examine official tracks of Hurricane Carrie's path and the positions of *Atom* and the ill-fated *Pamir* during the storm.

"From that day," Johnny informed his friends, "when the Navy lectures about the 1957 hurricane season at sea, they always mention the mighty *Pamir* and the little *Atom*. This is how I am known in the American Navy!" Years later Gau was again shown the tracks of the storm and "the little *Atom*" when he was the guest of the Naval Academy in Annapolis.*

Yet for years Jean smarted over a remark in a popular introduction to heavy-weather sailing. The author, who did not correspond with Gau, stated that in the absence of specific details he was not certain whether ketch *Atom* was "anywhere near the center" of Hurricane Carrie in 1957. Queried in later years about the statement, Gau replied, with hurt in his voice, "I was *very* near the center!"

---

*A recent (1975) search there to locate any chart(s) showing Carrie's and *Atom*'s tracks was unsuccessful.

But now, in New York, the voyage over, the seeker of winds faced the challenge of making a living, far from the distant sea.

9

Departure from Valras

More confident and self-assured than ever, "without any fuss" the fifty-six-year-old chef returned to his old job in the warm, pungent kitchen of the Hotel Taft. But, to the more prosaic job of opening cans or arranging celery sticks on a tray, he preferred telling his fellow workers about the stomach capacity of South Sea cannibals or the greed of Chinese traders. There, beside the huge urns of shining stainless steel, a white toque tilted back from his sweaty brow, with gray eyes flashing and his rough voice rising to briskly emphasize a point, Johnny energetically responded to artless questions about *la vie Tahitiene*. At other times, his lips pursed, he would spear a savory hors d'oeuvre, his eyes soft at the recollection of the exquisite Nanai.

Every evening, haunted by the warm recall of soft nights under the southern heavens on make-believe atolls, he caught the garish subway for Brooklyn and yacht club where nightly he boarded his faithful *Atom*. Occasionally, upon arriving at the club grounds, the old-timer was interrupted by a casual visitor asking

139

if he knew anything about "that little red and green ketch out in the harbor." Jean would nod to the visitor's "She's a salty little devil, isn't she?" and then step down into his dinghy and begin rowing toward the shadowy boat, whose bowsprit-nose pointed seaward as though smelling the good salt air.

With each pull of the oars he relived some small fragment of his dream—a drop of water falling from an oar's lip reminded him of dark opaline pearls; The *thump! bump!* of the dinghy striking *Atom*'s hull suddenly brought Taime's dusky outline, scented and sensuous, before him. Bright and strong was the lingering aura of his long voyage, and it would remain so.

But there had been changes.

"Jean began to neglect *Atom* after that first voyage." The speaker, a close friend of the navigator's, continued, "He'd become a real pack rat, stuffing all kinds of junk, worn pieces of rope, abandoned bits of plastic, stuff like that, in her." And he seemed to have neglected himself, too.

"I sold him a rifle that I'd paid eighty dollars for, for fifty dollars. Later Jean told his boss, Agnel, that I'd overcharged him! Said I charged him fifty dollars for a twenty-dollar gun!" The speaker paused. His face suddenly twisted with feeling. "Agnel confronted me. 'Why did you do that to Johnny?' I was dumbfounded! So I saw Jean and demanded to know why he'd said that. I was damned mad.

"Jean looked me straight in the eyes. 'Down on Chamber Street,' he said, 'there's the same gun for twenty dollars.'

"I went to look. I found some guns in the window and a sign that read, *Gun Holster, $20!*" The speaker was looking down at his feet. "That voyage did something to Jean." His voice had softened. It sounded sad.

Another man in the small group nodded. "Johnny always paid for things, y'know, but he never returned a favor. Never."

"Ah, he had no sense of business either!" Hunched over a kitchen chair, the third man waved a thick workman's hand to indicate Gau's attitude toward money. "That small hunting preserve his dad owned, and the family vineyards? Ahhh! Johnny lost them because he wouldn't act. Today they'd be worth millions!" Not waiting to be asked how or why, he thundered angrily, "I said to him, 'Johnny, please let me lend you ten bucks a week to keep up payments on the property. Keep the estate, Jean!' He said, 'I don't want to owe anybody anything.'" His face a portrait of anger, disgust, frustration, the man sat back in the simple chair. "All impulse." He shook his head. "No brain!"

One of the men suddenly smiled. "Oh, Johnny had a lot of funny habits.*. . . Well, whenever he was in port, no matter where, he'd close himself up in that damned boat. Every now and then he'd pop his head up through the hatch, look quickly around, then quickly disappear below." Thickset, ruddy-faced, the smile still brightening his face, he chuckled. "Just like a woodchuck!"

After Jean's return to the States, the Societé Nautique decided to honor Valra's adopted son by naming the small harbor on the lower River Orb Bassin Jean Gau. When he was told at work of the Societé's action, tears filled Johnny's eyes, reflecting the emotions within. He vowed that one day he would repay their faith in him. As his happy co-workers raised their kitchen glasses to toast "Le Bassin Jean Gau!" the small chef, his throat taut with emotion, fought to control the storm unleashed by the news.

But as he lowered his empty glass, Johnny knew suddenly how he could repay the honor. It would be a gesture that only Valras would understand, and it would require time; it was too soon. Chef Agnel, thinking of the challenge facing his small friend, cried vigorously, *"Au défi de la mer!"* Smiling, Jean accepted a second glass of wine. He paused and then raised it high. He bit off the words, *"La mer lointaine!"* But only Jean, in the year 1959, knew just how distant the sea was.

Three years passed before he felt that his bank account was sufficient to pursue his dream. In the spring of 1963 Gau told his supervisor, Eli Agnel, that he would be leaving his job in early May. The huge chef laid down a saucepan of truffles. Briskly wiping his hands, he looked at Jean. "Another voyage, *mon*

---

*When refueling *Atom*, Gau always insisted on carrying gasoline in containers, ignoring dockside pumps.

petit?" At Jean's nod Agnel leaned heavily against a steam table. He folded his arms. The sounds of a well-run kitchen surrounded the two men. "Jean, my friend, you're sure you want to do this?"

Looking up at the tall chef, Jean, nodding, said simply, "Yes." Both men knew that the real question was Gau's age, but neither spoke of it. Agnel, sparing of criticism except where food was the subject, nodded slowly. "I will inform the management. When, Johnny, will you leave?"

"I must get away no later than the middle of May." Gau pulled at his ear. "Eli, I can't wait any longer."

The easy-going chef laid a huge white hand on Jean's thin, muscular shoulder. "Of course not. I understand, Johnny, but will your friends?"

Gau's friends tried hard to dissuade him from making the voyage, arguing that the boat, at least, had aged. Their advice went unheeded. They suggested that instead of making a voyage he write up his journal and try to find a publisher. But Jean sublimely refused to discuss the matter, and began to prepare the little ketch for the long voyage. If in the eyes of many Gau appeared a lonely figure as he toiled at provisioning his boat, Jean, happily, was totally unaware of it.*

Of his fateful attitude about the departure, there is no more illustrative example than his manuscript's opening statement: "All being properly stowed and made ready for sea, I started the engine." With these simple words Jean Gau began his account of a circumnavigation that was to last nearly six years; he was referring at this point to his sixth crossing of the Atlantic, and not to the beginning of his world voyage.

To repay the Societé Nautique and the citizens of Valras, Jean had decided to begin his great voyage from the basin named for him. Before his return to Valras he witnessed bizarre incidents, any one of which would cause most sailors to abandon the sea.

---

*But if he toiled at provisioning *Atom*, he did not toil where her well-being was concerned. "One reason for Johnny's excessively lengthy periods at sea," commented a close acquaintance who often sailed in tandem with Gau around the world, "was *Atom*'s poor shape. Every time he'd pile on sail the boat would open up."

Bad weather, the Levante, and engine troubles plagued his sixth crossing. Arriving in Valras, he spent nine months ashore before departing on May 26, 1963. By starting and, hopefully, ending his world voyage where his childhood dreams had germinated, Jean hoped to achieve several goals: Valras would forever be identified with his second circumnavigation; he would have discharged an obligation (largely, we think, imagined) to redeem himself in the eyes of his fellow countrymen; and he would be repaying Valras for its decision to name its harbor after him. In that decision practicality was paramount.

Taking his departure from the basin that had seen "old Jean" depart many times, "only to faithfully return years later," he resumed his way, "the way of the distant sea." Memories flooded over him and he was "deeply moved, a phenomenon that surges from my soul at *every* departure." This sentiment unfortunately is seldom supported by his writings. But when uttered here, he was in his sixth decade of life. Perhaps the village rooster had grown wistful?

The account that follows lacks only that portion that describes Jean's transit through the Panama Canal, a small boat passage that has been aptly described as "beastly." Such accounts are legion and are essentially similar, broken bowsprits and smashed spreaders seemingly being a requisite for successful transit.

Jean Gau's Account of His Second Circumnavigation

From 1957 to 1962 I resumed my old job of scrubbing pots and pans to get the money necessary to refit *Atom*. But finally the long-awaited day arrived, and at six-thirty on 15 May, 1962, all being properly stowed and ready for sea, I started the engine. Freed of the mooring lines that had held her for four years, *Atom* headed for the channel as I cast a last look at the yacht club. But at this hour nothing stirred except a lone fishing boat heading out of the bay. I bore off to let him pass. It was the *Sea Pigeon*, whose skipper greeted me, "Fair winds, *Atom!* And farewell!"

After rounding Rockaway Point I steered eastward. At three in the afternoon I had sailed sixty-five miles, leaving behind Ambrose Channel's traffic and dangers. At last I was on the high seas, with an old acquaintance, looking for new adventures. But if I was glad to be leaving I was a bit unhappy also, for many good memories were being left behind.

For the first three weeks the winds weren't favorable. And squalls followed with a disconcerting regularity. Yet it was fascinating to see my small boat struggle against the rough seas. Swollen at the beginning, they became even higher as the winds rose. When taken aback by the wind *Atom* pushed violently against the waves which then broke over her stern. And as long as the sea would not run a normal course, though I set sails properly and adjusted the helm, she shipped green seas on all quarters.

During the night of May 21 there was some breakage, as, under reduced sail, *Atom* painfully made her way against a strong northeasterly, the anemometer indicating thirty-five to forty knots, with rain squalls thrown in gratuitously. The seas were heavy and dangerous and each minute big ones boarded her.

About two in the morning I was thrown violently onto the port side. Minutes later, when the waters receded, I looked out expecting to see the dinghy swept away by that awful wave. I found it still fastened by its ropes, but what I hadn't expected to see was a shroud swinging and swaying to port. A stainless steel turnbuckle had broken. Luckily, *Atom*'s mainmast is held by four and not two shrouds as shown in the builder's plans. At daylight the weather improved somewhat and I replaced the broken fitting.

Now I was alone once more and in the middle of the great sea . . . I was happy because I'd left behind civilization's meanness, happy to be free and my own master.

After thirty-seven days of freedom, suspended between sea and sky, I was nearing land. At daybreak, June 21, I was scrutinizing an overcast horizon when about nine o'clock the sky cleared and I saw ahead the outline of Flores Island, the end of the Azores chain. Though it wasn't my first navigating experience I was pleased to verify my ability with the sextant.

North of Flores lay Corvo Island, a mere speck on the ocean. A dark volcanic islet with green heights and vertical slopes, Corvo is a shelter for seabirds tired by their long sojourns in the open sea. Pretty as it was, I still had 135 miles to sail before reaching Fayal, where I intended to stop.

But the winds gave up and for five days *Atom*, courted by fluky breezes, crawled over a flat sea. On the twenty-sixth a noon sight placed me seven miles from Punta Comprida, but a horizon full of rain prevented my sighting it. At five o'clock the wind rose, veering northeast, and *Atom* gamboled along at five knots.

That night it was dark, as dark as a fisherman's drawers in a nor'easter, and I lacked a light suitable for signaling the land. And yet land was near, dangerously near. To continue at that speed was to flirt with death. So I hove to until daybreak. Before daylight, however, I was on deck, and saw in the dim light a strange landscape dead ahead. On a high black cliff stood an extinct, gloomy lighthouse, its base buried in volcanic debris. I finally recognized it as the Punta Comprida light-house. And then I recalled the 1957 eruption; well, the landscape had changed considerably! North of the structure now stood three new hills—to the south the terrain looked more familiar. It was Branco Castello, and for the first time in five years I gazed at its rocky mass. Beaten furiously by the high Atlantic swells, this huge rock pile pro-vides in its crevices and cornices quiet shelter for the wild Azorean pigeons.

Rounding the Guia Peninsula, I entered at five in the afternoon Horta's noted harbor. As I rounded a pier I saw a motorboat approach. I immediately recognized by his spotless white uniform the port pilot, my good friend, Joa Silveria de Faria. After a warm welcome he directed me to a familiar mooring in front of the ancient fort with its castellated walls.

Later, with my friends, I drove to the new island over a road bor-dered by blue hydrangeas, which are abundant here, passing white cottages with walls and window frames of black lava rock. We stopped for a splendid view of Fayal and the neighboring islands, especially the dark and majestic summit of Pico, a study in reds and purples, whose sharp upper profile contrasts sharply with its lower spreading base. Later we ate, using as a table a large flat rock. The meal over, we left for the western part of the island, where, as the road climbed, the circle of our horizon broadened the higher we drove. At one point we spied a cart dating from Roman times. Set on massive and solid wheels, it was drawn by soft-eyed oxen. We passed several hamlets half-buried by sheets of ancient sand and cinder. Finally the road stopped at the edge of a thick wall of black sand. Before us lay a wild scene: the extinct lighthouse and the three high hills which had puzzled me at sea. Having burst from the sea, they had eroded away but after two weeks had reappeared, growing in size until they formed a new peninsula.

Regrettably, I received more invitations than I could accept, for I had much work to do aboard *Atom*. The rigging had to be checked carefully and new turnbuckles fabricated locally. At last, seeing that

Atom was ready for the rigors of the sea, I said good-bye to my island friends where I'd spent ten happy days. Slipping my mooring on July 7, I wondered if I'd ever again see this picturesque harbor. The little town, hardly awake, soon disappeared behind a curve in the coastline. Under a cloudless and airless sky, with the engine running, I made good way sailing along Fayal's eastern coast, rounding its grim capes. Seagulls, resting on the water, lazily flew off one after another to let us pass, the cliffs echoing their laughter.

By one o'clock I'd sailed forty-two miles and was north of the San Jorge and Graciosa Islands. Dismissing the engine, I lay below for food and rest. *Atom*, no longer steadied by the winds, lazily rolled all night in the swells of the high seas, and her skipper slept like a happy fellow until daybreak. Then a light breeze kissed her sails and she moved ahead, her foot tearing a thin seam in the fabric of the sea. Gradually all land receded beyond the water's edge and we were alone.

Except for two rattling squalls when the wind reached fifty-three knots, the crossing was uneventful. On July 25, after eighteen days at sea, a sight placed me forty miles west of Portugal. By nightfall I perceived the powerful light of Cape St. Vincent. As I neared these frequented parts I sadly knew that the relative tranquility of the great sea spaces was over. I had to get up once an hour every hour of the night to scrutinize the gloom of space for dangers and to check the running lights. As the boat rushed into the black night I became anxious, for I heard the . . . boat vibrate, . . . sound waves from distant horns passing into her masts.

The distance from the Cape to Gibraltar Strait is 180 nautical miles. Once more *Atom* lay becalmed, but with the help of her iron stomach I finally reached, on July 30, the entrance to the Strait between Trafalgar and Spartel. But here I met an old enemy, the unavoidable Levante or easterly of the Mediterranean. And so I tacked for two days and nights, beating from the white cliffs of Spain to the black rocks of Africa and back. In this short, choppy sea *Atom* looked after herself, but her old man had to remain awake to avoid collisions in a seaway where pass the largest number of ships in the world. Finally the Levante abated enough to let a light and favorable southwest breeze push us through the Strait like a peddler's cart.

After four slow days I entered at noon Cartagena's fabled military harbor. There the local press dedicated a whole page of *La Verdad* to my sea exploits, which resulted in a crowd of visitors the next day. And it was with pleasure I welcomed them, for they, too, were interested in the world of the sea.

But on August 11 it was Up Anchor! I filed away on a northeasterly course, destination France. Five days later I sighted Taragon and, because of friends there, decided to stop. At three in the afternoon I dropped the hook off the Nautic Club landing. Club members gave me an official reception and that evening a hearty dinner. The next day I happily strolled the streets of this ancient and colorful city.

On August 18, at five in the morning, escorted by the Taragon fishing fleet, I sailed out of the harbor. That evening at five o'clock I was off Barcelona, but continued towards France. After weathering Capes St. Sebastian and Creux at sunset I was but forty miles south of Valras. The evening weather was kind, the breezes favorable, and I had but seven hours of engine time before reaching my goal, Valras. My calculations indicated I'd reach it by three in the morning. Such favorable weather reminded me that one must take advantage of a smiling sky, for it is like the smile of a whimsical woman—one must discern when her eyes call for a daring move. . . .

Weary, I went below, intending to resume course at four o'clock to arrive before noon. But at three o'clock it was not my alarm clock that made me leap from my bunk but the howlings of a northerly blowing at gale force. In minutes an enormous sea was created, which caused me to heave to under bare poles. Every fifteen minutes the garrulous waters broke on deck. To my surprise the waters took longer to wash overboard than before. *Atom* was slammed hard, but it had happened before. It would happen again.

The openings fast closed, the cabin warm, I lay in my bunk, but I was impatient as the anemometer . . . oscillated between thirty-five and forty-two knots. But on August 23 in the afternoon, though the seas remained heavy, the wind abated. In the Mediterranean such seas can rise in minutes but require twenty-four hours to calm down. I resumed my northerly course and in ten hours had regained the fifty-nine miles lost to that wind and its squalls.

On the night of August 26 I was fifteen miles off Valras. Taking bearings of La Nouvelle lighthouse to port and aft, and that of Sete to starboard, I fancied I'd arrived. I've learned, however, about that distance between the cup and the lip! At about three-thirty in the morning there remained but three hours of engine time before reaching Valras. An hour later the engine quit. Fortunately, the breeze, a headwind, was weak. . . . I entered Sete's harbor about noon the next day. Towed to the quay, within an hour I made several friends, and we repaired, as they say, to Le Nautique bar for drinks. The layover was made especially pleasant by a visit from childhood friends from

Serignan. During this time a mechanic repaired *Atom*'s engine, but, since it was a Sunday and a feast day, it took longer. Unlike my America, here time is not always money.

That fall and winter I spent in Serignan and Valras, but I visited also Sete, Montpellier, St. Guilhem-le-Desert, Beziers, Narbonne, and Pezenas in a period that elapsed like lightning. And at each yacht club I made new acquaintances. In Narbonne I saw with pleasure amateur sailors being well instructed in handing, reefing, and steering. And I visited their modern sailing school, which I herewith wish great success. During this same period several learned societies honored me by inviting me to talk about life at sea. This, I admit freely, surprised and confused me because, for one having no more than a minimal formal schooling, it is an honor. In my talks I tried hard to be interesting and they, for their part, were most indulgent with my difficult syntax. For my part, I've gotten from these efforts profitable lessons and pleasant memories.

It was now exactly twenty-one days since I weighed anchor at Valras to undertake this my second voyage around the world. And it was not without emotion that I departed from that dear little harbor that now bears my name. It has seen old Jean leave several times, only to return faithfully years later. With great joy I have always returned to be with friends and relatives, the former, sadly, the more numerous.

An excerpt from my logbook, dated Sunday, May 26: "The weather is beautiful. I cast off the mooring lines at 1030, and escorted by friends and relatives aboard numerous fishing and sailboats, I once more resumed my way, the way of the distant sea, new horizons, new adventures. But the call at Valras has lasted nine months! As on previous departures, I leave France regretfully and sadly, but I am eager to be at sea again. One may consider oneself a so-called citizen of the world, but one doesn't forget one's mother country.*

Swearing to return, I got busy with ship's work, which always brought me relief. The wind was feeble and under three sails *Atom* made her way south at five knots. After an hour my well-wishers turned back and only the yacht *Le Maraudeur,* skippered by my friend Miguel, lingered to film *Atom* underway. And then it, too, departed. I then noticed a small racing cutter belonging to a cousin, Christian Asperge. Accompanied by his lovely wife and a good-natured crew, Christian left grau d'Agde to escort *Atom.* Now at noon I see them in the cockpit

---

*"A Frenchman by birth, American by choice, a citizen of the world by God's help," was a favorite opening remark in his public talks in later years.

eating and a light breeze brings the odor of frying—perhaps they'd caught mackerel earlier? Their meal over, the cutter neared and I was offered several cakes. Finally at one-thirty, after moving farewells, they depart. Tacking, the cutter makes for Agde hill, barely visible in the northeast. She bears off fast and soon is but a speck on the horizon, a white dot against a blue canvas. Fascinated with this sight, my eyes continue gazing until I realize that, once more, we are alone, absolutely alone. And then the memories flood over me and I am deeply moved, a phenomenon that surges from my soul at every departure.

By the evening of May 30 *Atom* was wrapped solidly in a thick fog, the haze so thick that from her small cockpit I could not see the mainmast. Without any breeze, *Atom* stopped in her track, and on that deserted plain I sensed being someone Time had forgotten, if it had ever noted.

The dawn seemed to be the most radiant I'd seen at sea. As soon as it broke the fog assumed the shape of thick clouds that rose until the Balearics, a few miles south, were visible. When I reached the eastern edge of the islands the breezes freshened a bit. *Atom*'s sail bulged and she continued daintily footing, like a pregnant young matron, along the north coast of Majorca. With the first rays of the sun I saw the summits of mountains whose profile stood dark against a reddish sky. I was strangely attracted by this coast's wildness: rocks that time and erosion have hewn into myriad shapes produced strange visages in the quiet of a morning. Then, at sunset, the weather changed suddenly. A gray cloud sprang up that darkened as it developed. As the southwest wind rose I quickly dropped the main and mizzen sails and left *Atom* to herself, under jib alone in high seas. In minutes the storm burst and flashes of lightning tore across the cloud banks, lighting intermittently the indented face of the mountains with a sinister glimmer. Squalls, pregnant with pouring rains, continued nastily all night long. By morning the storm had decreased but a dull growling was heard where the seas, still swollen, set towards the coast on which they broke angrily.

For five days I tacked along the coast, taking the land tack in daylight, standing to sea at night. Patiently I succeeded in rounding Dragonera, Iviza, and Formentera Islands. Then, on June 10, a fair northeasterly rose and with all rags on *Atom* ran before the wind at a spanking five knots, her course westward. Progressively the Balearics faded away, leaving one of those pangs that strike the traveler urged on by the shortness of life.

The night of the twelfth there was a midnight storm, the anemometer hand jumping between thirty-eight and forty knots (force 7 to 8 Beaufort). One hour later I handed the mainsail and left my boat to sail before the wind under jib and mizzen. Later I saw dead ahead the twinkling eye of the Cape Palos lighthouse on Spain's eastern shore, which I weathered that morning, and . . . arrived at Cartagena's Royal Yacht Club. My stay there, however, was short, for I wanted to cross the Atlantic before the hurricane season. At eight o'clock on June 18 I was underway for Gibraltar.

Between headwinds, light and fluky in the daytime and completely dead at night, I made slow progress. And to compensate for the inflowing strong current I needed all sails on, for if I reduced canvas *Atom* hardly moved. And, of course, the nighttime calms would sweep me backwards. I began to feel as though I'd never get out of that damned Mediterranean by sail. Had I used the engine I could have reached Gibraltar in four days, but I wanted to save gasoline.

Seventeen days later I entered Gibraltar's dramatic harbor and dropped the hook at my favorite spot near the airfield. I waited there for seven days until an easterly sprang up. On July 14 at ten o'clock *Atom* and crew joyfully cleared the port and its monstrous brooding rock. But soon as we reached the middle of the Strait the bitchy wind jumped to between thirty and thirty-five knots. Running full and by with all sails aloft, *Atom* plunged into the waters in a forty-mile race against the strong currents. We had to get out of the area before nighttime with its awful calms, calms that usually leave windships stranded in the midst of a mercantile armada.

Near eleven that night I weathered the Tarifa headland, where, at 200 meters from the lighthouse, the inflowing tidal stream engulfs itself into the Strait at a speed between four and five knots towards the Mediterranean Sea. When opposed by the wind this stream produces a confused and very dangerous sea: the waves turn short, irregular, and deep. You must then steer continuously to correct the fearful lurchings of your boat, try to avoid jibing and collisions with countless ships.

At five the next day I was abeam of Cape Spartel, that bony finger of the African continent, and soon the Mediterranean and its harsh entrance were behind me. For my part, I missed them not!

Marie Louise Gau with Jean, about 1914.

Jean at the helm off Nova Scotia, *Onda*, about 1935.

Onda period drawing.

Onda period drawing.

Onda wrecked off Cadiz, 1937, as depicted by Jean Gau.

Ketch *Atom.*

Atom on delivery, 1945.

Jean Gau aboard *Atom,* 1947.

Atom self-steering on the River Orb.

Jean with his father, about 1947.

In the South Pacific.

The only known photograph of Taime, from an old newspaper clipping. "Une ravissant Taitienne . . . ," begins the caption.

Rose Island, Gau's Treasure Island near Tahiti.

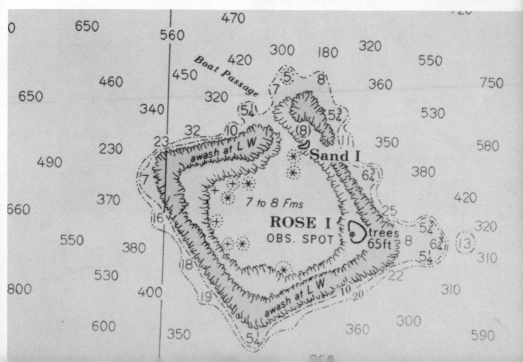

Skipper and *Atom,* about 1954.

Jean in Tahiti, 1954.

Sheepshead Bay
Yacht Club,
New York, 1957.

Claire Gau, Jean, and two
friends aboard *Atom* before
Jean's departure from
Valras, 1963.

Auckland, New Zealand, 1965.

Atom entering the River Orb, 1968.

Jean Gau in Valras, 1968, after
completing his second
voyage around the world.

Jean clowning in Valras, 1968. Note the mainmast sail track and the absence of parrels, indicating his switch to Dacron sails.

Atom and the mirthless sea, Assateague, 1971.

Aground on Assateague, November 1971.

Jean with *Atom* at Assateague.

Atom and rescuers
at Assateague.

Ocean City,
November 1971.

Jean and *Atom* in Ocean City, 1972.

Outward bound from Ocean City, 1972.

The wreckage of *Atom,* in a bight on the Tunisian coast. Note the broken oar in the foreground.

Jean Gau in his trailer, Valras, January 1975.

Gau in Valras, 1975.

10

"Atom! Are You Armed?"

      With the Atlantic surrounding and a good northeasterly, *Atom* and I agreed to stop the engine, make fast the tiller, and trim the sails. For her part, *Atom* took over and headed for the Madeiras 600 miles away to the west-southwest, gallantly and courageously working her way through enormous swells, not deviating a degree. The next day we were in the Spartel-Finnisterre seaway, where ships, always more numerous than are seen, are heading for ports around the world. But from now on it would be a wholly peaceful navigation, and I could enjoy reading books and magazines friends had given me in Cartagena.

      A sun sight on the twenty-third placed me fifteen miles off the Madeiras. Just past sunset I saw ahead the blinking light of the Sao Lorenzo headland, and that of Porto Santa Island to starboard. With regret I took the helm, which my hand had forgotten for nine days. And for the first time in some while I had to sit up all night watching *Atom* as she ran before the wind. Slowly we sailed away from these unfriendly parts, all the while closing the coast of Madeira.

      About ten that evening I rounded to starboard the Sao Lorenzo headland, where I spied village lights which seemingly hung from the sides of the mountains like lamps. And I imagined seeing a small cottage half-hidden in the foliage where a friendly family lived. I rejoiced at the thought of seeing again these old friends, of the fresh breads and fiestas ashore, of the Madeira wines. . . .

Rounding Cape Garajao at daybreak, Funchal's harbor opened before me. A haze blurred the hamlet while I lowered my sails, flaked out a good length of chain on deck, and readied my anchor. But as I started the engine the northeast breeze, which had accommodated us since Gibraltar, with no warning suddenly quit before an east-southeast wind that blew violently after a few minutes. Funchal's harbor, in this wind, is mediocre at best. During a previous call there in 1957 I'd cast a second anchor and that night the wind blew so strongly that *Atom* dragged both, as did a neighboring large schooner. The thought of spending an entire night worrying did not enrapture me. I changed my mind about calling and placed the chain, regretfully, back in the hawsehole, hoisted all sail, and departed for the West Indies, some three thousand miles across the distant sea.

At noon the following day my plot located me sixty-five miles southwest of Madeira. The transparent atmosphere let me see, far away and behind, the top of her high mountains. And I followed now for the third time the classic route of the ancient square-riggers. In the afternoon the wind veered northeast. What luck! For it was the trades, moderate it's true, but of a beautiful regularity, and the seas had a deep crystal blue color.

The afternoon of July 28 I had a pleasant surprise. Looking aft, I saw on the horizon a strange ship following the same course as *Atom*. I was puzzled because I was well outside the shipping routes. And the route of the old square-riggers is now abandoned, deserted, so to speak. Any encounter at sea, therefore, is a rare event in these parts. But any encounter at sea excites my curiosity: where is she going? And where from? What cargo lies in her hold? Most of the time such encounters fade with the ship over the edge, but this one soon approached *Atom*.

Through my glass I saw it was—an old-time square-rigger!

I wasn't hallucinating. *It was a three-masted bark!* I counted ten squaresails, four jibs, six staysails, a spanker, and topsails. My surprise, or awe, was even greater when I made out the American ensign at her mizzen gaff! I quickly hoisted my little ensign, according to tradition. On her great fo'c'sle a gang of youthful sailors waved. When abeam I took pictures and made film of the meeting. As she passed I saw her name, *Eagle*. Of course! The school ship of the United States Coast Guard. Soon I spied another ship in the east, making straight for *Atom*.

It was the American warship *W 377*. Two ships in one day in an abandoned part of the ocean? I was impressed.

Progressively her bow wave diminished as her engines were slowed. When within a few yards she began pacing alongside *Atom*. Sailors, leaning over the bulwarks, watched in silence, surprised to see my small sailboat romping along without anyone at the helm. From her bridge the captain hailed, *"Atom*, ahoy! Where from? Where bound? Can we help?" I answered saying I need nothing but thanking him for his concern. Shortly afterwards a small boat came off and drew alongside. I was handed a case of fruit juice.

A young officer asked permission to board my boat. Though the breezes were light, a swell was running and I feared what might happen. Finally he jumped onto *Atom*'s small deck and introduced himself.

"Lieutenant Dinninger, on behalf of Captain Garity, who begs you to accept this case of juice, and to let him know what would please you more?"

"Well, bread . . . " I began to say.

"You're lucky, sir, because the ship's baker makes fresh bread daily."

While the launch returned to the ship I invited the young officer below. There I learned that his ship was the *Eagle*'s official escort, that they'd departed Madeira a few days before bound for Bermuda, and that the *W 377* was an Ocean Weather Ship, one of nine on station in the North Atlantic.

I was as interested in the young man as he appeared to be about *Atom*'s long voyage. I asked him to relay a message to the *New York Times,* for I hadn't written since leaving Cartagena. Shortly the launch returned and *Atom*'s delighted skipper was handed a dozen loaves of fresh bread and photos of the two boats. The launch put off, we waved good-bye, and the escort steamed off in the wake of the beautiful *Eagle,* now a cloud on the far horizon.

For some time I followed their silhouettes with pangs of regret and then they were no more. For two hours I had had a pleasant interlude but now before me lay nothing but thousands of miles of empty ocean. And only a long crossing on a small boat adequately conveys just how immense and solitary are the world's oceans.

On August 9, having crossed the twenty-second parallel, I steered directly westward. The light in the moving immensity of my environment was splendid. My small boat's bow raised troops of flying fish, who soared out of their environment to escape determined enemies, but the dorados often leaped after them. Where did I, a mere onlooker, fit into this timeless drama?

In such pleasant weather my sense of time vanished and nine days later I'd reached the 45° West Longitude. I still faced 1,200 nautical miles before reaching Puerto Rico. But as we neared the West Indies I became anxious. The month's delay in my schedule had exposed me to a special risk more worrisome than all the others. It was the beginning of the hurricane season and I was now in the path of these mighty atmospheric perturbations. There were weather signs indicating a change, and the wind and sky, already suspicious, got my full attention.

Eleven days later sinister-looking squalls began to be seen, their evil outlines thickened into a yellow transparent haze or edge. The glass fell visibly and all around my horizon were half a dozen squalls simultaneously lashing the sea. Occasionally one would, without warning, dump a cataract on me. The air was moist and stifling and thunderous lightning bolts followed one another across the heavens. Was it, I wondered anxiously, the evolution of a hurricane? This condition persisted for five days. On the twenty-second Miami radio revealed that a hurricane, Beulah, was raging 520 miles east of Puerto Rico, with winds of ninety to 100 miles an hour. Happily for me, the bearings of the storm's center lay 480 miles southwest of my position. But I hadn't arrived and, I confess, I was not relaxed. Any day another disturbance might come along, an evil hazard for small boats at sea. I still bore in mind the grim sight of Hurricane Carrie whirling 120 miles an hour over the broad Atlantic, creating a high choppy sea whose enormous waves toppled onto other great waves. . . .

The trade winds returned, bringing nice weather, the breezes never exceeding ten knots, and I was pleased except for remembrance of the recent signs of a hurricane. But I was nervous also because of the slow progress, due in part to *Atom*'s dirty bottom and to a foul log line, both of which sensibly reduced her speed. As we neared Puerto Rico the trades turned unsteady, evolving into squalls and calms.

Tropical birds such as the frigate bird and the stormy petrel appeared, hovering for a better choice of dinner below. Screaming, they would fall on their victims, but just as suddenly stop their killing to fight one another until the defeated disgorged his meal for the victor's benefit.

As the dots accumulated on my chart *Atom* ticked off the miles. On September 11, a little after nightfall, I made out the glimmer of San Juan harbor lights reflected on the clouds overhead; the port still was thirty-five miles away. Not wishing to enter port at night, I hove to. The next day at three o'clock in the afternoon *Atom* moored to a buoy in front of the Club Nautic. This, my sixth crossing of the Atlantic, had lasted sixty-two days.

While Hurricane Flora was passing south of Puerto Rico and devastating Cuba I decided to return to New York by plane to see my friends there. With *Atom* contentedly moored, on October 3 I caught a plane; three hours and fifteen minutes later I was on New York's sidewalks and within a few minutes the guest of my friend, Joseph Cordonat. There I learned that I'd been reported lost because of a mistake by a Spanish newspaper! It reported me to have shipwrecked in the Azores but, in fact, it was another single-hander, Jean Lescombe of Bordeaux. Jean's body, together with the wreckage of his boat, had been found on Flores Island. You can imagine the surprise and joy of my friends when I showed up! Joe gave a merry party, inviting some old friends as well as members of the Slocum Society. I later visited the Sheepshead Bay Yacht Club and the hotel where I work between voyages.

After four happy days I returned to Puerto Rico. That island is not without charm and, were it not so stifling hot, would be an ideal place for retirement. Not far from *Atom*'s mooring were several American warships. Their officers came aboard the mighty *Atom* and invited *her* commander to dinner, [an invitation] accepted with alacrity. We later discussed voyaging.

At thirty minutes past nine o'clock on October 31 I sailed out of San Juan's harbor on a course alongside the ancient fortress San Felipe del More, noting the seas breaking along its stony base. Offshore under a cloudless sky and rippleless sea, *Atom* met with a mighty swell that raised her several feet high in seconds. From the north this swell was slamming the coast, where it broke with an evil rumble, sending showers of spray into the air. This prodigious swell was caused by the distant Hurricane Ginny, . . . raging between Bermuda and the States, 900 miles north of where *Atom* now sailed. Lighter airs followed calm periods but we did progress, little by little, along the island's northern coast. But the trades were no longer there and on November 3 I rounded the headland and entered the famed Mona Pass, a sort of strait, sixty miles across, which separates Puerto Rico from Hispaniola. I had now the Caribbean Sea to cross and a thousand miles of water before reaching Cristobal in the Panama Canal Zone.

But I now faced the dangers of a 756-foot-high rock called Desechea, which lacks any navigation lights or markings and is a real hazard in this area. For my part I might have allowed a margin of safety of a few degrees, port or starboard, of this menace when drawing my course on the chart. Too late! I had to keep my course. That night I spent straining to see through the heavy darkness.

About two o'clock a line of breakers suddenly foamed in front of me, covering and uncovering foul reefs—my boat was running straight onto them! *Atom*, I noticed, was close to the western extremity of the looming rocks. There was time to run to the tiller, and by sheering suddenly to starboard we barely avoided them. Regaining her speed, *Atom* footed closely the last reefs, which soon disappeared into the blackness of night.

Having escaped this danger, I felt that tongueless sensation which follows great emotions. I also felt a great fatigue. A cup of coffee and I slept until daybreak.

But the next night I was startled by strong blows against the hull. In two jumps I was on deck, where, surrounding *Atom* as far as I could see, was a chaotic mess: bean pods, planks, bamboo trunks, coconuts, stalked bananas, etc. Several hours of careful navigation through this vegetated sea and *Atom* reached open water.

During the evening of November 6 *Atom* was almost embalmed by the stillness. There simply was no breath of air. The sea, absolutely flat, resembled an enormous oilcloth and the horizon was lost somewhere in the sky. The air was clear and the stars reflected on the shiny oilcloth sea. *Atom* and I seemed suspended in a void.

As far as the tenth parallel the days passed pleasantly. Incessantly rolling, *Atom* was courted by a light northeasterly, hardly sufficient to lift her skirts. She was also escorted by a court of svelte dorados, who had performed this gallant service since leaving the Mona Pass. They were enormous fellows and I had difficulty lifting them on deck. During the night flying fish struck the sails and at dawn I found scores on deck. By now, however, I was sick, absolutely sick, of fish. Frankly, I was anxious to arrive in Cristobal just to have a steak without fish!

On November 15 a spell of rain set in. Some . . . squalls were impressive by their grimness, for they were literally aerial cataracts, brief and violent. In this period of foul weather *Atom*'s deck became a shelter for seabirds tired by the storms. Two days later the sky cleared, but after sunset the breeze blew such that it was Down the Main! Down the Mizzen! Under jib only *Atom* ran off before the wind. Despite her short sail area she ran ninety miles in twenty-four hours. Since leaving Puerto Rico I'd apologized to *Atom* for the lack of wind. Now we had far too much! Sixty miles from Cristobal the wind softened and on November 22 I sighted land. That afternoon we weathered Manzanillo headland.

With thirty-one miles to go and only a weak headwind to help, I started the engine. Thirty minutes before midnight we entered Cristobal harbor and anchored behind the west jetty. At three o'clock port officials woke me up to examine the ship's papers and to grant me pratique.

There being no space at the club for *Atom*, I careened her beside the dry dock. While at the club I met an old friend, Bob Grant. For more than a year Bob had sailed from island to island throughout Polynesia aboard the *Mandalay,* a yacht owned by James Rockefeller. Later in Tahiti he bought a thirty-foot sloop, *Korrigan,* and with a young Australian went off to the New Hebrides. I met them in Bora Bora and later in Pago Pago. It was there that his crew married a pretty Samoan while Bob sailed on, single-handed, heading for Port Vila. . . . a severe storm threw him onto Eromango Island, where he lost *Korrigan.* By a fantastic stroke of luck he was rescued the following day by natives and arrived, safe but injured, in Port Vila. A short time later he bought a motorboat, but a gas leak caused an explosion that killed his companion and horribly burned Bob.* Carried by plane to New Zealand, months later he recovered and married his nurse. Adventure excited them both so they went to Hawaii, where he bought a sturdy sloop, *Typee.* Now I found him again with his wife and child in Cristobal, where he drives a hoist in the Gatun sluice. "One more year," he told me, "and it's French leave, Johnny!"

The damages caused . . . in the Gatun lock worried me. But I don't submit long to the effects of failure. Mastering my spirits, I resumed with more gusto than ever this long struggle against adversity.

By an unlooked-for stroke of luck the bronze propeller arrived just as *Atom* was entering dry dock. I hired a shipwright and a mechanic and we started work pronto. Everything was finished the next day and you can perhaps imagine my joy at seeing my old lady ready for the sea again.

---

*An anecdote not recorded in Gau's manuscript concerns Bob and Jean in Cristobal. Bob, so the tale goes, wore an artificial ear made of plastic, a result of the explosion. The two friends would select a Chinese restaurant and order bowls of soup and mounds of fried rice. After the waiter left, Bob would surreptitiously drop his ear into the rice dish. Seconds later, as he prepared to ladle some rice, "he would suddenly scream like hell, jump up and point at the dish!" The wide-eyed manager and alarmed waiters would run to the table, where the almost hysterical Grant would stand shaking, pointing at the ear "peeking out of the rice." Often Bob had to grab the ear and help his laughter-weakened friend to his feet before they were noisily pushed from the restaurant.

Tahiti required the only visa for my voyage and in Panama it is the French consul who delivers them. On January 9 I went into Panama to get spare parts for the engine and to obtain the visa. I found what I needed in a shop but it was then too late to catch the consulate. I planned to go next day. Buses being on strike, I returned to Balboa on foot, strolling the streets satisfying my insatiable curiosity for picturesque scenes and unforeseen events. What struck me about this town was its diverse population. I walked through a throng of Panamanians, Negroes from the Antilles, Hindus, Chinese, Indians from San Blas, and half-breeds of every color. Everywhere I found cabarets ablaze with life. But poverty reigns, and everyone seemed to be selling hats and lottery tickets.

I passed in front of a university, where students argued with gusto. As I reached Balboa a brawl broke out between American and Panamanian students over a silly matter of flags. In minutes the streets had filled with police and soldiers, who had a tough time chasing the Panamanians out of the zone. Almost immediately, like a lit fuse, all Panama was in revolt, and during the riot American helicopters flew overhead begging the crowds to go home to avoid bloodshed. Being very tired and hungry, I went back on board.

That evening about eleven o'clock a red gleam lit the heavens near Mount Ancon: Panamanians were burning American buildings! While I rested in my bunk, following the incident over the radio, 200 were wounded and twenty killed. Then, about 2 o'clock in the morning, a blinding light played over my boat. In two jumps I was on deck. Nearing slowly was an army picket boat.

"*Atom*, ahoy!"

"Yes . . . what do you want?"

"Are you alone on board?"

"Yes!"

"You are incurring the risk of being attacked. If you want we'll take you ashore to the clubhouse where you'll be safe."

"I thank you . . . but I cannot leave my ship."

"Very well. Have you arms on board?"

"Yes. A .30-.30 carbine."

"Good. Keep it loaded near you and don't hesitate to use it if you're boarded. Good night. Good luck!"

That night I did not sleep.

The next day the situation had somewhat bettered and on January 13 I went to the harbor master to get my health certificate, which, I noted, was handed to me in minutes. There was nothing else to do other than to get my important French visa. American authorities gave me a special permit to get by guards at the Zone boundary.

Formalities weren't too complicated at the consulate but I lacked four photos. I had to go back into town to locate a photographer. Finally, on a shabby street, I found a dilapidated house with a weathered sign: CHINK LEE—FLASH FOTOS—15 MINUTES. I entered a dimunitive studio, encumbered by an enormous camera. A Chinese met me. He was old, very old, emaciated and ugly enough to scare me. Speaking a scraggly Spanish, he laughed a lot and showed teeth black as cloves.

"Can you make me four photos in fifteen minutes?"

"Nooo . . . but I can make you six photos in ten minutes. . . ."

The camera was unique. I'd never seen such a monster! It was huge and held by a solid tripod. The lens had a diameter the size of a stovepipe and the shutter was operated by a rubber ball the size of a melon. The tripod really caught my eye—an ebony figure representing Titan, with outstretched arms lifting the camera. I got my pictures eventually, and my visa, and returned to *Atom*.

All difficulties overcome, *Atom* was ready for the long haul. The faraway island of Tahiti, my next landfall, was 5,500 nautical miles off in the Southern Hemisphere. I made a last study of the currents and probable weather conditions that I might encounter between Panama and the Galapagos and then traced a rhumb line on the chart. From previous experience I expected a long and difficult crossing between these points. Indeed, a voyage by sail in that region becomes a fastidious adventure, a vexing affair known to mariners. The best solution would be to cross the Humboldt Current at its extreme limit, sailing south up to 2° North, then head west towards the Galapagos. It would be a navigation of over 1,000 miles with headwinds, calms, and interference swells.

I departed Balboa on January 16 at seven-thirty in the morning and by eight o'clock had rounded the last buoy. I stopped the engine, got the sails up, and hauled away for the south-southwest. A final glance back towards the Andes etched against the sky, and then the wind outside brought me a sensation of peace and freedom. Leaving behind the difficulties of land living, I threw myself joyfully* into this huge ocean.

---

*Fitfully might be a more apt term. A letter dated May 1, 1975, from Hein and Sigrid Zenker, a Canadian couple who sailed more or less in tandem with *Atom* around the world aboard their twenty-foot sloop, *Thlaloca*, says: "Jean was ready to leave the anchorage but he couldn't get the engine into gear. The tide slowly carried *Atom* down-channel and it

At sunrise on January 20 a small, somber island, inaccessible and tomblike, stood off to starboard. It was Malpelo, a rocky seamark feared by sailors because of its fog and nasty currents. Notwithstanding the lack of breezes, I happily noted how *Atom* shied rapidly away from this object, no doubt influenced by the Pacific countercurrents.

Tower Island emerged from the waters at nightfall on February 1 but I forewent calling at its Darwin Bay, where, because of the great depths, anchoring is almost impossible. We now approached a region of brutal atmospheric conditions and the navigation would be tricky. Overcast skies, rising winds, soaking rains, and hidden rocks increased my apprehension as *Atom* sought a passage through curtains of fog and sudden squalls. But I managed to keep her heading in the right direction for thirty-five miles. Twenty-four hours later, during a lull, I saw the silhouette of Pinta Island.

All dangers now behind me, I altered course and headed southwest, but a strong current daily carried me sixty miles off course. And the southeast trades, hauling south half of the time, forced me to sail close-hauled. An enormous swell which seemed to grow and to leap at *Atom* incessantly caused her to roll or to pitch her nose, each dip suggesting that something solid lay beneath her foot. As she labored to gain each foot heavy spray surrounded her. Except for minor adjustments from time to time I didn't touch the tiller. As we neared the Equator the weather grew colder because of a branch of the mighty Humboldt which here flows to the west.

At one o'clock on February 11 I cut the Equator at 100°12′ West Longitude. Polaris had already disappeared beyond the northern horizon and my boat now roamed in the Southern Hemisphere. Where, I wondered, were the mighty trade winds? Until February 20 the wind blew from the south during the day, shifting to the south-southeast at sundown. But gradually—feebly and intermittently at first—it blew from the southeast and then, moderate and fresh, blew confidently from the east. And with them good weather and flying fish to adorn *Atom*'s deck and my skillet. Dorados, I noticed, were scarce.

Pitcairn Island now presented great interest to me. I knew the story of the *Bounty* mutiny and here was my chance to visit the site of that tragedy. But to reach it, some 3,000 miles away, I would have to

---

was strange to see Jean in a complete panic. He ran back and forth muttering in French and English, thrashing his arms with gusto! 'Throw the bloody anchor!' we called. Nothing happened. Finally, Ron Russel dove into the water, swam to *Atom*, climbed aboard, tossed the hook over, and all was well. The gear was fixed and Jean pulled up the hook. We next saw him in Tahiti."

exchange the trade winds for bad weather, calms, and crosscurrents. Despite this and the knowledge of Pitcairn's unsafe anchorage, I laid out the course.

I cut the trade winds diagonally on a course south-southwest, but steering south to counteract the Equatorial Current, which drifted us sixty miles westward daily. In the afternoons a "reinforced" trade wind would often arrive, its outrider a huge regular swell that obliged me to climb rolling hills every ten seconds.

Atom slowly cut her way south in heavy rains. At the twenty-fifth parallel I headed her west on the night of March 24, a Venus sight placing us forty miles from the dangerous Ducie Atoll and 300 miles east of Pitcairn. As birds began to be seen I grew excited. One week later at sunrise tragic Pitcairn Island revealed itself fifteen miles away. After seventy-five days of plentiful sky and water I congratulated *Atom*'s navigator on his skill.

Pitcairn began to stand out like a wall with no discernible footholds. Soon, no phenomenon of nature could have impressed me more than this great barrier, at whose foot lay a chaotic heap of giant blocks, one of which was so beautiful and savage in character that it impressed me profoundly. From the base of the island wall where I sailed, the summit seemed to be falling into the sea 1,000 feet below. I saw a dense vegetation along the heights and in the ravines and rocky chasms. In one place the thin silver thread of a distant unseen waterfall flashed. Beauty, peace, and extreme solitude are Pitcairn's price for being forgotten.

Even in the midst of this spectacle the security of my boat was paramount. Hoping to find a safer landing, I regained the open sea, and in time arrived at a small opening between vertical rock walls. It was Bounty Bay! On its bottom lay the blackened hulk of Bligh's ship. The opening, strewn with huge rocks against which the waves broke unceasingly, tempted me, although I knew no boat could remain anchored there unattended in a southeasterly. The wind being light and favorable, under jib, mizzen, and engine *Atom* slowly threaded the needle. Inside a ribbon of sand circled the inner bay. Anchor at the ready, I stood in the bow, casting the lead without stopping. But I had to run aft frequently to correct the helm whenever a gust of wind slammed down off the mountain. Although I was in a hornet's nest I admired what I saw.

Failing to find bottom at ten fathoms, I didn't dare to sail any farther. When I was almost at the edge of the breakers I promptly tacked and stood out to sea again.

I rounded the southern point of the eastern coastline, and on a high hill I saw the antennas of a radio station manned by young Thomas Christian. Nearby a signal flag was being hoisted: WISH YOU BON VOYAGE!

I acknowledged it, ruefully, by dipping my burgee.

11

The Call of the Spray

My destination now was Tahiti, nonstop, by way of the southern edge of the dangerous Tuamotu Archipelago. As we worked westward the trades ɔecame more regular and the speed of the swells increased, which pushed *Atom* westward an extra thirty miles daily. On April 19 I stood off the uninhabited atoll of the Duke of Gloucester Islands, whose reef belt is partly covered by the seas. On its *motu* grows a rich vegetation which contrasts with the ocean's blue darkness and the whiteness of its surf. I cringed when I recalled how *Atom* had nearly wrecked on these reefs years before. But today the way was clear, with less than 400 miles separating us from Tahiti. Suddenly the wind veered and I tacked, which lengthened this distance considerably. Seven days later I succumbed to a strong emotion when the mountain peak Orohena towered above the distant clouds. Tahiti!

As I rounded the foreland, Papeete harbor opened to my excited eyes. A pilot boat directed me to the quay, where, with one anchor to seaward to keep *Atom*'s nose sniffing the good salt air and her stern held by pier lines, I was ready to greet the curious crowd gathered on the quay. I was anxious to join close friends who cheered me with cries of *"Ia ora na!"*

Tahiti had changed. A new coral jet airstrip now brought the rapture of the South Seas to far-off Europe. Despite the new buildings, ersatz Polynesian "culture," and higher cost of living, Tahiti's charm still entices the long-distance voyager.*

Among the yachts I saw was the *Dora* out of Marseilles, whose owner I'd met years before in Durban. There was also the cutter *Easterling*, manned by three young Floridians whom I'd met in the West Indies the previous year. These young fellows, incidentally, will long remember an encounter they had in the middle of the Pacific when a feisty whale scratched his backside against their boat. By temporary repairs and muscle—mostly the latter, for they pumped without ceasing—they eventually reached Papeete.

On September 29 I dropped *Atom*'s harness and waved farewell to friends, each of whom gave me a small present as well as the traditional shell necklace. I was saddened by the departure. I could have remained, of course, until the end of March, but the call of the spray was stronger. Impelled by an insatiable thirst for adventure, for sailing toward distant shores over great seas, I knew that I was leaving the security of quiet harbors, the pleasures of the hammock, the comfort of a life too calm for my temper. But I knew also that *out there* were exciting hills to climb, contrary winds to combat, cold, danger, fatigue, and, ultimately, goals reached with joy.†

---

*While in Papeete Gau was at a party where Marlon Brando, having drinks with friends, exclaimed, "Boy! It's hot." The famous actor, to Gau's button-eyed astonishment, suddenly stripped a toupee from his head and placed the "rug" in his shirt pocket!

† For Jean, however, Papeete held more than yachts, *tiare* flowers, and deep-sea tales. One day a clerk in the Indochina Bank refused to change $100 bank note saying, "Only smaller bills will I exchange. *Not* a $100 bill!"

"So," said Gau, "I returned to *Atom*, picked up $100 in smaller bills and went back to the bank. But I kept the $100 bill on me. When I got there a guy was ahead of me. I couldn't see his face but I saw that *he was holding a $100 bill!* I figured the clerk would give him the same treatments. He did. But this guy took a card out of his pocket and handed it to the clerk.

"I looked at the card — Oh boy! James Rockefeller — Jesus!

"He said to the clerk, 'I want to speak to the president.'

"That clerk say, 'So sorry. President not here. I will change bill for you.' And he did. So Rockefeller turns to leave and I'm blocking the way.

"Hello!" he say. 'You are the one on board *Atom*, aren't you? . . . Well, nice to see you. So longs!"

"*So* I say to that clerk, 'My name is *not* Rockefeller, my name is just Jean Gau. But I want to speak to the president!'

"That dumb clerk, he say, 'What's the matter with you, boy? Here, give me that bill. I will change it for you.'"

Atom entered a splendid sea warmed by a dazzling sun, and, making for Bora Bora, I watched Tahiti gradually vanish as her sister, Moorea, assumed a more precise outline. By sunset all was gone from the sea.

I didn't linger in Bora Bora but cleared shortly for Pago Pago in the Samoas, which I reached after 1,200 miles and twenty days of comfortable sailing. Not far from Pago Pago, of course, lay Rose Island with its barnacled bullion, nacre, and pearl. From my previous voyage I knew this island well and I was anxious to see it again.

A morning sight on October 19 located me two miles east of the island, which, but for an ink-stained squall on the horizon, would have been visible. As the squall dissipated and the horizon cleared I saw, dead ahead and a mile off, a clump of trees which seemed to step out of the sea. It was Rose Island! I sailed along its eastern reef, an unusually wide coral belt with heaps of black blocks rising above the brick-red reef, which encircled a lagoon two miles in diameter. At nine o'clock, north of the atoll, I lowered my sails and started the engine. As the seas boomed thunderously over the stony reefs I felt a formidable sensation. . . .

Atom entered a foaming whirlpool that boiled in the narrow cut. At one and a half knots, she appeared to be standing still until a coral head to port showed that we were progressing. At midpoint the current lessened and *Atom* slid into a jade-green lagoon. As the bottom rose and corals and sand appeared I anchored.

Placing some food in a bag, I rowed first to a nearby thicket. To a sailor any vegetation is a delight. Stepping ashore on the pulverized shell beach, I sauntered into the shadowy brush. The quietness there was so tense I felt I was violating a natural sanctuary.

Leaving this tiny forest by the sea, I wandered to a large tree, and found carved deeply in the trunk YACHT ATOM, J. GAU 1955. Refreshed, I pushed on to Sand Island (which, by taking the inside reef, wasn't far), seeking turtle eggs on the way. Thousands of seabirds covered the island and their stench made the air oppressive. Screaming wildly, several attacked me, forcing me to use a stick to drive them away. Finding several sand mounds, I dug until I uncovered the deeply buried eggs. Tired and enormously hungry, I returned to *Atom* about sunset.

That evening I enjoyed a good cigar while admiring the Southern Cross overhead. Out beyond the reef Old Ocean's great and deep voice roared and cursed while I slept the sleep of the just.

The next day I rowed along the inside reef to the south side, where in a corner of the lagoon there is a small bight. There, in 1955, I had found more than 100 pounds of nacre and several lovely pearls. I had heard, however, that Japanese fishermen had explored *my* lagoon. In Panama an American sailor* had warned me, "Don't stop at your island, Jean 'cause there's no nacre there. . . . Not only there," he added, "but even atolls without passes!"

I had to see for myself. While the dinghy playfully rubbed the lagoon's face I dressed in an old towel and dove into the lagoon's crystal waters. My friend was right—the oysters were rare and small, and only giant clams, capable of enjoying my leg, were common. Severing an oyster no bigger than a saucer, I placed it in my bag and came up for air. After a dozen dives I had only six nacres! Discouraged, I went fishing for lobster out on the outer reef, where I was more successful, hauling two giants in minutes. But sharks, swimming around in tight circles, diminished my interest.

As the sun rose I weighed anchor, and minutes later motorsailed out of the cut, helped by an outflowing current. The pass or cut behind me, the open sea ahead, I set the sails, killed the engine, and watched, pensively, as Rose Island became another memory.

October 22, off to starboard, I saw Tau Island, the first of the Manua group of islands, and later, despite light breezes and a flat sea, Ofu and Olozenga Islands. After sunset I spied on the western horizon the friendly tic of a distant lighthouse, but not wishing to arrive at night, I hove to. The next morning I sailed into Pago Pago's breathtaking bay.

Ashore, I found that it, too, had changed. Everything looked new and shiny, and women covered their breasts and men their tattoos. Five days later I cleared for New Zealand and distant points, marveling at the inroads of missions and civilization in the Pacific.

For the first five days in November I sailed along the Tonga Islands, keeping 120 miles east of them. The scattered Kermandec Islands were in the general vicinity on November 13, but I altered course to sail far west of them. My thought was that when I lost the southeast trades I'd encounter strong westerlies and currents which could set *Atom* onto these rocks.

On November 18, having crossed 180° West Longitude, I found the sky leaden and misty, and a rain full of volcanic ashes and cinders, smelling heavily of sulphur, dirtied the sea and my boat. Auckland radio later reported that the Kermandecs' Raoul Island volcano had erupted, that flooding lava had swept away a new met station there, and

---

*Most probably Bob Grant, who, contrary to Jean's manuscript, reportedly knew of Rose Island's wonders.

that Auckland's beaches were closed for fear of a tsunami generated by the eruption. But *Atom*'s crew had no fear, for my ship would be in danger only if she were in the vicinity of the epicenter, which she wasn't. Ships tied quietly at piers sustain far greater damage than ships at sea under these conditions.

We soon entered the area that separates the trade winds from the Roaring Forties. Dressed in woolies, sitting in my heated cabin, I was chagrined to learn that an Antarctic depression was moving northeast at fifteen miles an hour and carrying winds of forty-five to fifty knots. Sure enough, that afternoon the breezes veered southeast, the clouds increased, and the glass fell. That night, November 29, I was worried because I couldn't see the Cuvier Island lighthouse, which my midday observation had located sixty miles away. During the night squalls hit us at the rate of three or four an hour from the south, the anemometer reading thirty-five to forty knots every eight to ten seconds. Pointed high, *Atom*'s bow ran across a corrugated sea. By dawn I was forced to drop the main, an hour later the mizzen. Finally, I hove to under a taut jib, knowing very well *Atom* would drift badly, but I could [do] nothing else. Having secured my boat, I went below, where I was soon warm and snug in a sort of coziness, the more gentle as everything else was hostile and raging.

After three days of being hove to I managed to get a sun sight . . . . *Atom* had drifted backward 120 miles during that time. Because of the improved weather I was able to resume my southward course on December 2. Six days later an island stood off to starboard. But was it Cuvier Island? East and west of it were small helpings of coast that resembled islands. After sunset a lighthouse suddenly winked and, from the flashes, I knew it was Cuvier. At eight o'clock the next day *Atom*, attended by sunshine and a moderate breeze, rounded the eastern foreland of Great Barrier Island and happily entered the Houraki Gulf.

Needing rest, about twilight I decided to heave to when five or six miles from the Tirititi lighthouse. I was up every hour to glance topside as *Atom*, under all rags, drifted slowly toward the lighthouse. By eight o'clock on December 10 I'd rounded the foreland where the gulf narrows, forming several bays, and two hours later rounded up at Rangitoto Island to hoist the yellow flag. Under motor I entered the well-marked channel and proceeded, eventually, to tie up at Marsden Wharf, where *Atom*'s happy gang was welcomed by a crowd of nearly one hundred souls.

Atom's was in good company, her neighbors the ketch *Minerva* (San Francisco), *Tropic Seas* (Sydney), and the *Kismet* (Boston). We were joined a few days later by a nice little twenty-four-footer, single-handed by Major C. W. Bromley, an ex-RAF pilot, arriving from Sussex, England. Wherever *Atom* goes she makes friends, and such a friend was Toni MacGrenes, who came aboard to obtain some anecdotes and photos. Miss MacGrenes suggested I write an article for the Auckland *Star*, which, in time, brought me many visitors, invitations, and trips throughout this curious and interesting land. From these trips I'm forced to conclude that this charmed country is a packaged Riviera, Alps, African hunting ground, and—yes!—Norwegian fjord.

I'd expressed a desire to see the country's birthmarks, so to speak, its fabled volcanic landscape and undulating countryside, and its primitive forests. A young couple, the Ian Johnsons, having read the newspaper article and interested in sea travel, invited me to join them for a week's stay inland at Opotiki. Leaving *Atom* in Major Bromley's care, I gladly boarded Ian's car.

We arrived at nightfall and I was warmly greeted by Ian's parents. Over the door of my bedroom was a sign, WELCOME, JEAN GAU, TO OPOTIKI! Early next day we followed the shores of Of Plenty Bay, where, against the horizon, smoked the active volcano of White Island. Our first stop was at Hell's Gate, a small sulphurous town where nearby a vast geothermal zone boils. There, spectacular steamy geysers, bubbling muds, cliffs, and precipices were being orchestrated in a timeless drama by unseen hands.

At the Waitama Caves stalactites and stalagmites vied for my interest with the Glowworms Cave, where worms provided an eerie underground lighting system to the growlings of an invisible cataract. Later we stopped at the Waipona Forest, where we entered a truly green world, that of the giant Kawri tree. With amazement I gazed at the giant *tane malruta*, a tree that after 1,200 years still grows with commanding splendor.

Five days later we returned to Opotiki. The local media, in our absence, had published an article that began, "The dean of solitary voyagers, Jean Gau, world citizen, includes Opotiki in his voyages." Well, I *had* to accept several invites to parties as a result. Among them was a talk at the Arts School, where I demonstrated my drawing technique to instructors and students.

Back in Auckland I set to work. *Atom* was hauled so that I could scrape, brush, and paint her maidenly bottom. Invitations to parties continued to arrive but the call to put to sea once more was the greater.

On April 15, all being ready for the hazards of the sea, I dropped *Atom*'s reins after a stay of four months. Many persons, now friends, were present and I noticed that even the dock workers interrupted their labors to wish us Bon Voyage. With deep feeling I left this charmed island, where my visit was among the best I've ever had.

Under a dull, windless sky *Atom* soon entered into the Gulf of Houraki. By nightfall I took departure as a gentle breeze stroked the surface. *Atom*, enjoying herself on the quiet waters, barely cut a feeble wake. All night long Cuvier Island kept its friendly eye on her sails. At dawn, New Zealand was no more and the sea seemed suddenly deserted and dull.

Five days later there was a westerly blowing and the sea, dazzling beneath the sun, looked deep. Pointing her nose high, *Atom* wreathed in spray, stood her course for New Guinea. Four days later we reached a region of rough atmospheric variations where depressions from the Antarctic crossed constantly. At two that afternoon the sky darkened and rain threatened. Far away and to port an albatross, that prisoner of the Southern Ocean, hovered nearly motionless, gray against a grayish sky.

Near sunset the wind veered to the southwest, a bad sign. It is from this quarter that the squalls generally arrive on wet feet, so to speak. Later the wind rose quickly to between twenty and thirty knots. I dropped the mainsail and made all fast. Nearly at once a blast of air laid *Atom* on her side. Picking herself up, like an angered lady, she rushed ahead challenging the churlish seas. The Pacific now lost its feminine identity and youthful looks, for it assumed the visage of a wrinkled, angry old man, tossing his locks, driveling and drooling madly. Hours later, the raging sea changed completely, sweeping *Atom*'s deck from prow to pintle. Howling in the shrouds, the wind changed gradually from an evil moaning to a shrill cry, and the jib actually shook the mast with its motions. Unable to stand this pace, for it was straining my boat, I hove to under two sails, both taut in the middle, the helm lashed to leeward. The wind blew with force all night and big ones climbed aboard, trampling and knocking before leaving. Among the gale's thousand voices I heard distinctly the shriek of the mizzen gaff peak; I feared it might tear. And I regretted I hadn't lowered my sails much earlier, for I could not now go topside. I had to wait for the dawn to do this delicate and dangerous maneuver.

At six o'clock, weary from no sleep, I went topside dressed in a swimsuit. A chilly, strong northerly cut my breath. The sky was low and dark, the seas disheveled, enormous, hideous, and nearly black, everywhere laced with blowing spray. I looked upon a night-mare . . . and I can't forget it.

Patiently and slowly I got in the mizzen, tying it to the boom. The jib was quickly lowered by a downhaul, but to pass the gaskets around onto the club was difficult and painful. Astraddle the bowsprit, in a prone position with legs crossed, I fought that maniacal sail, which, for its part, gave me many harsh raps. At each plunge I let go the sail and desperately grasped the bowsprit for support, receiving for my effort an icy, compulsory bath that numbed me. Swearing like a madman at that wind-crazed, insensate cloth, I repeated the operation several times. With completely numbed hands I managed to furl the sail, but nearly got partly wrapped in the folds. Ages later I succeeded in making fast three ties, and, exhausted, slipped and stumbled aft and went below where bruised and shivering, I lit the stove and rubbed myself vigorously with methylated spirits. A cup of boiling coffee, fortified with generous splashes of rum, and I rolled snugly into my berth. Progressively warmth returned to my body, but my good friend, the sea (though I thought of her as a bitch at the moment), had given me a deserved thrashing.

For four days and nights *Atom* laboriously climbed impressive hills and then nimbly slid down them as they passed. The wind during this time howled, producing an extremely moving tone, as the anemometer nervously recorded gusts to fifty-five knots.

I climbed on deck the morning of April 27. A vicious wind was pushing ahead of it enormous breaking waves. I saw that the mizzen halyards were slack and was about to tighten them when, looking to windward, I saw coming from the horizon an enormous buster, more frightening and high than the others. It was making for *Atom*. A rogue wave! Fearing that I'd be knocked overboard, I jumped into the cabin, closed the washboards, and grabbed something. With the sound of thunder, making a terrible blow, the wave tumbled onto *Atom*'s deck and superstructure, submerging her and knocking her onto her side. She bounced back immediately. I held my breath and listened. When the waters cleared I popped open the hatch and saw that the tiller had broken across its middle. Finding no other damage, I started immediately to replace the broken stump with a spare, a task made difficult because of the tiller's motions. I was constantly afraid of being swept away, but as darkness and a torrential rain arrived I finished the job.

Two days later the winds softened. By noon they were blowing only twenty-five knots and I set the jib. The sky cleared sufficient for a sighting but the waves, looking at least forty-five feet tall, made this task difficult. Wedged between the mainmast and dinghy, a watch in one hand, a sextant in the other, I watched the sun's red disc reflect its outline onto the mirrors. Choosing the right moment, on top of a wave, during the fraction of a second that I saw the horizon in the telescope, I turned the screw of the micrometer so as to place the lower part of the disc tangent with the horizon. I shot the sun at five-minute intervals. Once reckoned, the data showed my position to be 31°58'6" South Latitude and 171°44'42" East Longitude. This meant that *Atom*'s drifting while hove to hadn't been too bad, for I was only twenty-five miles east of my last position of April 23.

On the second of May Sydney radio forecast that a band of high pressure coming from the Tasman Sea was slowly shifting to the northeast. The barometer, I gleefully noticed, was rising slowly, and I immediately informed *Atom*'s skipper: "Oh, *mon capitaine,* you shall soon have good weather!" But the damned weather was even more disagreeable, for the squalls followed so close onto others that neither the sky nor the horizon cleared. With some concern I considered how badly conditions were breaking as we sailed toward Norfolk Island.

Without warning on May 4 the wind veered southeast and blew into a gale. Could it be the trades, I wondered? Three days later, taking advantage of a clearing, I managed to get a meridian sight, which placed me at 25°28'32" South Latitude. I now was in the trade winds but they were blowing at gale force, probably because of the high-pressure system. The seas were big but not as big as they'd been farther south. New Caledonia being then my destination, I hoped to lay over in Noumea to accept an invitation at the yacht club there.

Six days later I lay several miles off the island's southern belt of hidden reefs, which, having neither lighthouse nor beacon to guide the hapless mariner, stretch more than fifty miles along the coast. These reefs are extremely dangerous in stormy weather. At least twenty-seven wrecks have been recorded on this wrack-strewn belt. In light of the weather I decided to forgo a call at Noumea.

Once I'd left the perturbed area the trades resumed their normal direction and strength. By stages the Pacific regained its beautiful mien of blue skies and tender seas. I wasn't upset at having to leave this period of ugly weather. Eighteen days of it was enough.

The mighty Coral Sea was entered on May 18 and several days later I was not far from the Louisane Archipelago, the farthest southeast point of land of New Guinea. Once again the relative tranquility of sea life was over. From now on an attentive watch was the rule aboard *Atom*.

For days and nights I sailed along an endless reef that lay level with the surface of the sea. As far as the eye could see huge green waves, stumbling their toes, so to speak, toppled and burst mightily along this invisible barrier. From sunrise to sunset I stayed topside, tensely alert because of the reefs' wavy pattern of bights and headlands. During the afternoon the watch became painful because the sun's reflection on the spray was dazzling. At nightfall I carefully tacked ship, gaining the open sea, getting away from this endless snare. So it was that *Atom* progressed slowly towards Port Moresby.

The weather clouded and the winds gusted, creating heavy seas. Finally on June 5, at eleven o'clock, I sighted the wreck of the steamer *Pruth,* which identifies the Nateara reefs. Four miles beyond this sad seamark is Basilisk Pass, and beyond it, Port Moresby's bay.

Soon the outline of the beacon marking the entrance loomed and the pass suddenly opened. As we sailed in the seas calmed.

Hidden behind a hill, Port Moresby cannot be seen from seaward. As we entered the port area a launch came off, and the two Australians aboard helped me anchor and put in a harbor furl. So ended a difficult passage that had lasted fifty-one days. My health, however, was excellent and I was excited to be once more in a strange and foreign country, one of the least known in the world.

A member of the Australian Commonwealth and known as the Territory of Papua, New Guinea, though an island, is nearly the size of a continent. In its way, it is beautiful and curious, for there the human head is still sought as a trophy.

Its jungle is almost impenetrable. Among its inhabitants are mosquitoes, giant snakes, and a species of bumblebee that can drill holes the size of a thumb through tree trunks. It has also a strange and incurable disease, the laughing death. Despite this the Australian government gets numerous applications from Americans wishing to settle somewhere in the interior, where Stone Age squats next to the twentieth century.

Today the Sepik headhunters live chiefly in the swamps of the central south coast. The heads, which they preserve with extreme care, are given the place of honor among a family's trophies. Sought for religious and ceremonial reasons, the heads are mummified to preserve what the Sepiks consider the real beauty of the victim. They hunt for heads beginning in June, paddling their canoes for days without stopping. Officials aren't able to stop this activity, which takes place far from their patrolled territory.

But in Port Moresby modern Papuans have exchanged their red and blue lap-laps for shirts and shorts to become traders, taxi drivers, carpenters, and clerks. But these represent only a small part of the total population of two million. The linguistic aspects are so varied that members of villages separated but a few miles cannot communicate with one another. In Port Moresby the white community communicates with Papuans in a colorful language called Pigdin English, with lessons given regularly by the radio station. Although New Guinea is not a great tourist spot, its gold deposits, and culture, still attract adventurers, some of whom venture into its interior never to return.*

Accompanied by three young engineers, I made a short trip into the jungle about Port Moresby. Driving to the edge of the jungle, about ten miles from town, we soon entered a wild and completely virginal region. Carrying guns, food, and sleeping bags, we crossed knee-deep swamps and encountered vegetation we had to circumvent. For eight hours we tramped through a green hell that has never allowed sunlight to penetrate, where the trees are commonly buttressed by huge tangles of roots and the floor is littered by a carpet of rot housing tiny venomous snakes. Pythons, enormous tortoises, and crocodiles live in its rivers. Among its insects, those harmful to man carry swamp fever and typhus. I saw also butterflies with wings the size of saucers. There is in this wildness a giant snail, the size of a human fist, which the Japanese introduced as a food during World War II.

At nightfall, tired but satisfied, we left the New Guinean jungle and ended the day with a good meal and strong cigars at the Grand Hotel.

---

*On his first voyage Gau met Michael Rockefeller. The two shared an interest in New Guinea's jungle and people. In 1961 the outrigger canoe in which Michael Rockefeller and a Dutch companion were sailing around the island capsized. Rockefeller, leaving his friend (who couldn't swim) with the canoe, swam off for help. "But," said Gau, "to seek for help in New Guinea! Snakes and sharks in the waters, crocodiles in the mangroves, cannibals in the jungle . . . " Governor Rockefeller flew with his daughter to New Guinea, hiring a helicopter to search for his missing son. Gau later met Rockefeller in Port Moresby and was asked for any information he had. The sailor mentioned a paper that speculated that the boy may have cut his foot, thereby attracting sharks. But in 1975 Gau remarked that he'd heard that missionaries, finding Michael's remains in the Stone Age world of New Guinea, "were afraid to tell the father."

12

Incident on Warrior Reef

The anchors were gotten aboard at six o'clock on June 29 and I cleared for the mighty Indian Ocean by way of the Torres Strait, Arafura and Timor Seas. My plan was to cross the Indian Ocean before the hurricane season, which begins in November. As I stood toward Basilisk Pass the trades were blowing high and ahead, as usual, causing *Atom*'s bowsprit to spear many a wave. Having navigated the pass, I altered course to the west and now faced heavy seas. One hundred and eighty-four miles now separated me from the entrance to Torres Strait, a bottleneck channel which separates Australia from New Guinea.

Two days later an Australian patrol boat, seeing the *Atom,* made for her. Because of the sea . . . the ship appeared to have trouble keeping course, for she zigzagged several degrees from side to side. Her great bow plunged into the heavy seas, trying, it seemed, to scoop the bloody basin dry, for she shipped tons of water across her fo'c'sle. Soon the powerful voice of a bullhorn trampled across the short distance between us. Waving my arms, I indicated that all was well aboard yacht *Atom.* Three great blasts of her horn and, turning, she bore off on her lonely vigil.

The first of July the trades degenerated into a gale, but one with character, which obliged me to lower sails and carry on under jib only. In spite of its small sail area I sailed too fast for my taste. I had intended to arrive off Bligh Pass and to reach Bramble Cay before sunset, where I'd hoped to ride at anchor for the night. The Pilot Book showed that the Cay has a luminous buoy, thirty-six feet tall, visible in good weather for several miles; its anchorage is mediocre to leeward. I read also that many shipwrecks had occurred on the islet's low, sandy shores.

Crossing Torres Strait by sail single-handed is tough mostly because it requires a constant watch. Lined by reefs of the Great Barrier Reef to port and by the Great Warrior Reefs to starboard, the strait itself has reefs of all sorts, some submerged, and is strewn with sand shoals. Currents are strong, especially in the season of trade winds (June to July), with a five-knot on record. Daytime navigation of the strait is relatively simple because one can moor almost anywhere to leeward of the islands. But these anchorages are precarious at best, often resulting in lost anchors and considerable lengths of chain. To sail Torres Strait at night, however, is to go seeking for disaster.

The weather allowed a sun sight on the second of July. My chart indicated I was sixteen miles from the Bligh Entrance. That afternoon, however, gales darkened the horizon and precluded my getting a bearing on the Bramble Cay beacon. Because of the tremendous tidal current I couldn't heave to: I'd have to stay awake all night, maneuvering frequently, awaiting the sunrise. I began tacking once an hour in order to remain in the middle of the strait. I was very nervous, not from lack of sleep, but from worry that the strong current was inexorably pushing *Atom* towards the Warrior Reef.

The winds increased constantly. I went topside often but couldn't make out a thing in that darkness. My wristwatch, which I'd hung on the binnacle, and had consulted often, showed ten minutes past five when, suddenly, with jumps and violent shocks, the metal shoe of my boat began pounding on coral! Seconds later *Atom* stopped, stranded on reefs I could not see. Quickly I got her sails down and secured my boat by heaving an anchor onto the coral.

As the seas receded *Atom* began listing until she lay thirty-five degrees from plumb. The face of the inclinometer disappeared into the blackness as I flicked the torch off. I sat, waiting.

By the dawn's early light I saw that a great stretch of reef had emerged. Eastward and windward, about half a mile off, a white line of breakers extended as far as I could see. And in that thickened line I imagined a shroud for Gau of *Atom* fame. This, I felt, was to be my fate. I prepared myself to accept it.

I began to examine *Atom*'s hull. I found no damage.

The problem then was to overcome a feeling of anxiety which was replacing thought. Action was what was needed. But what action?

I began to walk. My booted ankles barely covered by water, I walked for some distance along the sharp and poisonous reef. As I walked I noticed a large fish trapped and swimming with difficulty in the shallow reef waters. I saw sea snakes three and four feet in length darting over the coralline pavement on which I splashed.

I found completely unexpected shapes and unique geometries in the coral surface of the reef: cupolas, pinnacles, turrets, and terraces studded the reef while elsewhere other surfaces resembled petrified plants of red, white, and lilac. Reddish sea stars covered the ground of the reef, and moving slowly round the madrepores or corals, their giant round eyes watching me closely, were huge turtles. Farther on I discovered debris from a shipwreck that was partially buried by sand. Poking and lifting the debris, I recognized pieces of decking and bulwarks whereon living men used to run briskly.

Suddenly I started as I recognized the bones of human skeletons!

Detached skulls, misshapened by coral growths, yellowed and pitted by time and shifting sands, lay beneath my feet. *Horrible!* Deeply stirred, I imagined the drama that had been played, perhaps briefly, long ago. . . . *

The sun, casting its scorching rays over the reef, the strong stench of the coral, all made me ill. Decay everywhere was here mingled closely with life. A discouraging sadness overcame me and I returned to my poor boat.

Not having eaten since the day before, I was extremely hungry. Because of the boat's heeling I couldn't light the stove so I ate from a tin of preserves. It was probably because of the strain I was under that my hunger was satisfied with so little food. At any rate a good bumper of rum was necessary, for I had to preserve my strength as long as possible.

I wanted to know the exact position of the wreck so, at noon, I obtained three sights. My calculations placed it at 9°22′36″ South Latitude and 143°29′15″ East Longitude, or on the northeast side of Warrior Reef and a half mile inside.

---

*Gau later reported finding portions of nine skeletons.

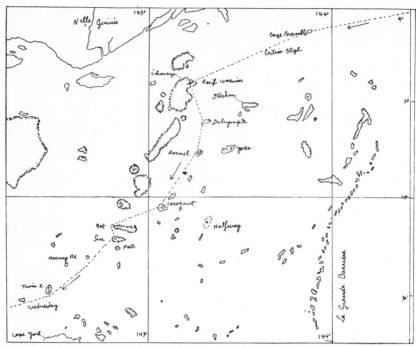

Figure 3. Warrior Reef—site of *Atom's* grounding. Traced from Jean Gau's manuscript

I knew that the reef extended for thirty-eight miles and that its greatest width was ten miles. Stephens Island, the nearest inhabited island, was about a score of miles southeast of where I lay stranded. It also lay in the direction of the trade winds, which, in season, blow between twenty-five and thirty knots, creating thereby a four-knot current.

What if I couldn't refloat Atom? Anxiety began to overcome reason. It would be impossible to use the dinghy against the trade winds, and once in the waters off the reef it would be at the mercy of a swift tidal current. Oh Christ! *Here*, not far from that wreck with its eyeless skulls, here it is, I cried, that *Atom* and I must end our lives, to be covered in time by sand and coral?

By ten o'clock the sea began rising and the waves, whose pounding against the boat's lifeless bow could cause it to slip and be lost, were getting bigger and stronger by the minute. By four that afternoon I noticed that it was slack water and that *Atom* lacked about a foot more before she could get off the reef. But I was not surprised because I knew that daytime high tides in Torres Strait do not reach their maximum, that about midnight they reach full flood. I sat back, knowing I could do nothing but be patient. And cling to what was left of hope.

Because of her old-fashioned long keel and her buoyancy I knew that *Atom* would float off at high tide. She had to! When night came I was worn out and lay back on my bunk, which slanted like the roof of a church. During those long sleepless hours I heard the winds chatting and whispering in the masts, the mocking laughter of gulls, the unnerving clamor of nearby breakers. I remember thinking how obsessing was the constant roar made by the waves in violent combat with the immovable barrier reef, the sound of a death struggle so very near. . . .

Through the half-opened hatch I watched large clouds majestically cross a sky wastefully strewn with stars. The Southern Cross stood proudly, brilliantly, in the absurd wastes overhead.

Later that night I felt *Atom* stir.

Lighting a torch, I glanced at the inclinometer—she'd righted twenty degrees! Another fifteen and she'd be afloat. It was about midnight when suddenly with tremendous urgings she started to pound the reef!

Not losing a moment, I got the anchor aboard, started the engine, and at reduced speed, steering at right angles to the reef, made for the still invisible edge of the reef mass. Each minute *Atom* struck her toe on coral heads, which yielded to the pressure—twice—thrice—four times she struck. Each time my heart nearly stopped, but it really beat furiously when I spied the ectoplasmic breakers in the darkness killing themselves in suicidal attacks on the reef. I headed into that fearful chaos. Flushed with anxiety, I wonder what would happen when I reached the extremity of the fringing reef. Would I find enough water to cross this last, final, obstacle? I envisioned tons of water falling on *Atom* once I'd reached the breakers. I sensed an impending catastrophe. Suddenly my boat had come to another standstill! I gave her full throttle and *Atom,* freed from the reef, moved quickly away and into the deep waters of the strait.*

---

*According to Bernard Moitessier, who met Jean months after the incident, his normally calm face revealed "horror" when the grounding was related. Sailors of modern design sailboats who have sailed single-handed through the Torres Strait tend to be critical of Jean's grounding there. "Jean gave me horrifying information regarding the passage. . . . In Port Moresby I rowed over to some Australian yachts with children playing on deck. They said they regularly spent their vacations sailing the strait," commented one prominent single-hander whose boat, he pointed out, sails much closer to the wind than little *Atom.* Unfortunately, the point overlooked is that Jean Gau sailed it at night; his single-handed detractors haven't, so far as is known.

Greatly relieved, at two-thirty I stopped the engine—*Atom* had been pitching in the deep waters of the strait—and, under reduced canvas, headed south-southeast. Exhausted, I lay on my bunk. But at dawning I was up and sighted Dalrymple Island about eight o'clock. Suddenly a shoal appeared about a cable's length dead ahead. Soon the white lip of breakers was seen. I was struck dumb—the chart had showed no reefs in this area! I recalled that the Pilots Book had mentioned a sand shoal, Pierce Cay, six miles northwest of Dalrymple, but its mile-long shoal emerges only at low tide. Fortunately, I caught sight of a narrow passage between the shoal and the island. With careful steering *Atom* sailed along the reef close-to, avoiding the corals which I surmised existed from the motions of the waters and visible changes of color. Seabirds by the hundreds inhabited the sandy shoal. When *Atom* passed, they rose curious and without fear to investigate the strange objects disturbing their existence.

Rounding the shoal, I headed for the island, and managed to stem the strong current. At eleven I reached the northwest headland, where I'd intended to anchor to leeward, but after a careful survey showed depths of 130 feet close ashore, a distance which gave *Atom* no swinging room, I "passed the word" to tack. We made for Rennel Island, about ten miles distant. At noon trees began rising over the edge—it was Rennel Island. Before I anchored I was surprised at finding no ships or boats at anchor. There seemed to be no movement ashore either. The boat safely anchored, I went below, ate, and fell asleep.

The next morning I went ashore and headed for the small village on the south side, where, as I recalled, about thirty Torres Strait natives lived. Of a very dark color, kind and courteous, speaking a kind of aborigine dialect, these friendly people had welcomed me during my first voyage. But now only inquisitive seabirds greeted me. A bit later I entered the village and in time found the cabin of my friend, Tom Savage. I went from cabin to cabin, finding each empty except for a few worthless items. I saw absolutely no one.

Stupefied, I stood motionless for a while, my actions seeming to have augmented the stillness which pervaded the village. Finally, I started back along the island's north shore, stopping frequently to look back at the deserted village.

Occasionally coconuts would fall on the ground—the coconut tree crabs were having a fling! I realized that a small fortune in copra lay at the foot of these trees. But I passed on.

About noon I reached the extremity of the island and found my dinghy being investigated by dozens of seagulls. Lighting a fire of driftwood and coconut floss, I tossed an enormous crab onto the charcoals. Of a nice blue color, sometimes attaining a weight of six pounds, these fellows have really vicious claws. Despite a slight taste of copra their flesh is comparable to lobster.

Atom rose contentedly at anchor in the perfectly clear water. I gazed at her with pleasure mixed with emotion, thinking of the joys and the fears she had given my life. My meal over, I lay back on the warm sand and smoked a cigarette while around me the seabirds strolled solemnly. Whenever they came too near I waved them off with my hand, but fearless, they soon waddled back.

Three days passed rapidly, during which I lived like Robinson Crusoe. But on July 8, fully rested, I weighed *Atom*'s anchor and took departure for Coconut Island, twenty miles to the south, which I reached about noon. Tree-covered Coconut Island is about one mile long, 600 feet wide, and inhabited by perhaps one hundred persons who deal in nacre, troca, and pearls. That evening two natives came aboard bearing coconuts and papaws. In exchange they accepted cigarettes. I opened a bottle of brandy and in the subsequent lively conversation asked about the mystery of Rennel Island.

I learned that because the bêche de mer (trepang) was declining part of the island's population had migrated to nearby York, while others, chiefly the younger divers, had settled in Harbour Cay to dive for pearl oysters.

At daybreak on the tenth of July I departed, after great labor, for I had 180 feet of chain out. Assisted by the trades and a current old *Atom* footed nicely along to the west towards the islands called Three Sisters, Bet, Sue, and Poll, lying twenty-three miles to leeward. After rounding Bet, I made for Sue. Finding our way amidst a host of ugly reefs, I came to anchor near a masonry tower in nine feet of water. This anchorage, suggested by my brandied brothers back on Coconut Island, is too close to the reef to be comfortable, but after a quiet night, refreshed, I took departure for Thursday Island, forty-five miles away.

Though the course is winding it is nicely marked, each island or islet or rock standing proud as real seamarks. As such it made for my easiest leg through the strait. Passing east of Seale Island, I perceived the curious rock called Nine Pin, a sort of pointed tower tapering twenty feet out of the sea.

At Harvey Rock, a black and gloomy outcrop atop of which stands a metal tower, I changed course several degrees to starboard. Upon rounding the Twins and Wednesday Islands in the early afternoon I made Thursday some time later, mooring among the fishing fleet.

Since it was Sunday I wasn't too surprised that no one came off to greet me, but at the harbor master's office the next day I learned that, at ebb tide, a strong current flows which reaches seven knots speed! I learned also that the master had been alerted of my arrival by Frank Casper (a retired American engineer undertaking a quiet trip round the world) some weeks before.

Part of Queensland, Australia, Thursday Island has as its capital a small town, Port Kennedy. Here, ships and houses are built of driftwood, but despite a rather bleak aspect it enjoys a certain prosperity due to the nacre trade. Its pearl-fishing fleet consists of about 100 sturdy ships, usually ketch-rigged, their crews mostly of aborigine stock. At nightfall I looked on as they came in from the sea, one after the other, anchoring near the wharf where Chinese merchants haggled for their crop. Torres Strait nacre, I'm told, is highly valued, and worth more than that from the far-off Tuamotu archipelago. The pearls and nuggets or swellings of nacre, from which jewelry is made, are magnificent in quality.

My neighbor was an elderly ketch, *Wera*, inhabited by an old captain and his wife. He came aboard *Atom* and over a glass of rum told me his story in perfect English. A pearl diver since he was sixteen, he said that in his youth Malayan pirates would enter the strait to rob the natives of their pearl oysters. He still carried a terrible scar on his left shoulder, six inches long, made by a Malayan kris or dagger. One day, diving, he found a big oval pearl and with the 5,000 pounds Australian he got . . . he bought *Wera*. He began diving, he related, in a diving suit to greater depths, bringing up more than 400 pounds of nacre a day. Business increased such that he bought two more boats which he'd recently given his sons. But having spent most of his life aboard a ship, the old man couldn't live ashore, even in a comfortable dwelling, and it was aboard the ancient *Wera* that he insisted on living.

That I understood well, having lived aboard *Atom* for a score of years. I would truly be miserable if I had to spend my old age in a house.

I spent an excellent evening among these simple, happy folk, listening with interest to their stories. But the day of good-byes arrived and at nine o'clock on July 15, saying farewell to the *Wera*'s captain, I left Port Kennedy. Pushed by a fresh following breeze and a favorable current *Atom* parted from the island at a good speed.

Now the mighty Pacific and the notorious Torres Strait were aft and ahead lay a mighty long passage, Thursday Island to Durban, South Africa, 6,700 nautical miles nonstop. I had planned to pass north of Indonesia to make a stop at Borneo. But in Port Moresby sailors warned me to "watch out for Indonesian pirates, especially north of Borneo. They'll appear suddenly from the coast aboard flat-hulled boats mounting fifty-horsepower engines!" Skimming over the reefy areas, they easily escape the slower police craft. Literally armed to the teeth, they shoot up small boats after boarding. To hell with Borneo and Indonesia, I thought. I decided to follow my old 1955 track, keeping the Australian continent to port and the Indonesian landmass to starboard, but at a proper distance.

That evening I rounded lonely Booby Island by sailing close ashore. Seldom visited today, Booby was formerly a refuge for shipwrecked sailors. Passing ships would leave supplies there in a cave, removing any letters they found. Today it features a lighthouse, some large houses, and radio antennas. I wondered, as I passed, what stories this small, obscure piece of ocean real estate was heir to.

We now challenged the great Gulf of Carpenteria and the Arafura Sea. Relatively shallow . . . the Arafura waters are mostly a light green color that as I progressed westward changed subtly from olive green to indigo blue, a reflection of the greater depths. Then on July 26 in the afternoon I rounded at a considerable distance Cape Van Diemen, Australia's northernmost headland.

Rotti and Timor Islands announced their presence to starboard several days later. But on August 2 I made out a two-masted sailboat about two miles off to the west. It appeared to be heading northeast, probably for the island of Java, which, because it was sixty-five miles away, I could not see. But I watched the ship closely.

There was something odd about her. In her motions, for example, I saw inexplicable singularities: she seemingly sailed along a curved path, which I surmised came from hapless efforts by her crew to hold their course. Her high spars swung heavily from side to side, the ship wallowing wildly in the heavy swell, then running. Puzzled by these and other aspects, I studied her with my glass.

My Lord! It was what I had feared. She was a Malayan proa, easily distinguished by her high stern that resembled somewhat a caravel of Columbus's day. As she loped near *Atom* I distinctly saw on her deck a large crew, a crew I felt too large for her tonnage. But having no wish to become more knowledgeable about this strange craft or her crew, for that matter, I changed course to port. To my relief she gradually disappeared, spars swinging and lumbering clumsily, in the direction of Java.

After sailing out of the Timor Sea I entered the mighty Indian Ocean. No longer sheltered by the Australian landmass, the trade winds sweep this vast region, producing extremely high seas. I began to encounter a long swell with troughs thirty to forty feet deep, their crests 300 feet apart, coming from the southeast. Every ten or fifteen seconds *Atom* shipped really frightening seas on her starboard side. For eight days the sky was overcast, dark and threatening. I failed to get a sun sight on several occasions. I wasn't too worried, of course, for I had too much sea room around me and no reefs to contend with.

The trades, I noticed, blew more now from the east than from the southeast, which obliged me to take in *Atom*'s main and carry on under jib and mizzen, thereby letting *Atom* self-steer. Under these sails her speed was checked, but the duration of the trip didn't matter for I was somewhat ahead of schedule. The galley was well stocked and I lacked nothing.* And my dishes were made tasty from the flying fish volunteering for galley duty. Satiated, I would lie comfortably in my berth, wedged between cushions, drinking coffee or cognac, and smoke cigars. The time I spent reading, writing up my notes, or listening to broad-accented radio stations in Australia, and the singsong voices of China and Indonesia. And I followed with keen interest the extraordinary voyage through space of the American astronauts, Cooper and Conrad, aboard *their* ship, Gemini V.

As I sailed westward the seas became larger, probably because of an anticyclone then moving towards Australia. An enormous swell, coming from the south, met another coming from the southeast, their mating producing gargantuan interference waves. The effects produced by the winds on the wave crests were truly impressive. [The waves] tended to be battered and to break in an odd fashion, giving the sea a gloomy aspect. From time to time one of them would cataract down, nearly burying *Atom*. I didn't stay topside, for there was the possibility of being ignommiously washed overboard like a straw. I quickly lay below to the homey comforts of my cabin.

On the twenty-second of August a gang of whales followed me the entire day. Mere babies measuring about twenty feet in length, they moved along very close to the surface, their cylindrical heads suddenly projecting out of the far side of a wave. They milled about a long time, seemingly in no hurry, disappearing from time to time to reappear elsewhere. This game soon brought them close to *Atom* and I began to worry. I was concerned that they might, playfully, touch *Atom*'s keel or

---

*At the start of his voyages Gau commonly had heavily salted hams swinging from the cabin carlings. On both voyages he carried hundreds of jars of preserves prepared by Joe Cordonat and his wife.

her rudder or, worse yet, tap them with their huge tails. But at twilight they headed south and *Atom*, relieved, continued her westward course.

Then on the eighteenth of October I sighted Cape Ste. Marie, Madagascar. I now sailed in an area subject to atmospheric pertuba-tions caused by the presence of the warm African continent. It is an area frequently disturbed by storms that appear absolutely terrible in aspect but are actually without teeth, if you're bare-poled at the time. And so the evening of the second day, having rounded the cape, *Atom* was sailing under reduced canvas. I was sitting on deck enjoying the air, deep-scented with the smells of land under a sky studded with naillike stars, when slowly in the west there arose a mass of distorted dark clouds.

As the darkness gradually filled the sky it snuffed out the stars in succession. I dropped the sails pronto and had finished putting them in stops when the storm broke. Dazzling flashes of lightning tore the clouds apart. Tremendous claps of thunder seemingly made *Atom* shake as if she'd struck an underwater rock. Suddenly the wind came like a whirlpool and knocked my boat on her side immediately. But she rose as quickly.

The first blasts of wind gone, the rains came. Indescribable! They didn't last long but they were terribly abundant, and in no time laid flat the swollen waters. Deafened by thunder and completely soaked, I locked myself in the cabin. Lightning flashed incessantly, lighting the cabin interior through the portlights as though it were daylight outside. I don't know how long the storm lasted, probably no more than thirty minutes, but it abated little by little. As it did the sky resumed its brilliant character and the little *Atom* made her way with all sails fully taut.

The next day I was south of the Mozambique Channel, a submarine gully that separates Africa from Madagascar, and not far from where the Indian Ocean hurricanes originate. This was October and the season begins in November. I decided not to linger because I might encounter a great wind in the making and then would have to cram on sail to reach the nearest land.

As I sailed southward the trade winds became less regular. Flying fish, I noticed, had disappeared, but several dorados still followed the boat. The variable winds, turning anticlockwise, kept me busy. And I contended also with interference waves caused by a swell from somewhere else. The nights, to add to the general misery, were cold and damp now.

Then, on the night of November 4, a violent southwest gale suddenly broke. And I mean broke! I had to put *Atom* under bare poles as the winds gusted to sixty knots. The following day the weather cleared some and, despite heavy seas, I managed to shoot the sun. My plot located me about ten miles off the coast of Africa. Finally, at daybreak on November 6, land lay ahead several miles off. About noon the tall buildings of Durban began marshaling on the horizon and an hour later I hoisted the quarantine flag. Warned of my coming by the signal station, a health service launch waved me to a buoy to await the arrival of the harbor master and the journalists.

Three months later it was time to put to sea and on the eighth of February I cleared for Cape Town. Friends accompanied *Atom* as far as the jetties aboard a fishing vessel belonging to Ray Cruikshank. Photographs and a hearty salute and once more I was alone. But I was solemn this time, for ahead I faced the most difficult part of the voyage, the rounding of stormy Cape of Good Hope in very heavy seas. From Durban to the Cape is about 840 miles, a passage I'd made in twenty-one days in 1955 and without trouble. This time it was to be something else.

To reach a line well out of the shipping lanes I sailed south and then laid a course westward forty miles from the coast. At this latitude the favorable Agulhas Current is weaker, but I could at least sleep calmly and not worry about ships. In face, most sailors going into the Atlantic keep close to shore, generally not less than ten miles off, to take advantage of the same current. And ships sailing in the other direction use the countercurrent closer to land. In these parts the seas offshore are always raging, however. I'd read accounts of ancient Portuguese sailors fighting these currents for many years before rounding the Cape. There exists also in these regions a frightening combination of gigantic waves and almost continuous gales which forced these early mariners to turn back. Da Gama finally succeeded and rightly named it the Stormy Cape.

The first two days the weather was beautiful. A light northeasterly pushed *Atom* along at four knots, but the barometer, I noticed with concern, was falling. In these parts barometric indications always fortell weather changes: a rising barometer indicating winds from the northeast to east. If the glass falls expect winds from the west, the ones most frequent and feared.

At nine o'clock on February 10 the east wind suddenly ceased and gave way to westerlies. Every hour this wind increased and about two o'clock in the morning the anemometer read forty-five knots. Reduced to two sails, *Atom* painfully fought heavy winds and towering seas, now steering towards land, now towards open sea.

For two weeks the gales from the southwest followed with a discouraging regularity. On February 20, however, I had reached 21° East Longitude, which meant I was only 180 miles from Cape Town. This I wouldn't have minded but for the threat of foul weather indicated by the falling barometer. Moreover, I was now fifty miles off Cape Agulhas, one of the most storm-exposed points in the world. Here the southwest gales are feared . . . they cause most of the shipwrecks that stud the coastline. Since my arrival in South Africa thirteen fishing vessels had been wrecked somewhere along the coast off which I now sailed.

At sunset on February 26 the sky had a blackish blue cast and a red stripe followed the horizon. Seldom have I seen so ominous an appearance of weather at sea. It communicated an inexpressible fear. Yet it was strange, I mused, that I was so much affected by it. I sensed, of course, that something was brewing. To reassure myself, so strong is the instinct to live, I postulated: These, after all, are but ordinary clouds which bring us the rain and the wind!

At ten that evening the East London meteorological station forecast a gale warning with strong winds from the west, and a little later, the west breeze began to freshen. I immediately lay to under bare poles. Shortly it was heavy going, for the waves changed rapidly, their crests now breaking at very great heights. From time to time one would break on deck. At four o'clock I got up to check the instruments. The glass had fallen to 980 millibars and the anemometer indicated a wind speed of seventy-two knots! *A hurricane!*

It was very serious. *Atom* was shaking vigorously, pitching and rolling as never before. Entombed in my bunk, I could not sleep. "Be calm," I commanded myself, "for we had worse weather in Hurricane Carrie in '57!" Soberly, I recalled how then the winds had reached speeds of 120 knots. Surely this was but a gale among gales? It will take more than *this*, I weakly argued, to break my courage.

I did not know then that my courage was to be fully tested.

13

Capsize!

Some time during the night of February 27 the catastrophe occurred.

About three in the morning I heard a strange noise approaching my boat. I could not believe my ears. What is happening? Probably nothing—or something. I thought: It *must* be a furious wave that is coming, head first, and about to tumble on deck? Instinctively I grabbed the side of the bunk. Suddenly in a terrifying din, like an explosion, an enormous wave hit the port side and tons of water fell on deck. I was thrown violently against the ribs of the boat, to be immediately covered by all sorts of items, sailbags, charts, books.

Atom had capsized!

Her keel now lay over my head!

All openings were tightly closed at the time except for a small porthole on the after wall of the cabin. Through that opening a powerful jet of water now spewed into the cabin. My heart sank for I expected this to be the last blow. I remained breathless for seconds. "I am finished." was all that I could think of. I had suspected that one day I would meet at sea one of those ultimate waves that would bury my boat and me completely. I now believed it was all over. Alone in the moving dark-

189

ness, entangled and nearly buried under debris, frightened, unable to get up and help myself, succumbing to an acceptance of death, I was suddenly aware that *Atom* had righted herself! Her heavy iron shoe had saved us.

In an effort to overcome my sense of distress and hopelessness, I decided that I had to get out of that cabin! Freeing myself, hurting and bruised, I hurried topside. A dreadful turmoil was raging about the boat. . . . Atom *had been dismasted!*

What a horrible sight—bowsprit, stumps of masts, spars, splintered booms, sails and lines torn and tugging to leeward, all held by tangled shrouds and halyards. Gone, too, was the dinghy. All had happened in a few seconds!

The dismal thought that there was nothing I could do overwhelmed me for several minutes. Then I began to collect my wits and to judge the situation a bit more calmly. I thought: this is *not* the time to be inactive, not with the hull being vigorously banged and smacked by the debris alongside. I felt there was still a chance to get out of this dangerous mess, because *Atom* and I had been united for a long time. We had always worked together. And, frankly, we were destined to sail on or to sail under. My boat had rescued me several times in the past. Now it was up to me to help her.

I had to get rid of that rigging. If it continued smashing and chafing it might have started a plank or staved in the hull. What scared me was the thought of having to go topside again, for the seas were now a tormented wasteland. And if another wave struck while I was on deck it would have been certain death. But, aware that hesitation wasn't going to accomplish the task, I cried aloud, *"Do it! Do it now!"*

Topside, I tied myself with a long rope to the broken foot of the mizzenmast. I worked quickly in the blackness, the work made very difficult by the boat's crazed rolling. The force of that wind was so great I had trouble breathing. I do not exaggerate but I know that those who have never witnessed the strength of a gale at sea are reluctant to trust an old sailor's tale completely.

Using a metal handsaw I tried to cut the shroud strands, but a wave, that nearly cost me my life, snatched it from my hands. I then had to use a small pincers to cut the cable strands one by one.

In that hostile darkness I didn't feel safe. My sou'wester was torn away by the winds, and because the decks were often awash, waves fell full on my neck. Busy with both hands trying to sever the cable strands, fearful of being swept away, I could do nothing to prevent this. My eyes, accustomed to the darkness, looked out on a swollen and torn seascape where waves phosphoresced on their crests. Moving and glowing, these crests rushed out of the darkness, rising high and bursting at great heights with noises that I cannot describe. Spray raked me as I worked, cutting away the tough strands of wire, one by one. My God! Would I never finish?

By daylight, after more than three hours labor, the job was finished. I looked at my boat.

It was a floating wreck, almost awash from seas both monstrous and magnificent. Later, I found a mess down in the cabin. The floor was under water but none was actually entering the boat. I tidied up a bit and then fixed a scratch meal. Exhausted, I threw myself onto the bunk, but I couldn't sleep because *Atom* rolled incessantly. All night she was swept by heavy sheets of water, which met little resistance for very little remained to resist.

The next day I rested. Perhaps oblivion is a better term, for upon waking I wondered where I was. I reasoned that I *had* to survive at all costs and this meant saving *Atom*. Only my engine could enable me to reach a harbor where I could repair my damaged companion. And now began the most morally trying hours I'd spent at sea. Would I succeed in starting the engine when the elements were *still* mauling the boat? Greatly worried, I crept into the engine space below the companionway ladder. With a wrench I tried to remove the sparkplugs but they were completely seized. My discomfort was very great . . . my body was bruised by repeated falls against the engine. I finally managed to unscrew the plugs. Placing them in my pockets, I crawled back into the cabin.

Atom was, of course, still dancing nervously. I reasoned that seawater must have entered through the engine exhaust pipe. I cranked the engine by hand to remove as much water as possible. Carrying rags, I crept back into the engine space to wipe water from the cylinders. This I did even though it was very difficult to do. I couldn't afford to neglect anything, no matter how tiring or uncomfortable.*

Back in the cabin, I heated the spark plugs in a pan to ensure a temperature that would enable them to start better. After spraying ether in the cylinders, installing the plugs, and replacing the wires, I paused to reflect: Would it start? Reeling and staggering after two hours of exertion and frantic worry, I pressed the starter button. At the

---

*Gau's sense of humor, especially his ability to laugh at himself, surfaced as *Atom*, dismasted, drifted towards Antarctica. "Boy!" he said to himself, "if you don't want cold feets, you better do something!"

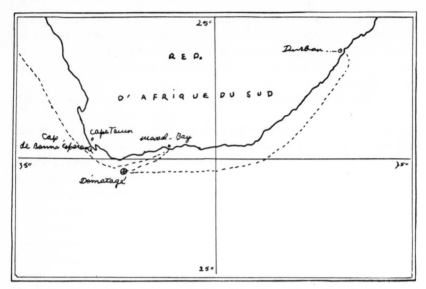

Figure 4. Site of *Atom's* capsize and dismasting. Traced from Jean Gau's manuscript

first try my little mechanic—wrongly despised by some sailors—started! I have never felt so much love for any engine! Her voice was a soothing note to the aggressive and shrill sounds of the elements outside. But my moment of extreme joy was followed by one of invincible anxiety when I remembered how alone I was, and on a small boat without masts, sails, away from the shipping lanes, drifting towards Antarctica. . . .

Fortunately, a sense of impatience overcame me. After a quick breakfast I steered for the nearest harbor, seventy-five miles away. That evening the winds let up and the seas calmed, and on the second of March, a sunny pleasant day, *Atom* motored slowly into the small harbor at Mossel Bay. Grim and gray, encrusted with salt, her starboard sides badly marred from her long pounding by wave and wood, *Atom* presented a bleak picture to the dock workers who stood silently, grimly looking on as we passed.* But the sound the anchor made as I moored completely transformed my feelings and I felt the relief one feels upon waking from a raging nightmare.

---

*As *Atom* neared the dock a woman cried, "Look! The *Atom* has had her wings clipped!" Gau, startled by the aptness of the remark, never forgot it.

There were no facilities for repairing *Atom* in Mossel Bay so I ordered masts, booms, shrouds, etc. from Cape Town and Durban. A friend, Ray Cruikshank, hearing of my presence in Mossel Bay, arrived and drove me to Wilson's Shipyard in Durban, where I made the necessary purchases.

Back in Mossel Bay the people were exceedingly kind. But work as I did, I could not estimate when *Atom* would be seaworthy again. And I felt this delay would not let me reach New York before the hurricane season started. It seemed likely that I would have to lay over in the West Indies or in the Caribbean until late September, then leave for America.

A friend in Durban kept me informed about the status of my new spars, which, when completed, had to be redone! Months passed. The sea life seemed more distant than ever. Frankly, this delay ashore became unbearable even though friends inundated me with invitations. I became exceedingly restless.

The coaster *Indoda* arrived on August 1 carrying *Atom*'s new masts and booms. I turned to and worked hard to refit and get *Atom* seaworthy again.* Late that month the masts were stepped and after a careful check I felt *Atom* ready for the hazard of the sea. But of course it was time for a gale to strike! This time the storm caused three large trawlers to break their moorings, and a Japanese trawler came in from the sea with two crew members seriously wounded by waves off Cape Agulhas. I could not depart because the seas still raged offshore and powerful waves were smashing against the jetties and nearby buildings in Mossel Bay. But shortly after sunrise on October 3, saying good-bye to my friends, I cast off *Atom*'s lines after a seven-month layover and motored toward the end of the jetty. A small crowd of well-wishers gathered there cheered as we passed and I was deeply moved.

Once away from the land, the distance to Cape Town, about 280 miles by sea, was not the problem. Instead it was the matter of rounding Capes Agulhas and Good Hope. Frankly, I began this short leg with real anxiety, but by evening the land had vanished, at once forgotten, and things resumed their normal routine. It was close to the end of the austral winter and the cold was sharp. *Atom*'s skipper was dressed like an Eskimo. The first day was calm with a light easterly. Normally, westerlies nearly always blow in gale strength at the rate of two or three a week here. Moreover, the proximity of capes and a mountainous

---

*Among the alterations made on *Atom* were new heavy-duty gooseneck fittings for both masts and a thick steel deckplate with welded bow chocks.

coastline combine to produce bad weather. In the vicinity of the Cape of Storms (Good Hope) the presence of two opposite and strong currents makes this region one of the world's most difficult to weather by sail. The Agulhas current, which flows from east to west along the eastern coastline, encounters at sea the east-flowing Antarctic Drift, a current generated by the eternal west winds. Once joined, so to speak, these permanent gales generate the world's largest waves, between forty-five and fifty feet in height. By comparison, Pacific storm waves attain heights of thirty to thirty-three feet, Atlantic waves from twenty-five to thirty feet, and Mediterranean waves twenty to twenty-five feet in height.

Fifty miles south of Cape Agulhas, when the wind blows contrary to the current, it generates a dangerous sea because the waves then assume an unusual shape. Such waves, meeting an obstacle like a ship, break at once and cause great damage. It was one of these monsters that had capsized and dismasted *Atom* on that dark February night.

The glass was falling. This could only mean a west wind. Suddenly before noon, after a rather long period of smooth water, the breeze veered and the sky instantly became gloomy and threatening. I prepared for a stormy crossing. Black, lugubrious night came, and a darkness in which no shape was discernible. Everything vanished in that complete blackness, a blackness almost tactile. And with it came a torrential rain that I actually heard moving across the sea. Huge drops soon hammered the deck and an icy wind fisted *Atom*'s hull. The ashen-faced sea suddenly turned white with spray and flying spindrift.

Under a storm trysail and heeled forty degrees, *Atom* fought against a wind that heaped before it huge pyramidally shaped waves. These upright towering and threatening masses gave me a sense of insecurity I'd never experienced before. Would this be another February 27? I was silent with worry.

The seas pounded the boat furiously, each wave receiving, so it seemed, a broken hand from the beating. Every hour I tacked ship. My hands, softened by the long stay ashore, were painful from handling the ship. At night I remained at the helm to keep the boat as close to the wind as possible. That first night was hard for I now had to fight against sleep, a habit I'd picked up ashore! It was very cold and I shivered in my fur clothes.

On October 17 the winds reached their greatest intensity and for the first time ever I tied myself in the cockpit. The probability of being washed out of a cockpit at sea when alone is a hazard of small boats. That is what happened to my good friend, John Pflieger, late com-

modore of the Slocum Society. He was sailing solo from New York to St.
Martin in his twenty-eight footer, *Stella Maris*, according to a letter
dated April 26 which I received in Mossel Bay. But on July 20 his boat
was found beached on Antigua, the jib set, the main properly furled
and the tiller lashed. His pipe, unlit, lay in the cockpit. Inside the boat
all was proper. His logbook showed a last entry dated July 10 which
placed him about 100 miles north of his destination. John Pflieger, in
my opinion, fell or was swept overboard by a wave.

The wind died a bit on the fourth day but the waves continued high
and dangerous. All sails on, I headed for Cape Agulhas, which was in
sight ten miles away in the southwest. For this leg I would say that *Atom*
crawled, not sailed, for her motions were violent and unpleasant, each
foot of way a struggle. The Agulhas current fortunately assisted me or I
don't know how we'd have gotten away from those hellish winds.

On October 18 the Cape Town radio announced, to my surprise, that
"Harbor authorities are worried about the yacht *Atom,* which left Mossel Bay fifteen days ago. We have heard no news. *Atom* should have
reached Cape Town by now, where an official welcome had been
arranged by the Royal Cape Yacht Club. Considering the bad weather
in the Cape region it is supposed that the yacht has altered her course.
Two South African Army airplanes are searching for the vessel." At
four o'clock the next day I had Cape Agulhas abeam to starboard,
where, incidentally, the coast has an extremely savage aspect and where
countless ships have gone to their deaths.

I was relatively close to the cape where the sea was breaking with
great violence. Too close, I realized anxiously, because I sensed that the
elements were setting *Atom* on shore. I had rashly ventured too near
land! And now the booming sounds made by the breakers brought me
to my senses. By nightfall I had weathered the formidable cape and the
nervous tic of its lighthouse was astern.

I now sailed in the South Atlantic, sailing "up" or northwest, keeping
a respectful distance from the coast. *Atom* self-steered and for the time
being there was little I could do for her. The next day, rested, I took the
tiller. *Atom* was being escorted by a troop of gamboling seals below and
by imperious albatrosses above. I never tired of studying their effort-
less flight, spending hours admiring this almost mystical bird. Cape
pigeons also hovered around the boat, at times perching on the
shrouds or spars. What fantastic thieves these fearless birds are! But
this same quality allowed me to catch half a dozen. Despite a faint fish
odor, their legs and breast meat are edible if scalded and thyme is
added before cooking.

I rounded towards midnight the Cape of Good Hope. Three days later two whalers changed course and, coming alongside, we gammed for some time. They agreed to radio my position to Cape Town, where, they informed me, planes had searched for three days but, failing to locate *Atom*, reported us lost at sea. Wishing us good luck, they soon were out of sight. That evening a South African radio station reported that we were 120 miles southwest of Cape Town. The next day a South African Air Force plane circled overhead before returning to base. Thirty minutes later the radio announced that *Atom* was but one or two days from Cape Town. Well, we'll see, I thought, nodding my head. And at midnight the wind suddenly veered to the southeast. The weather deteriorated and squall succeeded squall. The Cape Town met station reported gale warnings already foretold by my little nervous friend, the anemometer. It was what I had feared, for the southeasterlies, a strong gale of wind, often blow from October to April about the Cape. Instantly I lowered jib and mizzen, but *Atom*'s mainsail was blown out, rendering it totally useless. I hove to and thought about my boat, drifting slowly towards the northwest, away from Cape Town.

A sun sight the next day placed me sixty-five miles northwest of Cape Town. Aware that the gale might last several days, I raised the jib and set a course for the West Indies. *Atom*'s galley was well provisioned, her water tanks nearly full. I would sail "up" nonstop.

On the chart I drew a line passing the great circle as far as Fernando Noronha. Then a second line (Mercator) as far as Grenada which would be my landfall. The distance was 5,463 miles. The weather for the following two weeks was dull and, of course, ahead. At last, veering, it settled in the southeast, which meant I was now in the southeast trades region. Only stormy petrels, hovering in the swales of the sea, now followed *Atom*. Flying fish appeared, flinging themselves from the sea into *Atom*'s galley, so to speak.

Not especially interested in sewing, I chose to replace the blown-out mainsail with an old storm trysail, a mistake, as it later proved. With this smaller sail area *Atom*'s speed and distance fell off considerably. With a full suit of sails we would have made 100 miles daily; now we made between sixty and seventy every twenty-four hours. But I was in no hurry. I was glad to have the Cape of Good Hope behind me. And I now cooked excellent meals for all hands, whose appetites never seemed to flag at sea. Or ashore, for that matter!

Now, following the meridian shot, I would sleep for hours, something I seldom ever permitted myself, trying to recover those sleepless nights spent in the unsettled southern regions. On December 7 I passed 240 miles west of Napoleon's St. Helena. With the tiller adjusted and made fast, *Atom*, muttering to herself at times, at times chatting with the sea, looked after us both as the wind aft rolled her rhythmically along at a speed of three knots, her course northwest. Twenty-two days later we were not far from Fernando de Noronha, an island about 125 miles northeast of Cape Sao Roque, Brazil. I changed course a few degrees to make for my landfall, Granada.

At about midnight January 2, 1967, I passed from the southern into the northern hemisphere, crossing the Equator at 36° West Longitude. The good southeast winds decreased, the sky filled with huge cumulus clouds, and we were welcomed into the Doldrums by a gathering of old acquaintances: variable winds, rough squalls, thunder blasts, and downpours! Five days of this mess and the weather cleared with the arrival of the northeast trades, timorous at first, then confident and very strong. I was then off the Brazilian coast about 100 miles to avoid the coastal traffic and, believe it or not, the Amazon River! During the rainy season this mighty river debouches vast amounts of debris far out into the sea, which, encountered, cause problems for small craft.

At six o'clock on February 2 I discovered Grenada! Five miles off its port of St. George I started the engine. But after ten uneasy minutes of "breaking wind," it quit. With the trades blowing from thirty to forty knots I couldn't enter the harbor under the sails I had. The best I could do was to continue heading the westerlies, hoping to make a suitable landfall *somewhere* in the West Indies. Had *Atom* owned a full suit of sails, to make a landfall here or elsewhere would not be a problem, only a game. But being undersailed, I ran the risk of missing island after island before landing somewhere in the vicinity of Puerto Rico.

The fresh-water tanks were now empty. I had five precious gallons in jerry cans, but knowing from experience that a body needs half a gallon per day, and not certain when or where we'd make our landfall, I instantly rationed *Atom*'s crew to a quarter of a gallon per day. Let the logbook show there were no complaints!

On February 14 I was thirty-five miles southeast of Puerto Rico. I was also right in the middle of maneuvering American warships. A plane dropped three smoke bombs around *Atom* to mark our position. I took the opportunity to signal for assistance by hoisting the flag letter F, which means *I am in distress*. A ship approached and I explained that I lacked a mainsail, that the engine was ill, and that I hadn't been able to make the nearest port earlier. Shortly afterwards a submarine, the S.S. *Sea Cat,* popped up nearby, nearly taking away *Atom*'s new bowsprit! Asked if I needed food or drink, I signalled the latter. Forthwith, *Sea*

Cat produced two cases of beer, which came aboard the *Atom* at the speed of lightning. I was also given my position, which agreed nicely with my own plot. To round out the war games a tugboat arrived that afternoon and towed *Atom* away at a speed between six and eight knots—fortunately the sea was flat!

I was towed to a dock at the Roosevelt Roads naval base in Puerto Rico. Later, in the office of the base commander, I related my most recent adventures. A doctor examined me, finding me fit, except that I was badly underweight. It was true. I had never been so thin, but then it had been a long crossing.

The next day *Atom* was towed by the Navy around the Isleta Marina near Playa Fasardo Village. Frankly, after 123 days at sea I was glad to shake hands with the land. But only for a while, because sixty-nine days later, after writing articles for the San Juan newspaper, I was ready for sea. My stay had convinced me, however, that Puerto Rico is indeed the Pearl of the West Indies. In some ways she reminded me of the South Seas. . . .

While fixing *Atom* at Isleta Marina I was helped by an old skipper, an octogenarian, who'd sailed on windjammers. With his expert help I cut and sewed an old leg-o'-mutton sail into a Bermudian mainsail. The Palmer Engine Company shipped a new carburetor that encouraged my engine to start on the first try.

In the village there was a retired American mechanic. He began to invite me to his house on Sundays. One day he asked, "Johnny, would you mind going to church with me?"

Somewhat hesitantly I replied, "Well . . . not at all . . . "

The church was Episcopalian, and what impressed me was its plainness. Unlike the churches I'm familiar with, where gold and marble are displayed lavishly, here I found only bare walls, and in the back of the church a large wooden cross. During the service my friend asked if I wanted to take communion.

Embarrassed, for I did not want to confess my sins, I demurred.

"Don't worry, Jean. Here they don't confess."

Wishing to escape this duty, the necessity of which I failed to see, I whispered, "But I had a large breakfast. I'm not prepared to take communion . . . "

"Don't worry," he replied. "Here it doesn't matter."

Faced with this blunt statement, I capitulated and went with him to the railing. Later, as we left the church, the vicar introduced himself.

"So! This is Jean Gau, the sailor!" He smiled broadly. "I have a favor to ask, Jean. Would you please agree to speak next Sunday about your adventures?" He paused. "We'd be happy to pay you."

"Yes, of course I'll talk, but I'll take no money. I never take money for my talks."

"Quite all right, Jean. Quite all right! Don't say any more." He nodded emphatically. "See you next Sunday!" He held out his hand.

During the week this good man informed his entire parish about the talk, and when we arrived a crowd was gathered in the churchyard where a buffet was laid.

After the service, in which I again had to sacrifice myself at the railing, the vicar introduced me. While I spoke I saw him, armed with a long stick and a box at its end, passing from row to row taking up a collection. (Cover your faces, my fellow countrymen! At least those among you who, protected by anonymity, drop a mere one-franc piece, when it is not fifty cents, into the curate's alms purse! There were five and ten-dollar bills heaped in that small box!) When it was over the vicar took my arm and led me to his study.

There on a table stood a pile of bills he had gathered during my lecture. He pointed to the pile. "You see, Jean, what happened while you spoke?" I said nothing, but nodded.

"Now I can restore the roof of the church!" He was laughing and I laughed too.

He then opened a desk drawer and withdrew a one-hundred-dollar bill, which, despite my protests, he thrust into a coat pocket. "Don't say any more, Jean!" He shook his smiling face. "You offend, if you do."

Taking my arm firmly, the vicar led me back to where my friend . . . waited.

On the twenty-sixth of April I departed San Juan for New York, the final leg of my second voyage around the world. . . . [with] a cloudless sky and a calm sea, although a moderate northeasterly was blowing, we faced the 1,400-mile voyage with a peaceful mind, in sound condition and contented at being underway. By nightfall Puerto Rico, if it ever existed, was now something no longer evident.

While New York streets lay under one foot of ice and snow, *Atom*'s deck was burning under a scorching sun. Forty-eight hours and about 130 miles after departing San Juan the breeze suddenly stopped. An absolutely flat calm ensued, a condition rare in these parts where the trades blow regularly at force 4 to 6! In my cabin the temperature soared to 35° Centigrade, while the radio reported a trawler in distress off Boston in seas enraged by pummeling westerlies blowing at hurricane force. I began to think about Isleta Marina, about San Juan . . .

Now, with the weather so beautiful I had nothing to do. *Atom*, her tiller fastened as usual, looked to herself. On this voyage, as on the others, when she behaved nicely I talked with her and even sang to her! Ah, but when she misbehaved, she heard from me as well. But now, with nothing troubling us, I read and slept as much as I liked. Occasionally I would step on deck to pick up my dinner or to get a sun sight and then return to the brightness of my cabin home.

By May 11 we had reached, at midpoint in our journey, the Horse Latitudes, an area of high pressure, flat seas, and light variable airs. No longer supported by the breezes, *Atom* rolled badly; her sails, slatting, created a jarring and unsettling noise, and the chafe on her sails kept me busy with needle and palm. The sea was streaked and matted with weed from the Sargasso Sea. As the swells diminished the carpeted surface became exceedingly calm and sparkling, but at heart it was a deserted, monotonous, and desperate sea. Rarely a light puff was felt and I trimmed sails immediately, only to retrim a few minutes later. Five days of this agony passed with *Atom*'s only progress the result of unseen fingers of the Gulf Stream.

But on the morning of May 15, for more than an hour, a spanking breeze from the northeast broke my torpor. Compared to the desperate length of the previous days *Atom*'s speed was mad! A silvery moustache curled from her nose and the winds whistled and sang in the thrumming shrouds. Then, in less than five minutes, it weakened and died. Five days later a big northwest swell arrived to battle the southwest swell, but it was a hopeless cause.

As we slowly emerged from this placid quarter the fleecy clouds of the trades were replaced by cirro-stratus, a sure sign the Tropics were escaping. Besides it was cold and wet. I broke out the ship's issue of woolens. Several days later we weathered that Atlantic graveyard, Cape Hatteras, passing 120 miles east of its sands and turbulent shoals, and entered the playground of atmospheric variations. At any moment, day or night, we could expect heavy weather.

On May 30 the breezes freshened and I dropped the mainsail, as the swells were growing under the breath of the rainy season. Vast foaming waves broke with a terrifying noise, completely inundating *Atom*'s deck. Seven days later we left this violent waste, only to be becalmed for ten days, 200 miles from New York. The unadulterated monotony was broken by a tanker, *American Eagle,* which offered to report my position to the *New York Times. Ambrose* lightship hove into view the night of June 9 and I grabbed the tiller after forty-five days of neglect. But because of the heavy traffic I was on deck every hour, day and night, firmly believing that it was better to see than be seen!

The next day *Atom* was wrapped in a fog so dense it was actually tactile, while around her, like bellowing ghosts, sounded the great-lunged foghorns of invisible ships, *Atom*'s small voice adding to the general din. Suddenly a ship, the *Ashanti* out of Genoa, stepped out of the mist and fog close aport. *Atom*, like a badly frightened hare, leaped to another tack.

At noon the sky cleared and New York's awesome skyline confronted and then enveloped us as we ticked off the channel buoys. One hour later quarantine officials in uniforms with stripes to their elbows welcomed me to their offices . . . thereafter, customs, police, and immigration were cleared. The questions were unending and sufficient to require a ream of paper! But the goal was free pratique and with this precious document in hand, I took departure for the Sheepshead Bay Yacht Club, seven miles away. Arriving, I temporarily moored *Atom*, now five years and 40,000 miles older, and went ashore to be welcomed by the club members as only Americans know how.

But now I face the monotony of shore life, the monotony of routine and regulation, and the worst of its evils, resignation. These now lie ahead.

But it had been a good voyage! Peril. Fatigue. Adventure. Intense satisfaction. And now that I no longer have *Atom*'s wake to study, at times to marvel at, memories rush in. . . .

Well, I must face what lies ahead.

At least for a while.

He would also face life without the sympathetic support of Claire Gau, who had died while he was away at sea. Claire had been one of the two or three women who had had some influence in shaping Jean's life; her advice, logical reasoning, and strength of character had appealed to his strong and independent nature. Now, with her death, he was truly alone. Her adopted niece, Andrée Pierret, seeking solace, wrote Jean.

The reply of the sixty-four-year-old sailor, still recovering from *Atom*'s dismasting off Durban, provides a glimpse of his religious belief and his growing concern for financial security in old age. But that concern is infused with his love of adventure, still bound by an unbroken thread, his love of the sea.

Mossel Bay
July 4, 1966

Dear Deede!
    ... Auntie is better off where she is for she no longer suffers
.... You say you are so unhappy that you wish Auntie would come
and carry you away. Such thoughts can only lead your spirits from
bad to worse. ...

I mentioned in my *Midi Libre* article that I must reach the States
and work for several months to be eligible for Social Security. If all
goes well I'll sail for France in the autumn of 1967. ...

Kisses,
Jean

This is not the simple letter of an aging navigator of the
world's oceans. It is the testament of a confirmed stoic.

Four months later he would be reported lost at sea. Describing
the unsuccessful search for the missing sailor, *Midi Libre* (October 20, 1966) wisely remarked that those who knew Jean
"believe that his loss is but a stage in his great adventure." Within
several days he was sighted.

Although the report of his demise at sea was dramatic, as was
Atom's capsize and dismasting, there had occurred an earlier
incident, unrecorded in Jean's manuscript or in his newspaper
articles, that was for him far more meaningful. As with other
significant matters in his life that he did not write about, but
discussed openly with individuals and before crowds. Jean
quixotically kept silent about this one. The incident that stirred
Jean deeply was seeing a small child in Tahiti.

One day, so Jean's telling of the story goes, as he worked
aboard *Atom* in Papeete's harbor, "I saw a little girl watching me.
I asked myself, 'What's that little girl want?'" The child was about
ten years old and had beautiful black hair down to her waist. The
aging sailor studied the child's face slowly, the child's even gaze
meeting his. Then he noticed a woman standing behind the
child. It was Taime!

They kissed warmly and embraced, and Jean was startled
when the little girl, looking directly at the wiry, silver-haired
navigator, asked, "Are you my real father?"

"No!" I replied. "No, no." I looked at her mother.

"Yes, Johnny, This is your daughter, Atomie . . . "

He drew the small child close to him, inhaling deeply the heavy scent of the *tiare* flower held by a tiny ear. Emotions in kaleidoscope fashion filling his mind, he suddenly fell to his knees. He held the child in a tight, passionate embrace. Passersby, looking, pointed. Someone laughed.

Taime had married, she told Jean, and her husband had adopted Atomie, who stood holding tightly the sailor's rough hand. Later, below in the cabin, never leaving her father's side, Atomie opened her eyes in wonderment at the ketch's colorful holdings as her mother explained the visit. Taime's husband, hearing of Gau's arrival, had urged her to visit Jean to show him his daughter.

Later, a thick seabag across his shoulder, the old sailor led Taime and his laughing daughter ashore to an aunt's house. And there they remained for the duration of his visit in Papeete. Once more there was a feminine presence in Jean's self-constructed Spartan existence.

"Atomie," Jean later recalled, "*never* left my sight. In the mornings she woke me up. 'Daddy! Get up! The sun is rising!'"

"Eh? It is still dark, Atomie!"

"Yes, but it is *about* to rise!"

"Well, it can also rise in one, two, or three hours—let me sleep!"

". . . . Do you want your coffee, Daddy, with the coconut milk that you love so much?"

"I was surprised! 'How you know that, Atomie?"

"Mommy told me!'"

His eyes and face reflecting reverie, Gau continued, "Atomie and I would go fishing in her little canoe." He laughed. "She showed me how to set the sail. I acted like I know nothing! Then we went to sea while her mother cooked the fish. . . . We swam in the lagoon. . . "

Telling the story years later, Gau often paused. "Yes, it was—wonderful," he said, obviously moved. "The day I left, a lot of people on the pier waiting for a schooner; pigs, goats, flowers, mattresses, everything . . . " The old man shook his head. He could say no more.

"And the people, they saw my little girl . . . Atomie . . . was crying." Gau took a deep breath. He shook his head briefly, tears on his hollowed, tanned cheeks. "It hurt . . . everyone was so sad. . . . "

But inexorably the call of the spray overcame, in Jean's words, "the comforts of the hammock." He never again saw his daughter or Taime. Years later he told a reporter that seeing his daughter was the highlight of his sailing career, but to a close friend he wrote, "Taime should not have done that to me! Atomie was crying."

If, as Gau has since maintained, Atomie ("conversant in French, English, and a little Chinese") continued to write to him, we have not located the letters. Our efforts to find mother and daughter have also failed. One report is that Taime and her husband, a plantation manager, moved with Atomie from Takaroa to New Zealand; correspondence with New Zealand officials has been unfruitful.

But if this scene is omitted from his writings, there remain three puzzling matters connected with Gau's second voyage that continue to engage readers' attention.

Did Jean reclaim the silver bars from the Rose Island wreck? We think that his account was written to encourage readers to infer that Japanese fishermen may have discovered the treasure and removed it. Although Jean carried scuba diving gear on his second voyage, he does not mention it in his manuscript. Nearly ten years after the voyage, the seventy-two-year-old navigator told his cronies in Valras, "Now, boys, we've got to organize an expedition to Rose Island! It's my only chance to regild myself, make a little money." Does the treasure still lie in the shallow lagoon waters of Rose Island? Did it ever? We don't know. But we like to think that one of those little markings that shows either rocks or wrecks on the Rose Island chart "marks the spot" where Jean Gau's barnacled bullion lies.*

---

*In March 1975 Jean was shown a large-scale drawing of Rose Island and asked to identify the location of the treasure wreck. "It was," says a friend, "a very moving scene. He could not take his eyes off it. He blushed, trying hard to recall the location. He gazed longingly at it. He asked if he could keep it. His honesty was amply demonstrated when he refused to plot a point that he really could not recall with certainty."

Why didn't the internal ballast tear *Atom* apart when she capsized? Having learned from his first voyage to fear the probability of a capsize, Jean had secured the ballast by nailing all the floorboards tightly to the bilge members. It was impossible for the internal ballast to shift. Nearly ten years later, according to an official U.S. Navy document, volunteers removed about 4,000 pounds of lead pigs from *Atom*'s hold in an effort to refloat her.

Why does the Warrior Reef photo not show an anchor holding *Atom* to the coral as described? By his account, Jean struck the reef at night and got the sails off and an anchor out. Examination of the available photos, however, shows only that a stiff breeze was blowing, riffling the thin layer of water on the reef; no anchor is in sight. The next evening Jean recovered the anchor and fled from the reef. One guess is that with the extreme drop in waters over the reef, the anchor line fell limp, and is thus not visible in these poor quality photos. A possible but unlikely explanation is that as the flood tide began covering the reef, Gau hoisted *Atom*'s anchor, quickly photographed his boat, and prepared to start the engine smartly as soon as the boat righted.

But poignancy and puzzlement, however intriguing to researchers, were lesser stones in the path of Jean's lifelong pursuit of adventure. As before, he returned to the Hotel Taft thinking ahead to the day when he would commence his third circumnavigation. In five years he would be seventy.

Jean's ninth transatlantic crossing, a voyage of 106 days, with stops in the Azores and at Cartagena, Spain, began on June 20, 1968. He had reshaped his bank account after one year's employment, and, more importantly, had qualified for Social Security benefits. Now Jean put aside the dishes that occasionally recalled distant lagoons and quiet waters. Exchanging his soiled toque for a cracked sou'wester, he departed, almost unnoticed,* only to be hailed by the New York Harbor Police—who accused

---

*The only sailors to note his departure were Heinz and Siggie Zenker. Johnny had previously invited them to moor their sloop at the Sheepshead Bay Yacht Club, and for seven days they did so. During that time Gau would not permit them to see *Atom* saying, "It's a shambles." Yet one year had passed since he returned from his second great voyage.

him of leaving "just like that, on tiptoes!" and gave the elderly skipper a friendly handshake and a bottle of whiskey.

His ninth crossing, encompassing the usual gamut of variable weather, entailed also a brief visit by a sea-weary pigeon, the uneasy presence of a silent Russian vessel, the news at sea of the French Navy's rescue of Edith Bauman (whose racing sloop had disintegrated in the third transatlantic race for single-handers), and the presence of a buoy marking the site of the mysteriously lost American submarine, *Scorpion*.

During the voyage *Atom*, whose daily course was at times as short as forty miles, was compared by her exasperated skipper to "an Atlantic turtle," to a "Mediterranean snail." Jean's superb skill at deep-sea navigation received a rough jolt when he landed at Terceira and not at Fayal as he had intended—the seventy-five mile error, his first major navigational error,* was probably due to eight days without a sun sight. It was fortunate that *Atom*'s track was not in the paths of two hurricanes; their far-off presence gave the storm-scarred skipper considerable worry.

If this voyage had begun with Jean breathing deeply the "fresh, pure air and smelling heavily the sea's iodine perfume," it ended under reduced sail in thirty-knot winds on October 9, 1968, when he arrived off Valras, France. "So ended," he wrote, "in my sixty-sixth year a second voyage around the world and my ninth Atlantic crossing." By this gesture he had repaid the Societé Nautique for its decision to name the little basin in which he now resided. At last Jean Gau was home.

---

*Back in New York, Jean had visited sloop *Panic*, where he had impressed Gordon and Jean Moore by casually mentioning that he'd used the same nautical tables for many years, "allowing for Leap Year."

14

A Wild and Savage Name

Gau remained in Valras for a year and a half,* writing his sea journals aboard *Atom* and giving talks before enthusiastic businessmen's luncheons in the neighboring small towns or in the larger city of Beziers. He also lectured at the Arts Decoratifs Museum in Paris. Little or no national attention was given him during this period. But many of those who heard him talk about his adventures fully agreed, with one listener, that the evening with Jean Gau had been the most fascinating program of the year.

According to a *Midi Libre* article dated February 13, 1969, the aging circumnavigator was busy writing the story of "his thirty years of fascinating adventures," and making plans to edit a book

---

*While he was there a ceremony was scheduled to commemorate Gerbault's calling at Valras before departing on his world voyage. Unfortunately, the ceremony was held at 0800 on a weekday. Six people attended, including Jean, who helped place a wreath at the street sign named for Gerbault. A speaker briefly alluded to Gerbault as "an example of courage, virtue, patriotism . . . for youth!" The little ceremony ended humorously as the local vicar dryly noted that "the only youths present" were sixty and seventy years old.

of his *Onda* period paintings. But the art book was never started. The *Onda* paintings remained stowed aboard the damp and aging *Atom*, their presence (or absence) constituting a mystery several years later.

The sixty-seven-year-old skipper was depicted by *Midi Libre* as having "features tanned by the sea breezes, his bearing athletic and physically youthful. Born in Serignan, his first boat was a camel . . . and his first voyage the Sahara." To achieve balance, the article also reported that Gau had "no special qualifications so had to begin as a dishwasher before becoming a cook."

When asked, inevitably, "What was your greatest danger at sea?" the quiet seeker of winds replied that his involvement with the three phases of Hurricane Carrie in 1957 was the most difficult, echoing remarks he'd made to the *New York Times* reporter twelve years earlier. Gau was quoted also as saying that when dismasted off South Africa, "two whaleships rescued" him. This, of course, is a reportorial error; Jean's manuscript states the case otherwise, and is corroborated by the South African search efforts to find him.

We find the omission in the article of his grounding on Warrior Reef surprising: most people, given the choice of death at sea by hurricane or the agony of death on a forgotten reef, would likely choose the former. Perhaps this omission was intentional: Jean seemingly preferred not to dwell on the grimmer and more awesome aspects of his voyages. He was, at heart, a great teller of tales; such gifted individuals can be serious in their art, but never somber.

Still enamored with Tahiti, Jean revealed to the *Midi Libre* reporter that he had considered retiring there, having "bought a piece of land but later reselling it. . . . As long as I feel good," he added, "I'll keep on sailing. Later, we'll see." He would, of course, "keep on sailing" even when no longer physically able to hand, reef, and steer.

Eligible for Social Security benefits and "no longer caring to make a living," Jean remarked that he still felt young, because he had "salt water in his blood"—a poetic way of indicating that even in his beloved Valras he was restless. No longer able to contain his feelings, Jean admitted that he planned to have *Atom* hauled and painted at Agde before attempting his tenth transatlantic crossing. "But where will you spend next season, Captain?" the reporter inquired.

"Cruising the West Indies," was the reply, "and then returning to Valras."

"To retire?"

"Certainly not!" Gau ran thick fingers through his silvery gray hair. "If I were to retire anyplace it would be Tahiti." Weak, faint intimations of a third voyage, signals that the reporter failed to read. But then, was Jean hearing the mocking laughter of the Fates?

Fortunately, the reporter caught something fleeting, for he noted "a smile, serene and philosophical" as Gau, now nearly seventy, said, "You know, when I die I'd like it to be at sea. I want," he added, "no other grave."

Gau's manuscript was finally completed, only to be rejected by a publisher.* The navigator's reaction to this defeat is not known, but some insight is provided by a comment he had made years before in a letter to his aunt. "My pen," he wrote, "is not as clever as my brush." And it was during this long layover in Valras that *Atom* began to deteriorate, neglected by her master as he struggled with the cruel demands of preparing his manuscript.

Sensing again the call of the spray, Jean bought an expensive plastic sextant, which a longtime friend and master mariner promptly checked out. He reported to Jean that the instrument was imperfect, that the reflected sun did not coincide with the true sun when the alidade was set on zero. But Jean refused to accept his findings, saying that the chandler, a former Merchant Marine officer, had approved the sextant.

Finally, on or about May 24, 1970, Gau left Valras bound for America, his quiet and little-noticed departure the prelude to a

---

*An offer to provide secretarial assistance to condense and improve his rough manuscript was firmly declined. Gau's response, "I couldn't be bothered," seems a defensive reaction, his ego having been bruised by the rejection. More probably, it is another example of Jean's total detachment from the demanding realities of life ashore. Jean's writing, a critic has said: "lacks a sense of time; they have no period . . . an absence of details necessary to present the impression of life . . . the writer seldom expresses himself." Again, it is an apt portrayal of Jean's uncommonly detached relationship with life.

mystery and the beginning of a series of trying and near-fatal mistakes. More than two months later, on August sixth or eighth (there is conflict regarding the exact date), a French customs launch on patrol found him in difficulty north of Leucate, about twenty-five miles south of Valras near Port Vendres. The launch towed *Atom* back to Valras harbor.

When hailed by the customs launch, Gau was tired "and strained from two sleepless nights," having, he explained, encountered problems near Cape Palos. He told the customs officers that, knowing it was then too late to reach America before the hurricane season began, he had decided to put in at Cartagena below Cape Palos. But "engine troubles" prevented his landing and he was forced to run before "a very strong gale" for five days, drifting part of that time hove to under a storm jib. Blown "more than 200 miles" off course, to the vicinity of Monaco, he later reached an area north of the Balearics.

Captain Gau stated that on the night of July 15 a huge wave had smashed in *Atom*'s fore hatch, flooding the cabin halfway up his thighs, and that he had bailed for three days and nights with a pan (he later explained that a bucket was too heavy for him to lift). When hailed by the customs launch, *Atom* was still hove to.

These constitute the facts of the incident. For reasons not clear, Jean appeared to be humiliated over this 1970 failure to reach and to pass the Strait of Gibraltar.*

The actual distance from Valras to Cape Palos is close to 400 miles, which, even at a very slow rate of, say, twenty miles a day, he could have covered in twenty days, or by about mid-June. If, nearing Cartagena (Cape Palos), a strong mistral or north-northwest wind had surprised him, he should have been able to run easily under the wind and reach Cartagena.

One of the launch officials, a Gau fan and longtime friend, René Paletta, believes that Jean may have reached Cape Palos within two weeks after leaving Valras, but that bad weather, after

---

*Subsequent medical data suggest Gau most probably had a "blackout," a period of near-unconsciousness that enabled him to eat mechanically, lie in his berth, grasp railings. After a "spell" he'd have no recollection of time lost. Although no witnesses exist for this period at sea, periods of near-unconsciousness *were* recorded on land in early 1976.

July 7, could have pushed *Atom* as far north as the Balearics, and that a severe gale on the fifteenth then pushed *Atom* to Monaco in five days. For some, however, this two-month period raises uncomfortable questions. There was exceptionally bad weather in June and July, and that there was a severe storm during the latter part of July is not doubted—Boussiere was sailing his ketch during that period, and encountered the same storm; he acknowledges that it was capable of smashing in *Atom*'s hatch. But even with bad weather between July 7 and July 22 it is hard to deny that any competent sailor could have reached a port in the Balearics or in any of the numerous small ports along the French and Spanish coasts.

Furthermore, a question about the condition of *Atom*'s engine seems proper. Jean, of course, was trained as a mechanic in his youth. But according to certain individuals, his attitude toward engines was quixotic. Having sailed twice alone around the world, having had his life saved by a working engine off Cape Town four years before, having had nearly a year and a half's rest before departure, and now undertaking his tenth transatlantic crossing, it seems appropriate to ask *why* Jean reported "engine failure." The boat was now more than thirty years old, the man nearly seventy, both seemingly victims of the maxim that harbors rot ships and men.

They also rust motors. *Atom*'s engine at the time was faulty and deemed unreliable, according to René Paletta. After *Atom* returned to harbor, Paletta subsequently discovered small pieces of the cabin rug in the engine clutch assembly!

Valras was stunned. At the time *Atom* was ignominiously towed into harbor, most citizens assumed that she and her dauntless skipper were nearing New York. Jean never afterwards spoke about the incident with comfort. Normally loquacious with fishermen and visitors (although a notoriously poor listener), he seemed in subsequent recollections almost to ignore this failure.

There is some evidence that Jean, even at this late stage in his seagoing career, did not know all of *Atom*'s capabilities: once, under power on the lower Orb, he refused to come about, fearful there wasn't enough water under the keel. His only passenger suddenly grabbed the tiller and spun the boat completely around in the broad river. "Jean," the passenger said, "was astonished."

If Gau were a heavy drinker, one might conclude that at the height of the gale—the after hatch smashed, waters sloshing and surging throughout the small ketch, the winds shrieking above the sluggish *Atom*—he could have done what many sailors, believing themselves about to drown, have done in the past—drink liquor, lie down, and in a last very human gesture, meet death at sea without terror. Who could have blamed a tired old man, one who had espoused and practiced a stoic attitude most of his life, for wanting to face eternity with some degree of defiance of death? But this was probably not the case.

Alternative explanations are that Jean could have had a period of lapse of memory, or could even have been unconscious* at the height of the storm. Of course, examination of his logbook might have resolved the matter. But as long as the incident remains open no one can say with certainty just what happened. We know only that Jean, sensing that the storm was subsiding, managed to bail enough water to appreciably lighten *Atom* and improve her buoyancy. And it was thus they were found, drifting hove to, man and boat protecting each other.

One year later, several weeks out of Valras, Jean wrote Andrée Pierret from Cartagena, Spain.

June 25, 1971

Dear Dedee:

A quick note to tell you of my arrival after twenty days of a slow and rather difficult passage . . . . Each day I thought the weather would improve . . . This bitchy Mediterranean is a demanding sea for the single-handed sailor. I reached the harbor yesterday about noon. Friends at the Yacht Club helped moor *Atom* and, wearing my sea clothes, I joined them for a drink and meal.

Jean was now sixty-nine, and beginning his tenth transatlantic crossing. He concluded the note: "I am in excellent health, good shape, and very happy to realize again my dream—adventure."

---

*In 1974 Gau was diagnosed as a pre-diabetic, and with advanced age his fainting spells became more common and sometimes serious (broken clavicle, late 1975).

Four months later he would be stranded on a distant beach, his beloved *Atom* almost destroyed by his own hand.

Shortly after the note was received, *Midi Libre* printed Jean's log notes:

> *Atom* was making seven knots on a well-oiled sea, her tiller lashed while below I fixed lunch and stored gifts. After thirty-one months ashore adventure was beginning! On June 8, north of the Balearics—not a wrinkle anywhere, and in the luminous haze the tortoise lumbered along . . . in the afternoon Majorca's barren cliffs sighted . . . June 10, sunset an ugly red as the breeze rose and barometer fell. Radio Madrid forecast a gale north of the islands, which worried me; I dropped the main. About 2 o'clock the storm hit and I got the mizzen down pronto! It was hard work because of the lightning, which made things hard to see. *Atom,* jib only, ran before the storm, but the lightning began to alarm me—what if it struck the anemometer which friends in Valras had given me to replace the one struck there in the basin? A lacerating rail fell and I ran to *Atom*'s cabin as the lightning . . . began striking the nearby waters.
>
> With the dawn the storm broke and left only its offspring, a heavy swell—it took only ten minutes to form but it would take twelve hours to subside. *Atom* rolled like she was demented . . . . June 12, at night, the wind gusted between forty-five and fifty knots. *Atom* was a straw on that huge sea. A trying night, a disconcerting sea.
>
> Radio cross-bearings the next day placed me two miles east of Del Aires islet lighthouse. That night darkness invaded the sea, and the moon, rising, showed the horizon. I shot Aldebaran several times . . . . June 24 I tied alongside the Spanish destroyer *F36* in Cartagena, and in the clubhouse read a telegram from my Valras pals: "Did *Atom* make it?"

Jean's account of the 1971 passage, Valras-Cartagena, is accurate and reasonable; it raises no questions. The only allusion to the difficulty (failure) of the previous year was the telegram query. But because of later occurrences, we think it necessary to recapitulate:

Date of Departure	*Duration*	*Date of Arrival*
24 May 1970 (Valras)	two months	24 July (Valras)
4 June 1971 (Valras)	three weeks	24 June (Cartagena)

"Engine troubles" were mentioned in the 1970 newspaper article as the cause of Jean's inability to put in at Cartagena. He then had to run before the wind for five days, for more than "200 miles," to the vicinity of Monaco. But the actual distance between Cartagena and Monaco is closer to 400 miles. If we assume a drift of three knots (possible under a jib in a gale), in five days the distance covered could be almost 400 miles. But we're told that it was a mistral (northerly or northwesterly) wind that "pushed" *Atom*. We conclude that *Atom* was *not* running, but was sailing off the wind, perhaps as much as eighty degrees and hove to, and could thereby make Monaco from Cape Palos.

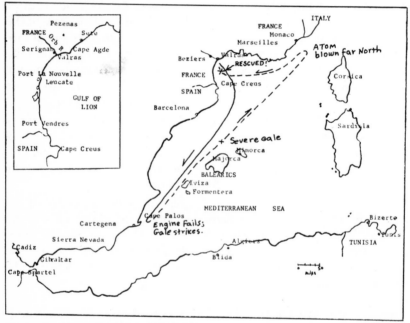

Figure 5.   Generalized plot of 1970 failure

We are puzzled by the lengthy period of the 1970 incident. We conclude, therefore, (1) that the 1970 newspaper account was in error respecting the distance reported, 200 miles, and (2) that Captain Gau was, for reasons not yet clear, badly adrift during a large part of the two-month period. It should also be pointed out that in this same evil triangle (Cartagena-Balearics-Monaco), Jean suffered disastrously several years later, again "hove to for five days and five nights."

Our concern here is to develop a working hypothesis that might explain the trend of subsequent events. Weather conditions during the 1971 voyage were less dramatic than those of the year before, but were still of sufficient malice to require three weeks for passage from Valras to Cartagena. If we assume that similar weather conditions obtained for the 1970 voyage, we find Jean off Cape Palos at the end of three weeks only to be met by a gale that blows him toward Monaco for five days. This still leaves him with another month at sea unaccounted for.

If by July 15 or 20 he was off Monaco, it would then have been too late for him to attempt an Atlantic crossing that season; a year later, in 1971, he shortened his stay in Cartagena for this reason. Why not come about and make for Valras? Jean could have sailed along the coast and in time reached Valras; why did he make for the open waters of the Mediterranean? And what of the information that he was next north of the Balearics, drifting to Leucate, where the customs launch found him "strained and bailing"?

That Jean did not put in at Monaco, or elsewhere on the Riviera, wasn't surprising. According to knowledgeable persons, for him to have done so *would* have been! "He dreads nothing at sea," one of his closest friends has stated. It seems natural, therefore, that he would steer directly for Valras via the dangerous Gulf of Lyon—which, had not the customs launch found him, he might very possibly not have succeeded in crossing.

People who have known him for decades have always been deeply impressed by Gau's lack of fear, and by what they call his "absoluteness." By this they mean that there was never any compromise or equivocation in his belief that ketch *Atom* would survive whatever surprises the weather or the seas held. This confidence existed because Gau knew just how soundly Bjorn Egeli had built *Atom*. He knew also her limitations.

To round out this cursory analysis as a prelude to understanding subsequent events, we must mention that Jean's sailing tactics were very simple: he dropped the main when the winds rose above thirty knots, set the jib taut, lashed the tiller to leeward, and let *Atom* drift. And drift *Atom* surely did!*

Since we have discounted the possibility of drinking, mental lapses, or unconsciousness to explain Gau's apparently "lost" period in 1970, we are forced to acknowledge that this grand navigator—whose life at sea is for some a model, for others less than a model—does not pass muster when compared with many conservative and competent sailors (See Afterword for further discussion).

Gau was less willing than most sailors to seek shelter in a storm, an attitude, it seems, of pure obstinacy. But we submit that without this obstinacy—another word for it is determination— Jean Gau would never have achieved the grand feats that he did. Because of his determined nature, he had twice sailed alone around the world, following adventure wherever it led. Less obstinate, thicker-waisted men, in the comforts of their clubs and homes, rail against the world's "sea-stained misfits." They do not achieve what Gau did.

But this so-called flaw, we feel, is to be an outward manifestation of Jean's obsession with the sea. He is, at heart, not a yachtsman but a mariner, a man of the sea, a waterman whose relationship to the oceans suggests an ancient biochemistry almost forgotten by the memory of our race. Jean put it much more simply when, on several occasions, he said, "I'm not a sailor. I'm a navigator." And he understood that on a long ocean passage one does not run for shelter. Truly Jean Gau is a spirit of the sea world, a seeker of winds.

Some time during the early morning hours on a day in late October of 1971, a beautiful thirty-eight-foot ketch with three young men aboard, after several days of rain, haze, high surf, and northeasterlies blowing twenty to thirty knots, was stranded north of Ocean City, Maryland. The youthful sailors abandoned

---

*If, as some sailing experts have pointed out, *Atom* was such a good performer when hove to, why did she drift so badly? Their argument is that small craft, when properly hove to, generally do not lose ground as rapidly as it appears *Atom* often did. Their conclusion: Gau simply didn't care where he was, or was going.

ship, and by swimming and wading eventually reached the beach, three miles distant from the stricken ketch. Later that day, as they watched helplessly, breaking seas utterly stripped and destroyed the sand-trapped yacht.

Two days later, not far south from the hulk of the thirty-eight-footer, another ketch, smaller and—to discerning eyes—with something of a deep-sea mystique about it, went aground, its keel deeply buried in the shifting sands of an island bearing an Indian name. Nearby, her white-haired skipper, wide-eyed with hurt and alarm, stood trembling with the gut fear of having lost his home and boat of twenty-six years. He stared at the stern name board as though for the last time: "ATOM New York." Behind him, elegant spears of sea oats whispered as they nodded before a stiff easterly sweeping in from the Atlantic's darkened wastes. This small figure, in leaky fisherman's boots and an overly large rubber suit, a seabag resting across his bony shoulder, was of course Jean Gau. The time was near two o'clock on the morning of October 25, 1971.

The grounding of this fat-hulled, old-fashioned, salty little ketch with its quaint ratline and garish Christmasy colors created headlines and stirred public interest as no other small boat grounding has ever done. Ironically, its elderly owner and master was a person who had avoided public attention and notoriety all of his adult life. But now television, radio, newspaper, and yachting magazine representatives trekked every day for weeks to the forlorn, sandy site to photograph his boat, or went instead to the hand-me-down-looking motel in distant Ocean City to interview, analyze, pester, and admire its owner.

But of all the extensive coverage the stranding produced, the most essential was an article by the skipper, which appeared in *Midi Libre* on August 17, 1972, almost one year after the incident was on the way to becoming a local legend. "It is almost *pure* Robinson Crusoe!" commented a French adventure freak, a Gau fan and avid adventure book and magazine reader. We think it's *pure* Jean Gau.

Being late in my schedule I didn't linger in Cartagena, but departed after four days on June 27, 1971. The evening of July 10 I rounded the

Rock of Gibraltar and six hours later Morocco's Cape Spartel. After two weeks of sailing I reached the Madeiras, but proceeded southward to 23° North Latitude, where, meeting the trade winds, I changed course to the west.* It was pleasant "lady's weather," and at night flying fish fell regularly on deck, and as regularly were eaten.

Day after day *Atom* plowed the seas until on September 7, sixty-eight days out, I was forty miles below Cape San Juan, where I had intended to spend the winter. My pleasure, however, was interrupted by a radio announcement: Hurricane Edith was stamping across the West Indies, devastating the Yucatan Peninsula with winds up to 122 miles an hour, and it was heading for Puerto Rico. Fearful that I might be too close to land, I tacked and stood for New York and the sea's open spaces.

Sixteen days later, when 600 miles southeast of New York, I learned that Hurricane Ginger, then developing off the Bermudas and packing 120-mile-an-hour winds, was heading in my direction. I had already noticed that the glass was falling slowly and continuously, the sure sign of an approaching hurricane.

I knew then that I could not avoid it, but I knew also that *Atom* had faced, and survived, formidable storms before.

For several days the sky was overcast, dark threatening. Each hour, according to the radio, the storm grew nearer. Then on October 23 I hove to under bare poles, and, mounting a pierced oil can on *Atom*'s windward shrouds, closed myself in the cabin, where the heat and humidity were oppressive.

At six o'clock the next day a gust suddenly laid *Atom* on her beam end with such force that it seemed she would remain forever in that position between the waves. The inclinometer read 60° to 65° during the gusts and I worried that the internal ballast of 4,000 pounds might shift and start a plank. In that position her deck was under water constantly and I had to man the pump, every thirty minutes, night and day.

From time to time I carefully opened the hatch to quickly glance around. Appalling waves were broaching *Atom*'s starboard quarter, their towering crests breaking in succession along her hull. It was a terror-filled sight.

The morning of September 25 the wind suddenly veered several degrees and began screaming in the shrouds and rigging. Suddenly a formidable shock! From the violence of the impact I imagined how it

---

*Some sailing experts don't agree with Gau on his choice of route. A single-hander, they say, ought to have taken a direct route, landing in New England or even farther north. Their reasoning is that he would thereby have avoided the turbulence of the Gulf Stream and the tricky near-shore countercurrents.

must have looked as the wave rose above my boat, broke, and then collapsed like a waterfall along her starboard planking and deck.

Suddenly everything turned black—I thought we were sinking! But as suddenly *Atom* rebounded and the infernal dance—suspended for seconds—resumed. The water still leaked in and I pumped without stopping. I was exhausted and hungry, but because of the boat's list, I couldn't light the stove. I managed to open a tin.

On September 27, without warning, the wind ceased blowing, which meant that I was now in the central axis of the hurricane. My skin crawled at not hearing the mad voices of the storm. Instead, the only sound was that of waves rushing from everywhere, meeting in angry confrontations around the boat. The barometer read 940 millibars— never had I seen it so low. I nervously climbed to the deck to check the extent of damage.

The ugliness of the scene terrified me! As far as I could see the entire ocean was white with spray and foam and *Atom*'s deck was under water. I couldn't move from the companionway or I would have become a part of the sea that spent itself vigorously on deck. But in the tumult everything appeared to be in order except that the oilcan had emptied. No longer protected by the oil slick nor steadied by a sail, *Atom* gyrated clumsily and randomly.

Suddenly rain, accompanied by hail, fell. The noise of the hailstones on the cabin top was so deafening that I quickly went below, where, despite the boat's struggles, I finally lit the stove and fixed a good meal. I needed one for I hadn't eaten in two days. Later, as I lay on the bunk, I had the sensation of it seeming to recede, to give way under me. But wedged in with pillows, completely fatigued, I slept deeply.

That night, however, the boat suddenly heeled and I heard that awful cacophony of wind crying in the night, moaning one moment, whistling the next. Quickly I switched on a torch—four o'clock. *Atom* had changed course and was now receiving the winds on her port side, which meant that I was now in the safer semicircle of the storm. The torch also showed that the glass had risen to 960 millibars. *Atom* now heeled 50 degrees. With time the winds let up.

Hurricanes move slowly at sea; not until the fifth day could I set my sails. The seas were still ugly and I had to pump ship once an hour. Before long gales arrived from the west-northwest with varying strengths, setting up interference swells.

But on October 24 the sun broke through, and my sights, when plotted, located me fourteen miles from the American coast in the latitude of a barrier island called Assateague. This meant that the storm had blown *Atom* 200 miles westward. After laying a new course to the northeast I lashed the helm and set jib and mizzensail. We soon entered a blanket fog and it was not long after that the catastrophe happened.

All was proper at the time. On October 25 at 0130 I lay in my berth listening to the radio (Dean Martin was singing) . . . suddenly I *sensed* danger. At the same instant I heard the terrifying noise of breakers! The cabin compass showed that *Atom* had changed course and now headed west—the damned wind had veered 180 degrees and now blew from the east! *Atom* had automatically changed course to accommodate the wind. Moments later she stranded and began listing on the sands of Assateague Island.

Several hours later, filling a sack with foodstuffs, clothes, sleeping bag, and other necessaries, I jumped to the beach and began walking in a northerly direction. Later I was to learn that had I walked south I wouldn't have met a soul for many miles. It was with a deep pain that I left my faithful companion stranded high on the sandy beach, the ocean breaking not far off.

The sack was heavy. Every 300 feet I had to stop and get my breath. I looked back at the boat on one of my stops and saw that she was disappearing in a haze.

Would I ever see her again? I swallowed hard and turned away.

Three deer, standing on a sandhill, watched me trudge past in the deep sand. Later a small herd of wild horses, their manes flying in the sea breezes, galloped along the gently sloping shore.

The beach was littered with pieces of wood, and at one place, on the lee side, I found the remains of a very old wreck deeply buried in the soil. Sea wrecks have always fascinated me—how many have I seen around the world! And now at my feet lay the wormy beams and rusted keel bolts of another wreck. Chiseled on the hull remains I found: "XI ● IV ● 1550."

Dragging the heavy bag, I began walking, wondering when I would find help. But walking in the deep sand tired me greatly so I decided to find some kind of a shelter. . . . I chose a hill higher than the others and settled down on its lee slopes. I decided to climb to the summit for a last look around.

To my great joy I saw in the distance a tall cottage whose image was distorted in the early morning haze. Leaving the bag, I slid and stumbled down the slopes and began jogging along the beach in the direction of the cottage. After what seemed hours I reached it but it looked abandoned. "Hello!" I cried, "Is anybody home? Hello!" A dog barked. The front door opened and a man, dressed in a robe, faced me. I told him my story but he naturally was reluctant to believe it. It seemed fantastic, an old man coming in from the darkened beach, ranting about a boat trapped nearby, a boat that had carried him from Cartagena, Spain, in 108 days at sea. Single-handed? If these were his thoughts, he nevertheless said, "Come in. Have something to eat."

I climbed the steps with difficulty for I was exhausted from the hike along the beach. The man sat me in a comfortable chair and handed me a large glass of whiskey. His dog lay quietly on a thick rug at my feet. As I swilled the comforting liquid the man introduced himself as Robert Clements of Washington, D.C. "You're lucky to find us here," he said, "but today is a holiday and the schools are closed."

Clements waked his family and after introductions we ate breakfast. At his advice I lay down while he drove off to alert the Coast Guard. That evening, after sleeping soundly, I spent pleasant hours with my new friends.

At five o'clock, near daybreak the next day, the horizon glowed reddish and a full moon descended in the west. When we arrived at the site a group of about ten men, journalists, photographers, television cameramen and reporters, were warming themselves in front of a driftwood fire. A young woman was passing out sandwiches and boiling coffee. I looked away toward *Atom*, who lay like a stranded baby whale. A portable searchlight brightened the scene and in its powerful glow I could only see the rust-streaked whitish hull of my poor boat.

Some time later four jeeps carrying Coast Guard Auxiliary volunteers arrived. These men, under the direction of Lt. Comdr. Andy Anderson, examined the boat, which lay on her port side at a 22-degree angle, and reported no visible damage. Her starboard side, which had warded off breakers at high tide, needed only caulking. A Park Service bulldozer stood by to push *Atom* over onto her other side, where mounds of sand had been placed to soften the impact of her fall. Then the machine's large jaws were placed against tires lining her port side. As she rose stiffly and then fell slowly to a 40-degree list on her right side, I felt a pain in my stomach.

Exposed by the light of dawn was a large hole in which *Atom*'s ribs lay indecently exposed. Fortunately, they weren't damaged, although much of the internal ballast had broken through the planking at the moment the boat struck. The hole stretched nearly three-fourths the hull's length. *Atom*, it was obvious, was finished.

The men of the Coast Guard Auxiliary, however, were optimistic. The next day they returned bringing three large plywood sheets and a special quick-setting glue. As men nailed the sheets to *Atom*'s side others began the awful job of hauling out the sand from inside the boat. There was in *Atom* not only most of her ballast but another ton of sand that had drifted in during the high tides. Several men worked in cold water as high as their waists rigging a nylon towline around her hull. A large beach fire and hot coffee warmed these hardy men, who had spent the previous day working at the site. Their work had to be timed with the tides . . . after midnight, with only a few hours' sleep, armed only with sandwiches, coffee, and beer, they reappeared and for six backbreaking hours hauled sand and ballast from *Atom*.

At six o'clock the morning quiet was harshly broken by the voice of the bulldozer, whose monstrous eyes stared blindly into the darkness. Before sunrise it had dug a trench two feet deep and ten long into the sea, forming a canal. As the waters entered the canal, sand would be eroded from *Atom*'s buried keel and the terrible suction would be broken. As the waters entered, the machine constantly filled its mouth with dripping sand.

Thirty minutes later a golden sun rose over the Atlantic, gilding the crests of waves breaking on the beach. At high tide the waves slapped and jostled *Atom* as they broke. By 0715 I'd begun worrying that we wouldn't get off because of the ebbing tide, but a trawler, the *Janet L*, arrived and stood close ashore in the breakers where she fired a one-pound brass lead carrying a 1½-inch nylon towline. The men placed the line around the boat and as the slack was taken up I boarded *Atom*. But the strain was too great and the trawler's cleats were ripped out.

The men then fitted a bridle so that *Atom* would be pulled simultaneously bow and stern while being pushed by the 'dozer. The signal was given and the strain began. *Atom* pivoted slowly and sluggishly, her bow gradually facing seaward, when suddenly part of the rudder broke and was hurled through the air. That canceled the day's effort. Helped out of my rope harness, I jumped ashore. We postponed the operation for a full day.

A radio telephone call from Commander McNiff of the Norfolk Naval Base picked me up. He said that the story of *Atom*'s grounding as reported in the media had stirred interest at the Pentagon.

"Cap'n Gau, what's the situation with *Atom*?" he asked. "Is she badly aground?"

"Yes, and if the weather turns bad she'll be smashed by the breakers at high tide."

"Roger, Cap'n. Don't worry, sir."

At three o'clock a helicopter landed on the beach near *Atom* and a naval officer and four salvage divers climbed out. Commander McNiff introduced himself and the other men, each of whom shook my hand vigorously. They carefully examined the hull and inspected the temporary repairs made by the Ocean City volunteers. Satisfied, Commander McNiff turned to me as I asked, "You think, sir, we can rescue *Atom*?"

"Cap'n Gau, I had an order to refloat *Atom* tomorrow morning at high tide. 0745 sharp! Don't worry, sir." The men lifted off in the helicopter and were gone.

His confidence and manner reassured me and made me extremely happy with the thought that my faithful *Atom* would find her element soon.

That afternoon a small convoy of naval vehicles loaded with gear roared across the beach and up to the site. The most important gear they carried was a powerful rotary pump capable of sucking the wet sand from *Atom*'s foot, and making a canal to the sea. That evening we all met at Bob Clements' cottage for an unforgettable evening.

At low tide on November 9, long before sunrise, the operation began with zest. The bulldozer and jet pump excavated a canal. Offshore stood a forty-four-foot Coast Guard cutter out of nearby Chincoteague, Virginia. As the rising flood tide spilled onto the canal and broke the suction along *Atom*'s keel, the cutter's launch brought a strong hawser ashore. At 0715 the tide peaked and the cutter sounded her horn. The hawser stretched taut. In successive stately jerks *Atom* slowly walked into the sea, leaving behind Assateague's gritty embrace.

After two weeks trapped on the hard beach *Atom* was free. Once past the breaker zone, she was towed swiftly to Ocean City, where a crowd had gathered around a large sign that read: CAPTAIN JEAN GAU— WELCOME TO OCEAN CITY!

15

Of Tears and Wine

Captain Gau remained for nine months in Ocean
City, where local businessmen generously provided him a place
to stay and a free slip at Captain Bunting's Marina. The presence
of this solitary man—an aging New York chef and a mariner
little known to the yachting community—had a profound effect
on the resort area. Jean's quiet and often frustrating sojourn
there has produced information that can be divided into three
parts: first, the grounding, which, when examined, raises
questions; second, the phenomenon of his appearance in small-
town America and the impact it had on individuals there; third,
some new insight into the skipper's personality.

Jean's account of the Assateague incident, though admirably
brief and clear, does not tell the entire story. We think it important to do so, because more than any other incident in his
long seafaring career, Assateague gave him an enormous press
coverage. For the first time national attention was drawn to his
exploits at sea.*

---

*Prior to Assateague, Gau's exploits were very briefly mentioned in four books.

The grounding by the aging navigator on a virtually uninhabited island, dramatically reported by the media, ignited long-smoldering fires of adventure in many secret hearts. Perhaps this is nowhere better expressed than in a subdued but thoughtful paragraph in an official United States Navy publication. The Navy's Naval Sea Systems Command *SALVOPS 71* annual report states that: "The recovered *Atom* was worth nothing to anyone except its owner. The recovery effort, however, meant a great deal not only to its civilian and Navy participants, but also to the thousands who learned about it through the news media. It was an occasion in which the many turned their attention to the one, recognizing something in the plight of the solitary Frenchman that touched upon their own lives." In short, many people, smarting from the packaged blandness of their own lives had a new and, if not virginal, interesting hero.

Why did *Atom* go aground? "All was proper at the time," Gau wrote. But was it? That the sixty-nine-year-old sailor was fatigued after at least five days of manning the pump every thirty minutes to an hour because of Hurricane Ginger and the subsequent heavy weather is obvious. Not mentioning his tiredness, Jean got a sun sight on October 24 (the same day the large ketch with the three young men aboard grounded north of Assateague) that placed him "fourteen miles . . . (off) Assateague," and apparently 200 miles off course. But according to Bob Clements, Gau stated that he'd gotten a sun sight the day before (October 24) at noon that placed him off Norfolk! This seems to be a truer statement, because then the grounding thirteen hours later (the winds having veered easterly) is very plausible.

Gau states that when he heard the breakers he noticed that *Atom* was heading west, although he had laid a northeasterly course the day before. But if it was heading west at the time of impact, *Atom* ought to have stranded at some angle to the northeast-trending island, and all photos that have been examined, including several made only hours after the grounding, show *Atom* parallel to the beach. The significance of this is that *Atom* must have drifted onto the beach while hove to, tiller lashed, jib and mizzen set, her bow pointed northeast.

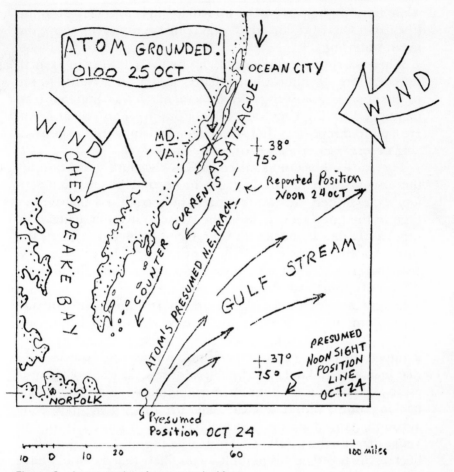

Figure 6. Interpretation: Assateague incident

Jean's account mentions that *Atom* was holed on her port or beach side; had she rammed onto Assateague heading west, she would first have bulged as she struck a submerged bar (exposed, according to Clements, only at neaps), thereby weakening planks on *both* sides that would be subsequently broken or loosened by the shifting ballast. Only the port or beach side was holed. We conclude that the ketch drifted onto and parallel with the beach while hove to, helped by the unusually high tide then running (the Coast Guard reported *Atom* as lying twenty yards above the mean waterline).

When Gau introduced himself, his first words were in French. Furthermore, he almost immediately asked for a chart "to see where he was," according to Bob Clements. It was then that Jean mentioned having been off Norfolk the previous day at noon. He later told reporters that Assateague had appeared to him as a "big desert"—in other words, *where was he?*

There are other points raised by Gau's account. For example, there seems to be a puzzling gap in his time at sea after September 27, when, during the night, he recognized that he was then in the safer semicircle of the storm. The next actual date reported is almost one month later, October 24. On that date the three youths reported northeasterlies—which, presumably, Jean had encountered, although he states that *during* the night of the twenty-fourth the winds veered easterly.

Examination of photographs made shortly after Gau returned with Clements to the stranding show *Atom*'s jib firmly set. Clements later recalled seeing two sails; presumably Jean dropped the mizzen before the photos were taken. It seems odd that Jean, who did not abandon *Atom* for several hours (Clements estimated that it was about 0645 when he was awakened by the barking dog), didn't get the sails off once *Atom* had gone aground. Nor does he indicate having considered trying to kedge off with the windlass, or using the engine. Lastly, had *Atom* been badly holed at this point it seems likely that he would have known it.

The skipper carried two bags ashore, not one. Once he had waked Clements he had to return to the rise to reclaim the second bag. If either bag held his valued *Onda* drawings, the Clements family did not see them.

We are puzzled at Jean's mention of the early date chiseled in the hulk found on the island's lee side. Rusted keel bolts from the sixteenth century?

An interesting oversight in Jean's account is the absence of any mention of what actually transpired for most of the first day after he waked Clements. For instance, Jean returned with Bob to the site, convinced that *Atom* was hopelessly lost. With tears in his eyes the old sailor said that he would burn *Atom* with gasoline from the engine. Bob Clements, his big, open features suddenly grave, argued that Gau ought to let the Coast Guard Auxiliary in nearby Ocean City have a hand at salvaging the stricken vessel. "Let them do it for an exercise," he argued. Gau finally agreed, seeing that he had everything to gain by the effort.

A United States Coast Guard team arrived later in the morning and made a cursory survey of the vessel. Finding starfish inside the hull, they stated that the ketch was too badly damaged to be rescued. Furthermore, because "no danger to life and limb" existed, regulations prevented them from further assisting the stranded sailor. Learning of their evaluation, the old man wept. Again it was Bob Clements who offered consolation; he put his arm around Jean. The Coast Guardsmen silently climbed into their vehicles and drove off, leaving the two men alone.

That afternoon a Bureau of the Customs official arrived at the site. Growling pleasantly about "sailors who wreck their boats so far from his official station," he donned white overalls to poke about the badly damaged little boat, searching for contraband, while the Coast Guard Auxiliaries aided the skipper in offloading his possessions, including two bottles of champagne.

As the report of the grounding reached the wire services, members of the various media began arriving. In the small crowd were ultimately several hippies, who pitched in out of interest and sympathy for the slight figure whose wispy white hair, blowing in the stiff ocean breezes, animated a face terribly grave, lined, worried. The efforts by volunteers to aid this "stranded ocean sailor" were as stirring as the task was formidable: access to the site, which lay a mile and a half south of the Maryland-Virginia border, was either by foot or by four-wheel drive vehicle. Only two houses stand on the narrow forty-four-mile-long island.

There subsequently arose various versions of how the Navy became involved in aiding Captain Gau. Each version is interesting. The one we prefer, although we have no basis for its accuracy or veracity, goes like this: "Seems like after them Coast Guard fellers said they couldn't do nothin' fer Jean, they was a

Admiral who was so embarrassed by them Coast Guard regulations that he called a buddy in the Navy and said, 'Can't you fellers do somthin' fer that old man?'" The speaker paused to scratch his head, as though the action improved his memory. "Well sir, the Navy Admiral sent his legal fellers to their books. They found a regulation or somethin' sayin' that 'private property on government property shall be removed by the Navy.'" The speaker beamed. "'Y' see, Assateague bein' a Wildlife Refuge, it's government property!"

One reason *Atom* did get off the beach was a 1,600-gallon-per-minute pump used by the Navy salvage team to jet wet sand away from her keel. The team's equipment also included a large neoprene flotation collar like the ones used to float recovered space capsules, in case *Atom* started sinking once she was at sea. For the record, the trench that launched the little ketch was thirty feet long, eight wide, and four deep. When rolled over, *Atom* revealed a hole fifteen feet long. She had obviously struck hard, or had pounded as she lay in the surf.

Before the Ocean City volunteers had been replaced by the Navy salvage experts, Jean, to show his appreciation for their unselfish efforts, opened the bottles of champagne. There, on the windswept beach, the air brisk with the scents of ocean and a driftwood fire, the small band raised their paper cups with the vigor given only to sailors. Several in the group affectionately patted the little boat's bottom as her skipper, his gray eyes dancing, smiled with deep feeling.

Regrettably, *Atom*'s two tons of pig-iron ballast, painstakingly removed and stacked on the beach, were eventually stolen, and Jean had great difficulty in finding a suitable replacement. It is interesting to note that, according to the *SALVOPS 71* report, *Atom*'s internal ballast of lead pigs "shifted as the days went by and pounded holes in her port bottom," a view contrary to that expressed by the skipper, who felt that the ballast had damaged the hull at the moment of impact.

Finally, the discussion of why *Atom* stranded must take into consideration the fact that Jean has always been an astute observer of weather.* His writings amply show that he seldom missed changes in wind direction at sea. It is difficult for us to understand then, how this weather-sensitive skipper missed a wind change of 180 degrees when close ashore. He was, he wrote, listening to the radio when *Atom* struck. One can't help but wonder, however, if perhaps he was not a victim of fatigue, a result of nearly a month of the "west-northwest gales" which appear to have succeeded Hurricane Ginger. Could Jean have been asleep, thereby missing the wind change and his ship's change of course? Lying in the dark cabin, extremely fatigued, he might easily have failed to check the tell-tale compass, something he invariably did when pummeled into wide-eyed attention during a storm. But when *Atom* encountered the Assateague sands, the storm had long passed.

It was not a cleat that failed aboard the fishing trawler, as reported. A knot slipped. At that point Jean, according to an observer, "lost all hope. He wept. He just collapsed, feeling certain that *Atom* was a wreck for sure."

SALVOPS 71 again: "Under maritime law the first person to reach an unattended, stranded boat and move it to a place of safety can claim salvage rights for a handsome reward. A salvage lien slapped on the uninsured *Atom* would have been the end of everything for Gau. The watermen of nearby Ocean City threatened reprisals against anyone who thought of attempting it, which averted that problem." Still, some looting occurred.

The anxious skipper was late in getting to the rescue. Seeing *Atom* afloat, he said, "I'm dumfounded. I feel like a million dollars. I can't believe what everyone is doing for me!" Capt. Robert Moss, Deputy Director, Ocean Engineering, later explained. "The Navy got involved because of the old gentleman's history with his boat." The Assateague incident, officially, was closed.†

---

*Nor did he lose his weather sense once he was beached. An Ocean City friend, sitting aboard *Atom*, was startled when Gau said, "Oh, oh!" A squall struck minutes later.

† Six months later Gau learned from Donald Nixon that the President, informed of the sailor's plight, had ordered the Pentagon to act. According to our source, Gau would have been a guest at Camp David, had time permitted.

How did Jean Gau and Ocean City view each other? Captain Gau's presence made a considerable impact on the seaside resort community, on the Washington, D.C., area, and on the United States Naval Academy in distant Annapolis. If the impact was considerable, it was also informative. We were able to interview people who got to know Jean Gau as few Americans have, except for his New York friends.

First, we think it inadequate to state that the chief reason for the stouthearted efforts by the Maryland volunteers was the plight of an elderly mariner in their midst. And to suggest that they responded merely because of the pressures of the media coverage is patently false. Ostensibly they participated as though it were an exercise in salvaging a stranded boat.

But another view of their participation—and of the vicarious interest of thousands of interested persons—a view difficult to portray with precision, is that modern life lacks heroes. Where today are the Lindberghs of yesterday? Our astronauts are team players. And in a culture that increasingly pays lip service to self-reliance and to the virtues of rugged individualism, the man who dares to differ is marked as rocking the boat, a trouble-maker.

We submit that Jean Gau, though not physically cast in the mold of the stereotyped rugged individualist, is just that—a really rugged individual. And the great-hearted recognize it. Frustrated with a system that rewards only with material goods, such people respond quickly and generously to men of daring in distress. And when in their midst there appears a figure of uncommon bravery, who may lack all of the stereotyped physical attributes of the hero but who breathes courage and spirit in every breath, they respond with their hearts. And so it was with the people of Ocean City, who possibly more than most shore livers still retain a keen sense of adventure. But, of course, their reply must be, "It was just an exercise . . . "

In the nine months he spent ashore, Jean was a guest speaker before numerous organizations: the Boy Scouts, sailing clubs, businessmen, and service groups. At first he was a town celebrity, but with time he was accepted as a person. Once settled in the Alamo Motel, during the off-season, Jean established his routine. He was driven to *Atom*'s slip or to the nearby boatyard, where he spent the day aboard cleaning out her grim interior, washing away the grime of Assateague's harsh memory, or chatting with visitors. Although he was outwardly friendly and responded to most queries, he seemingly never sought friendships.

In time the townspeople began to form opinions about the old salt.* Chief among their observations was the skipper's sense of humor, not always gentle. One day he was digging wet sand from *Atom*'s hold and carrying it topside to dump it overboard. A large woman standing on the pier called out, "Hey, mister! What's it like, crossing that there ocean?"

Gau replied curtly, "I don't know." Tired and sweaty, not looking up, he briskly dumped the stinking ooze. "I was asleep!"

Part of Jean's humor was his ability to laugh at himself. But this was because, uncomfortable speaking English, he preferred to use his face, body, hands, any part of his anatomy to emphasize, to make a point, when telling one of his stories. Jeff Davis, the young carpenter who repaired *Atom*'s broken rudder post, recalls asking Jean about storm anchors. Standing in *Atom*'s small fo'c'sle, Gau suddenly raised his thin arms above his head, making the sweeping motions of a breaking wave. His raspy voice whistling in imitation of the wind, he ran back through the cabin to the companionway to show the startled Davis how waves broke over *Atom* at sea. "Storm anchors?" His mobile face revealing the answer, he cried emphatically, "No! No! No!"

In January of 1972 Captain Jean Gau spoke before a large audience at a northern Virginia high school. For two hours,

---

*As reportedly most deep-water sailors are, Jean Gau was very superstitious. In an awed voice he once told about a prominent French sailor, who, when asked, "When will you stop sailing?" replied, "When I'm not able to climb a mast." Gau later saw a friend who said, "Johnny, Bernicot died. Did you know?"

"Well, he was old, wasn't he?"

"Yes, but you recall how I said he would die?"

". . . Yes. He would fall from a mast," Gau cautiously replied.

"Well, Johnny, he did."

After a long pause Gau, visibly moved, said, "There are such odd things in life."

Another time he remarked, "Being shipwrecked on the twenty-fifth of October (1937) is one thing . . . but being twice wrecked on the same day (1971) . . . is surprising . . . and a bit strange. . . ."

according to a newspaper account, the audience was "mes-
merized" by his tales of skulls and bones on sullen reefs, eighty-
year-old pearl divers, Atlantic storms and Pacific nights. Yet,
strangely, minglers in the crowd afterwards reported the dis-
satisfaction of many small-boat sailors. "They wanted to hear a
technical lecture, I guess," sadly commented one observer. "You
know, which jenny to use in Force 7, that sort of stuff."

"Even the dinghy sailors?"

She nodded. "Even the dinghy sailors."

The point here is that Gau's uniqueness as a storyteller, in the
finest tradition of a Robert Louis Stevenson or a Jack London,
was unrecognized by the more gung ho racing and technical
types; they were looking for expertise, not tales of adventure.
But ketch *Atom* was hardly a flat-out racing machine. And Gau,
they quickly learned, was a wonderfully old-fashioned adventurer who preferred to accommodate the winds of the world,
not fight them.

On the occasions when he dined with Ocean City friends or
spoke in public, Jean wore a very old dark blue serge coat, a buff
or red turtleneck sweater, and a small sailing club pin. His
insouciant manner, salty remarks, body English, and sporty
appearance as he strode to a table or a lectern impressed many
men and women.*

A good example of how the media coverage affected individuals involves H. K. Arnold, a Hyattsville, Maryland, attorney.
Impressed by the newspaper accounts, Arnold drove to Ocean
City to meet *Atom* and her skipper. Returning home, Arnold
wrote to the Superintendent of the Naval Academy to suggest
that "this incomparable gentleman" be invited to speak before
the Cadet Corps. "His accomplishments appear to be matchless
in the annals of the sea," Arnold warmly wrote, adding, "Where
in the world would one find his peer . . . ?"

Accordingly, Captain Jean Gau was invited to speak before the
entire student body of the Naval Academy, by, as he put it, "the
Admiral who commanded the Polaris submarine that went

---

*Jean, incidentally, was the Thanksgiving Day guest of a Maryland senator the previ-
ous year. And while in Ocean City, Le Blanc had at least one date.

under the ice. It was my seventieth birthday and I spoke before 4,300 midshipmen. Some of them," he wrote subsequently, "were planning to cross the Atlantic by sail. So they asked me to bring my sextant and demonstrate it since they don't use them anymore. . . . Later, French Admiral Geleinet was invited to see a film made of me showing the cadets how to use a sextant. The French Admiral was v-e-r-r-r-y proud!" The captain's relation of this event, probably the highlight of his long stay in Ocean City, was given with a great grin of pleasure, for he always enjoyed the company of naval professionals.

Jean's wistfulness surfaced occasionally. One day he mentioned to a friend, Joe Pettus, that he couldn't understand why he hadn't been granted the Cruising Club of America's honored Blue Water Medal. Jean shrugged. "But, Joe, I don't sail for that reason."*

After months of looking for a shipwright to repair his boat, Gau was becoming discouraged. In late March, because he had earlier met President Nixon's brother, Donald (then Vice President for the Marriott Inns Corporation), Jean was a guest of honor at a gala Buccaneer Ball at the Crystal City Marriott Inn in Arlington, Virginia. But the ball, undertaken to raise money for refitting *Atom*, was not a success—it had been scheduled for Good Friday.

By April the skipper was feeling that he might never again put to sea. Then a friend, whom he knew harbored a dream of one day sailing his own small boat across the Atlantic, picked the old salt up. Saying little, they drove to the Ocean City inlet and, leaving the car, strolled across the white sands to the water's edge. There was no need to speak; each sensed the other's feelings. Looking seaward across the breezy beach into the blue haze of a late spring afternoon, observed only by seagulls, the friend said simply, "You think I can do it, Jean?"

Gray eyes measuring the rhythmically moving gray waters, the

---

*According to the CCA's medal committee chairman, William W. Robinson, Jean Gau was among the candidates considered in 1975. "When so informed," says a friend, "Johnny was extremely pleased and moved. He blushed. Nodding slowly, he whistled to show his appreciation of the honor." But after forty years afloat as an ambassador of goodwill, Jean Gau failed to be awarded the American medal.

white-haired seaman said quietly, "Yes." He nodded gently. The two men, close friends, returned to the car. But as he opened the door, the friend saw that Johnny's eyes were filled with tears.

At the Alamo Motel, Gau dined often with the genial manager, Bob Cross. "Johnny never offered to cook. Said he'd had enough of that!" recalled Cross. Gau's favorite meat was steak, and he also concentrated on Tang, for vitamins, and peanut butter, for protein. "Old Jean really gorged on vegetables," said another friend.

Not surprisingly, Jean's favorite Ocean City haunt was an old-fashioned hardware store, since removed. But this time, a change from other ports where he'd called, Jean did not visit the fishermen's section of town, West Ocean City.

During the long period ashore Gau never attended church, was never sick, never tried to get part-time work. "He only lived for that boat," said Bob Cross. "He'd go down there about eight o'clock, work all day, fixing, cleaning, dreaming, I guess." The kindly, easy-going motel man paused. "'Course, he'd stop to chat when someone would drop by. Jean 'specially liked Saturdays and Sundays, 'cause of the crowds."

One day a visitor aboard the ketch saw Gau, grinning broadly, emerge from *Atom*'s small fo'c'sle. He had discovered something stowed long before in the fo'c'sle, which the visitor described as "an old-fashioned attic, just full o' junk!"

In May Peter Egeli,* the son of *Atom*'s builder and a portrait painter like his father, arrived at the marina with the competent shipwright, John Swain, of Cambridge, Maryland. After seven months of enforced ennui and considerable frustration, relieved only by removing sand and washing down *Atom*'s formica-layered cabin, the seventy-year-old Gau, working side by side with Swain, threw himself enthusiastically into repairing his home. The men eventually replaced the missing planks, re-fastened the hull, repainted the little ketch, and installed a new Palmer 45-horsepower engine. Swain charged $1,000 for his honest labor and the engine cost $2,500; Gau was close to pen-

---

*Hearing of Gau's plight, Egeli tried, unsuccessfully, to arrange for a cargo helicopter to lift the ketch from Assateague Island. The cost was prohibitive.

ury. He would have to return to his old nemesis, the kitchen stove at the Hotel Taft.

"What'll you do, Cap'n Gau, when you leave here?" a reporter asked one day.

"Go to New York, work in the damned kitchen for a year, then cross the Atlantic for the last time. They named a little basin there for me," Johnny smiled. "I'll just retire there and live aboard *Atom*." Confident, nimble as a monkey, the aging skipper returned to his job of painting the little ketch's cabin top. The thoughts of deep-water sailors are long, long thoughts—and often impossible ones.

As time neared for his departure, Ocean City began to comment about Jean's influence. "He's a compulsive teller of his tales. He'll listen to women but to no one else," said a large, fleshy salesman. He frowned for an instant. "For instance? Well, once I had him down to my place where the boys, all successful professional men, some of 'em admirals, were playing poker after bird hunting that afternoon. Jean quickly told his bag of stories. The group, anxious to tell theirs, did so. Jean just got up and walked off, but not in a huff or angry-like. I later found him in the library skimming through a book." The salesman, after a career spent studying human psychology in action, twisted his face in thought. "The point is that Jean has *got* to be the center of attention. Period!"

Her face pale in contrast to the smart tweed suit she wore, his wife smiled. "Jean was always interesting, no matter what the subject."

Her husband suddenly leaned forward in his wing chair. "That's right! The only time Jean was boring was when he repeated himself."

Boring? How, we pondered, could a *real* adventurer be boring? The answer, of course, is that Gau does not hunt, fish, play cards, golf, make small talk, drink heavily, or pretend. The absence of these social imperatives has removed him from an easy association and relationship with many people. Quick to admire his feats of courage, they still, like his closest friends, were puzzled by Gau's detached air and impersonal manner.

But if a conversation contained the briefest element of ad-

venture or excitement, Gau would perk up and be visibly interested. It's hard to avoid the conclusion that when life dulled in
Ocean City, as it must have for this challenger of the ocean, he
turned inward and found relief by recalling with photographic
clarity the most minute details of exciting times past. A "bona
fide Gau watcher," as one Ocean City resident and close friend
styles himself, has perhaps best depicted the solitary navigator:
"Only at sea, only in the deep sea, was Jean a *complete* person." A
long, thoughtful pause followed. "We never saw the real Jean
Gau."

Others recall that Jean had a pronounced shuffle when he
walked, and that he always wore slippers except when speaking
before audiences. Of his gait Peter Egeli has remarked, "Jean
walked fairly well when I last saw him. But, oddly, aboard *Atom*,
when she was stationary in the slip, he seemed to totter or sway.
He seemed to expect the boat to be heaving and he'd compensate
for the motion in his gait."

One writer, after visiting Gau in Ocean City, departed convinced that a "hard, concrete profile" of the man was impossible
to do, that he could only be portrayed by impressions. More
elegantly stated, and entirely appropriate, we think, is a recent
United Press International news item:

> Visiting French winemaker Baron Philippe de Rothschild signed a
> bottle of 1905 Mouton-Rothschild Bordeaux wine for the benefit of
> a school auction, then waxed eloquent when asked if the seventy-
> year-old grape is really drinkable.
> "Wine," he said, "goes through many ages."
> "First, it is a baby wine. Then it comes to adolescence, then to full
> adulthood. After that, it has a phase as sort of an old executive.
> Later, it becomes an old gentleman who goes about with a stick, yet is
> very elegant, and with whom some ladies still fall in love.
> "Just so," said the baron, "there are wine connoisseurs who delight
> in wine perhaps 100 years old, knowing it is no longer what it was, yet
> savoring what it is for its charm."

But now Johnny was ready to leave Ocean City. At seven
o'clock on a Sunday morning his close Ocean City friends, Joe
Pettus and John Sherwood, joined him for a short voyage to test
Atom's new engine. Returning to the wharf, *Atom* touched the

soft bottom nearby. Jean gasped, "Oh, no, oh, no!" But the little ketch bore quickly off the mudbank.

"The people had been good to him; they wanted to see him off. . . . So he sat on top of his green cabin . . . to shake hands and answer questions and pose for pictures. . . . But he was restless. He kept asking, in his French way, with lifted eyebrows and hands outstretched, 'So, what we wait for?'" So wrote Tom Huth, one of the more perceptive reporters who covered Gau's activities in Ocean City. "The . . . old mariner, his sagging chest bared and his sails furled on this sunny and windless day, bade farewell in a simple and self-conscious way and went back to the sea in his boat. . . . He didn't look back. He sat small at the tiller; and in only a few minutes his bare twin masts disappeared into the ocean haze." The date was July 20, 1972.

To the romantic mind, the ocean haze Huth noticed might have held something foreboding, something suggestive, as the little *Atom*, her master preoccupied at the helm, footed nicely into the mists and disappeared from sight. It was as if Jean's impatient mistress, the sea, had flung a cloak for her long-awaited lover.

Haze and morning sun, silent sea and a clean wake—and a mystery. *What became of Jean Gau's drawings?* Among the puzzles we've encountered, this is one of the hardest to solve. According to friends, Jean always carried his *Onda* drawings in a plastic bag aboard *Atom*. Assuming that the eleven-by-fourteen-inch drawings were safely aboard *Atom* when she grounded on Assateague, it is difficult to understand how they could have been damaged. There can be no doubt that among the personal items the stunned skipper hastily loaded into his two bags before abandoning the stricken vessel were his "little masterpieces." Yet, asked by Peter Egeli to show them, Gau replied that "they were ruined by the salt water. I threw them away." Others who asked were told the same story. No one—the Clements family, Bob Cross, the motel maid, Joe Pettus, or anyone else—ever saw the *Onda* drawings after Assateague.

Johnny managed to salvage color prints of the drawings. If he did destroy the originals, when? Before abandoning *Atom*? At the motel? These drawings, which had "nearly kept the company of sea urchins in Torres Strait," followed Jean on two world voyages. He could have sold them, many times over. He preferred, instead, to sell eleven perfect pearls when desperate for money. But never would he have sold his drawings. One theory is that the drawings, tightly sealed in a plastic bag, floated out of the stricken ship and were lost. Alternatively, they might have been stolen; Jean's .30-.30 rifle was stolen while *Atom* lay pounding in the Assateague surf. But neither theory is sound. We can only speculate.

In what must have been the most desperate act of his life, Jean Gau, sobbing, trembling, stood in the vessel's darkened cockpit and deliberately tore to pieces, one by one, the sea-ravaged drawings. He flung them, now scraps of soiled and vile-colored trash, into the mirthless sea.

16

Gray Is the Wave,
Harsh the Rock

Just before Jean's ill-fated departure from Valras in 1971 an uncle of one of his boyhood friends approached him. "Johnny," he asked, "why do you continue to sail when you are old, eh?"

The old salt shrugged. "Because the sea has me."

Soon after his arrival in New York from Ocean City, Jean found work in the Bienvenue Restaurant; his friend Joe Cordonat had gotten him the job. While *Atom* was being restored to minimal live-aboard condition, the two men shared Cordonat's apartment on 73rd Street. But Jean's heart was no longer in his work. In late May he quit, saying that he had to ready *Atom* for his last Atlantic crossing.

"What'll you do, Johnny, when you get there?" asked his friend.

"Live aboard *Atom* in the harbor," replied the gaunt, wrinkled sailor. His thin frame registered the restlessness aggravated by his long Ocean City layover.

241

Two weeks later Cordonat received a call at work. Gau's deep voice, now slurred, filled the telephone receiver: "Joe, I'm sick. I can't move one of my legs. If I try to walk, I fall." A slight pause, and Gau continued. "My leg, Joe, is dead!"

Cordonat's son, David, immediately went to the Sheepshead Bay Yacht Club. He boarded *Atom*, and after a costly trip by taxi, brought the sick man back to the apartment. The next day Cordonat accompanied Jean to a hospital for examination and tests. That evening the door to the apartment opened and Gau, having painfully climbed the apartment stairs, entered. The two old friends looked at each other. Gau spoke slowly. "The doctor says that I have to learn to walk again . . . I have a blood clot."*

Johnny stayed in the apartment for a week. The second night, while Joe was at work thinking his friend was keeping a hospital appointment, the tough little sailor left in a downpour to go to a movie. He later returned to the yacht club, where friends, having walked nearly a mile after leaving the nearest subway station expecting to find him aboard *Atom*, helped Jean board his boat. He had been waiting on the pier for someone, anyone, to give him a hand.

His New York doctor, an intern from the Ivory Coast who was worried about Jean's refusal to return to the hospital, sent two letters imploring him to return for medical treatment and further examination. Gau ignored them. Learning of his refusal, Cordonat left work to see the doctor to explain that Gau intended to sail soon for Europe. "He's crazy!" replied the doctor. "Really, Captain Gau is a *very* sick man."

Joe hurried to the yacht club the next day and confronted his ailing and stubborn friend. "Johnny, come with me," he pleaded. Shaking his white head, Gau refused. "No. I have a good doctor in France."

"Dammit, Jean!" Wide-eyed with anger at his friend's stubbornness, Cordonat said, "If you don't go back to the hospital I'll burn this goddamn boat to the water! You understand? To the water!"

---

*Gau's French doctor thinks the clot may have started during his 1970 failure.

Standing before *Atom*'s small galley, Gau said nothing. He poured coffee into a mug without a handle, and his weakened and shaking arm spilled some. Leaving the spilled coffee on the stove, Gau turned slowly and limped to the starboard bunk, where, with difficulty, he sat down. He said nothing.

Deeply upset, Cordonat watched as his old friend sat staring into space, the constancy of his gaze suggesting unseen visions and images. "It's stupid! You're committing suicide, Jean!" cried Cordonat. He hurried up the companionway ladder. Angry, frustrated, he could do no more.

On the morning of 21 June 1973 Jean ate a cheeseburger at the yacht club bar with his boyhood friend, Henri Sauzet. As they ate and reminisced, Henri was "hurt to see Johnny dragging that bad right leg."

"When do you plan to leave, Johnny?"

Gau shrugged. He ate his cheeseburger. He did not look up as his friend asked, "Have you enough food for the voyage?"

His gaze seemingly drawn inward, Gau shook his head. "Oh," he said, "the sea will provide. I eat very well at sea, Henri." So the two old friends who had shared their youth in a faraway place in a far-off time ate their last meal together.

His passport and health permit had previously been stowed aboard *Atom*. The next morning Jean Gau quietly motored out of the Sheepshead Bay Yacht Club anchorage. He soon exited by a familiar route into the heaving Atlantic, his mistress sea.

His mistress sea! A popular definition of an obsession is, "A persistent and irrational idea, usually unpleasant, that enters the consciousness and cannot be banished voluntarily." Jean's obsession with the sea clearly parallels the recorded case of a schizophrenic patient who volunteered for the demeaning job of cook aboard a cargo vessel because only at sea could he make any sense out of existence. His reward was a peace that cannot be further analyzed or clarified. Although man's reasons for going to sea are as varied as the sea itself, the thoughts of a deep-sea sailor are less crowded than those of shore people. At any rate, Jean followed the sea, the inexplicable lure of the sea, as long as he had a boat.

On November 22, 1973, the Washington *Star News* carried the headline SEA HERMIT LOST AT SEA! But in fact, after eighty-eight days at sea, Jean Gau had miraculously reached Cartagena in September. Several days later he left for Valras. *Atom*, seaweakened, her poor condition evident to all, followed her ill and crippled master. Once more they would test the Mediterranean's evil triangle.

In November, Gau's niece, worried at his failure to reach Valras, contacted the French Coast Guard. A search of French and Spanish seaports was started immediately. A message to the U.S. Coast Guard—"Gau is not in these waters. Have you any information?"—received a negative reply. *Atom* and her master had disappeared.

And then word came that Gau was alive. But his boat, *Atom*, was lost. The message came from Tunisia.

The old man was obviously tired, very tired. His sunpinkened, parchmentlike skin, furrowed and deeply wrinkled, showed cuts and scratches. His ears and his aquiline nose seemed too large for the shrunken, withered-apple face. But the reporter, sensing a story, pressed for details, and so the old man, pausing frequently to recall or to regain his strength, rasped out his story.

Again the events were pure Jean Gau—and their telling in the manner of a great storyteller, one whose life is inextricably woven into the threads of his tale.

On June 22, 1973, I left New York for Valras. Having made the wise decision to cancel a project very dear to my heart (a third voyage around the world), I put to sea telling myself that this would be my last cruise, realizing that when one has to struggle alone against the elements during a long cruise, such adventures become more difficult with age. But nothing retained me in New York. I was no longer working, living on a scanty Social Security retirement pension. . . .

But my resolve to abandon the voyage caused me great sadness. I saw it as a surrender not worthy of a sailor who has, during his lifetime, told his closest friends that he intended to die at sea. Well, we shall see later. . . .

The ease with which *Atom* reached Cartagena* on September 21, 1973, was remarkable, and reinforced my conviction that I was not finished as a man. My health was excellent and I could still master, with a strong hand, my boat. The welcome in Cartagena was generous and hearty as it has been these many years. But a few days later I put to sea for Valras.

If only I had known what was waiting for me off Barcelona, I would not have proceeded. Nor would I have been ashamed.

Suddenly, when nothing had foretold it, a wind of extraordinary violence arose. In seconds the sails were torn off. A large wave thundered aboard and broke, drowning the engine. Under that condition I had no means of fighting back and for five days and five long nights *Atom* was a toy on the sea. I knew only that we were drifting. During a lull in the storm I managed to get a sun sight. When plotted it showed me to be about ten or fourteen miles south of Sardinia. I got up what sails I could find and bent them on. But Aeolus hadn't blown his last breath. It was a new tornado that blew. *Atom*'s sails were torn to ribbons.

On December 3, about ten o'clock, I knew that my final hour had come. *Atom* was being set towards the coast at a tremendous speed when I saw ahead a jagged cliff, perhaps sixty feet high. *Atom* would be hurled against that cliff.

I was cold. I was hungry and my only reflex was to wait for the end. But a miracle happened. I view it as a miracle, this happening in a forlorn, deserted place.

As I looked about for what I felt was a last look I saw a man standing atop the cliff waving, trying to get my attention. But at that moment I felt an explosion and I was hurled onto the reefs. Half conscious I lay for perhaps fifteen minutes or more, I don't know. When I became conscious I was not able to move at first. Again I felt that death was at hand.

As in a dream, I sensed that I was fainting again when a rope swung into view above my head and beyond my reach. Painfully I raised my head. I saw that the man was holding it out to me. He would be the only man to witness *Atom*'s loss. And his rope was a long flannel belt that shepherds wind around their waists. He could climb no lower, but he

---

*For the first time in eleven crossings, Gau did not stop at the Azores. According to Mark Parris, American Vice-Consul, Azores, "I must inform you that I have been unable to discover any record of Mr. Gau's having stopped . . . on his 1973 crossing. . . . " Why he did not stop is not known.

showed me how to seize it. I grasped that belt with all my strength and the climb began.

I tried to help him the best I could but the coral heads were as sharp as knife blades. I was cut several places over my body and I lost much blood. I don't know how long it took to climb that cliff.

When I reached the top of the cliff the man, an Arab, leaned over me without speaking. After examining my wounds he said that I was "on the coral coast near the Bay of Bizerte." He offered me a cigarette. We were a day's walk from the nearest village, where he lived. He put his fingers to his mouth and whistled. A small donkey trotted to where we were.

"Now," the shepherd said, "I will help you to get on the donkey. The only thing you have to do is to let him alone. He knows the way. You will have to go along the cliff for a long ways. Don't look at the sea. When the donkey tires he will stop."

We started. It was ten o'clock and the donkey began pacing at a small clip. Sometimes when it mistrusted the firmness of the surface it would stop, tap with its foot, and then move on. After several miles I felt I was fainting. I did fall. When I regained consciousness I saw the donkey sitting next to me, licking my hands. Several times this happened and I had to climb down to rest. Each time my faithful companion would sit down near me and lick me! Today I realize how incredible all this sounds but it's not a joke nor a romance, this odyssey.

About five o'clock the donkey arrived in front of the shepherd's dwelling. Without asking who I was, but knowing where I came from, three young girls and their mother helped me into their house, put me near a fire, removed my clothes, and rubbed me energetically. They fed me soup and rolled me in a sheepskin coverlet and I fell immediately to sleep.

The next day the Berber arrived. He had warned the police and later three policemen arrived by jeep and drove me to the Bizerte hospital, where I stayed three days.

I then went by police vehicle to the American Consulate in Tunis, where all necessary steps were made to get me a copy of my passport, identity papers, Social Security card, and an order for my bank to send me $500. I had lost everything in the wreck.*

---

*Only his wristwatch and briar pipe (carved with a Legionnaire's head) were saved. His passport was discovered next morning, "the cover torn off and the first six pages missing . . . very moving to handle it, all stained with tar . . . little grains of sand and even dried seaweed stuck to it . . . " (personal letter).

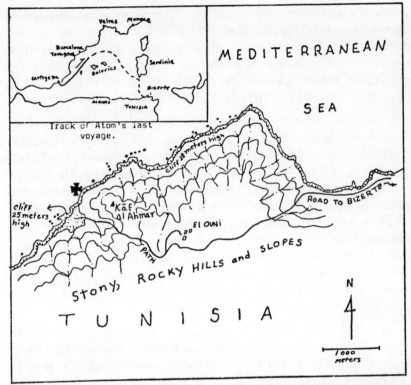

Figure 7. Sketch map of the approximate site of *Atom's* foundering, December 3, 1973

On December 28 I took a French jet to Marseilles, having written my niece in Beziers that I was arriving. But a delay in the mails caused me to arrive before my letter. I could not appear so weak at her door so I stayed a night in a hotel next to the station.

The next day, in rags, I knocked at her door. When she saw me, pale and poorly dressed, she cried. I did, too.

Wearing a large cast-off sweater, his wavy hair now silvery white, his lips trembling, Jean said, "Thus I ended the last and saddest of my adventures on the seas and oceans of this world. . . . " His eyes reddened. "My last," he repeated, "and my saddest."

When the article appeared in *Midi Libre* on January 7 and 8,

1974, it concluded with a call for "generous contributions in honor of one of the most accomplished sailors in the world." Southern France responded immediately, contributing a small trailer, clothing, a heater, a stove, a radio, and other items. An old friend kindly allowed the little trailer to be parked on her property in Valras so that "Johnny could be near the sea."*

Jean Gau, *Atom*, and Valras—inextricably tied for all time. True to its seafaring spirit, little Valras, recognizing "old Jean's" worth, had accorded him its greatest honor in naming the Bassin Jean Gau, and for one of the few known times in his life Johnny had been deeply moved. Now windswept Valras responded again. In nearby Serignan, busy with its grapes, it was different.

"Rose Island?" The elderly Serignan's eyebrows lifted, revealing dark brown, marbled eyes. He blinked, more from age than from the few shafts of late afternoon sunlight that penetrated the shadowy streets and dark alleys. "*If* the silver were there, why didn't Gau make it to another island, get explosives, and return?"

He stood beside a winter-naked plane tree planted close to the arched doorway of the thick-walled garage. Many years before he had been a Navy man and "had seen something of the world." His face reflected sincere doubt, and he muttered, "What's that rot about having a child, and not knowing it? Eh!"

The interviewer shrugged. He must proceed cautiously.

The Serignan, thick moustache as white as his eyebrows, placed a gnarled hand on the edge of the doorway. He did not move a muscle in his expressive face. "And in 1974"—his voice sounded strained by the thicket on his lips—"what's that business about a shepherd and an ass!" It was obvious that, like thousands of persons throughout southern France, he had followed Gau's adventures closely in *Midi Libre*.

---

*In America, *Yachting, National Fisherman, Chesapeake Bay* magazine, the Washington *Star News, Boating, Argonaut, Pacific Skipper,* and others ran pleas for money and letters of cheer. Radio stations WMAL and WNAU made sympathetic broadcasts. The public responded generously; letters enclosing checks and dollar bills poured in. But the letters of encouragement from adventurous men and women, mindful of the last hurtful days of Joshua Slocum, were magnificent. Typical of the depth of the response was a five-page handwritten letter from an elderly widow in New Zealand, who, unable to offer money, prayed for Jean's well-being.

Again the interviewer attempted to suggest sympathy with the man's viewpoint. He nodded.

"Monsieur," the retired vintner faced the interviewer and briskly shook a thick forefinger for emphasis, "Gau is an *adventurer!*" The words were torn from his hidden lips. "Such men are very hard, *very* hard to believe. *N'est-ce pas?*"

Of all Gau's voyages, this, the last and saddest, has been the most difficult to collect additional information on, chiefly because of his inability to recall or to explain clearly certain details. To date, however, our research has produced several pieces of data that either elaborate on Gau's short narrative or pose worrisome questions.

A study of pertinent literature on the Tunisian coastline showed only a rocky and sandy environment; Jean had originally described the cliff as a sand dune. He refers to reefs and corals, but we have not located references to these in the literature. Jean states that a "huge wave" drowned his new 45 hp. engine; we must accept this explanation. Nonetheless, the incident stirs wonderment. How *did* the waters reach the engine compartment? Assuming that the wash boards were in place, the wave(s) must have smashed in the fore, as happened in the 1970 incident. In subsequent interviews the captain could not provide additional details.*

He did not have aboard or could not set another suit of sails, even a jib, after the engine was drowned. He was thus at the mercy of the winds for "five days and five long nights." His use of "tornado" we've retained, although it seems inaccurate.

Finally, he mentioned to a friend (but not to the reporter) that when he was south of Sardinia a Dutch tugboat, responding to his distress signal (again, not mentioned), offered to tow *Atom* to Sardinia for $1,500. Jean, of course, refused the offer. The crew reportedly gave the elderly sailor some fresh bread and sailed away. This incident, like certain others in his remarkable career, has a faint echoic quality—fresh bread from the American escort to the USS *Eagle,* a Dutch tugboat in the Azores, five days adrift off Monaco . . .

---

*See footnotes on pages 210 and 212.

In reply to a letter requesting information about the shipwreck, the American ambassador to Tunisia, Talcott W. Seelye, wrote, "Tunisian authorities advise that Gau was discovered extremely exhausted on the shore by a shepherd named Salah Ben Hamida El-Ouida at Ksar Lahmar, Haicher Region, on December 3, 1973. The shepherd alerted the Garde Nationale at Bizerte and a Lieutenant Hassen Zarrouk took charge of the case.* The case was later taken over by the Bizerte Port authorities since the accident took place at sea. An officer by the name of Habib Turki handled the case and alerted the Embassy. Unfortunately there was no local press coverage of the incident."

In late January of 1974, a doctor in a Bizerte hospital wrote to Gau's doctor in Beziers, "Gau did not show any mental or physical difficulties. . . . no examination was made nor any medication given." We are advised, however, that medical treatment in Algeria can be very poor. When Gau was released he was exhausted and had many superficial wounds on his hands and face. Had he been examined, his partial paralysis would have been noted by the examining physician.† Nor was there any reference to his speech impediment—yet we know these physical problems existed when he departed New York.

Jean often told friends, "I don't care. I am a fatalist. I say, one time it is going to happen. I don't care." Although related to Gau's outlook that one day he and *Atom* would not survive at sea, these words relate also to his spiritual convictions. In a letter to Claire Gau in 1946, six months after he had bought *Atom*, he clearly and succinctly states his religious belief and, in a final passage, his philosophy:

> Your letter of January has upset me somewhat. For example, I will quote one passage: "This is the only reason why there exist convents and monasteries. Men and women sacrifice their lives to obedience, poverty, chastity, and the salvation of sinners. . . . I also know that the parent's sins (since Adam and Eve) are expiated by their children."

---

*Ksar Lahmar we think to be a phonetic variation of Kaf al Ahmar. A letter to Lieutenant Zarrouck, requesting details, went unanswered.

† In a letter to Cordonat dated March 25, 1974, Gau stated, "I'm beginning to take the hair of the dog that bit me. I think I'll soon walk without a cane."

I cannot agree that some must suffer for another's guilt. This is not right, and reminds me of that madman, Hitler, when he massacred hundreds of people for the fault of one unknown saboteur.

When I think about these horrible things my faith is seriously shattered, and I think that it is absolutely absurd to suffer on this planet for the salvation of sinners. Don't be cross but, you see, we don't see life from the same viewpoint.

Let us speak of something else, do you mind? About that matter which interests me most, the sea and my boat.

What can I say to you except that I am totally unable to express my passion for the sea with its beauty and fright? My pen does not equal my brush. So I am very eager to show you what I call my "little masterpieces." When you admire my Sunset, Dawn, Northeast Gale, On The Crest, Encounter At Sea, Moonlight, Lightning, Atlantic Wave, The End of *Onda*, etc. . . .

Then, perhaps, you'll grasp why my happiness is boundless when I am alone on the Atlantic. You will approve of my love for my boat, why I consider it as a live being, intelligent, sensitive.

That sentence will perhaps make you smile, but once, on a stormy night, I let *Onda*, her tiller lashed, look after herself while down in the cabin I tried to sleep. I often was waked by the shock of the waves and the boat's heeling. And yet I managed to sleep, and to rest. When I went on deck in the morning my gallant boat had kept her course as if my hand had been on the helm all night.

Landsmen? If only they knew they would not wonder that a lone sailor loves his boat and treats her as his best friend.

I know that I speak without meaning because you have no feel for the sea. Perhaps Grandad Fabre, were he alive, could understand me.

I end this letter with a little verse:

> They understood nothing of this great dream
> > Which charmed the sea of his voyage
> > Since it was not the same lie
> > That was taught in their village.

The lines poignantly portray the life of this grand old stoic of the seas. "They," of course, are the villagers of Serignan, "his voyage," a reference to the still cherished *Onda*. "The lie" is Gau's magnificent and scathing epithet for the spiritually empty culture that seeks only ease, comfort, and fame. These lines could only have been written by Jean Gau.

In a sense Jean's life, though turbulent, was poetic and fraught with romance and adventure. His creative efforts, even if termed insignificant, have value in that their roots were founded in experience.* Once Jean could, through activities of his own making, escape the question, Why Life? Now, ill, crippled, and often confined to a sickbed, he cannot escape. Now he must ponder answers to the question.

Today Johnny's hair is full, perfectly white, wavy, still parted on the left side. His well-formed forehead is deeply lined, as are his cheeks. His light gray eyes are seldom without depth and a quality of expression that startles; one is easily distracted from talking with him because of those eyes.

If intangibles can be sensed, one detects in his face honesty, straightforwardness, and a sense of essentiality. There is in his features, if not the glow of a man of action, a subtle aura of energy. It is not inaccurate to say that one feels, meeting Jean, that he has met with truth and with the presence of spirit.

Although his frame is small and wiry, even spidery, in old age Jean still exudes strength. He has a sailor's habit of moving with his hands ready to grasp for support; the result is a tension that one detects even when he is relaxed. His gait is that of a man who has had to walk with care. Although the stroke has partially paralyzed his right side, causing the leg to drag and the right arm to weaken, Jean retains an attitude of seamanly caution about deck.

His speech, once vigorous and deep and rough with a marvelous richness, now drawls. When he repeats himself in telling a story, thoughtful observers become aware that perhaps the old seaman is acting somewhat, playing a role for their amusement. This awareness at once destroys the charm. The spell no longer exists. One concludes that he is facing a rather ordinary individual.

---

*"Your adventures are of a time nevermore," stated the famous Swiss sailor and adventurer, M. Mermod, in a recent letter to Gau. "Your voyages were more epic than most. Your sailing . . . was a human experience that is precious because now man faces Bureaucracy, Profit, Organization. Consequently, the average person in search of an impossible dream, now more than ever, is forced to read adventure stories to escape his condition."

"It was moving to see Jean last Saturday," wrote an admirer, inadvertently providing the most poignant and telling summary of Johnny's present state. "No light in the trailer. All dark at eight o'clock in the evening. I called, 'Ship Ahoy!' A cheerful and immediate answer. He had recognized my voice. Fumbling for a light. Tiny interior like the cabin of a boat. On a shelf a few tins (beans, lentils). On the table the *Spray* magazine. His pipe the only thing rescued from the shipwreck. I give him the news. Some hope re your generous call in American yachting magazines. It was touching the way in which Jean welcomed this news. No greedy questions about money. Much mute recognition for all who strive to help him grasp once more his life's dream. No words but a faint and growing conviction that all is not over."

The letter ends, ". . . to an exceptional person like Jean the only difference between life and death is a boat. By boat I mean a hull in which he could exist, dream, and die. Really, that man deserves not to die in a hospital room."

This last thought echoes that expressed by another great lover of the sea, Edna St. Vincent Millay, in her passionate and moving threnody "Inland Sea".*

> People that build their houses inland,
> People that buy a plot of ground
> Shaped like a house, and build a house there
> Far from the sea-board, far from the sound
>
> Of water sucking the hollow ledges,
> Tons of water striking the shore,—
> What do they long for, as I long for
> One salt smell of the sea once more?
>
> People the waves have not awakened,
> Spanking the boats at the harbour's head,
> What do they long for, as I long for,—
> Starting up in my inland bed,

Beating the narrow walls, and finding
Neither a window nor a door,
Screaming to God for death by drowning,—
One salt taste of the sea once more?

Accompanied by Andrée Pierret, Johnny went for occasional walks along the shining beach of his youth. He seldom spoke, having only one thing on his mind—the sea. Once, after nearly an hour of silence, he called out softly, "Andrée, look!" The white-haired seaman, leaning heavily on her arm, nodded at the dancing waters. "Is she not fascinating?"

"Old sailors, when they no longer grow barnacles, grow roses," goes an ancient saying. For the courageous challenger of distant seas, Jean Gau, it would be neither.

In December of 1975 he was taken by a friend to stroll the docks in Cape d'Agde. Dragging his useless right leg and dressed in a heavy blue jumper and woolen cap, the old navigator seemingly ignored the sailboats tied to the docks. But left alone for a while, "Johnny paused in front of a store window. For some time he coquettishly readjusted his sea cap on his silvery head . . . The village rooster again!" His friend's letter concluded, "At least, Jean Gau, deep-water sailor!"

But, sadly, it was only a trace of vanity. Shortly afterward the old man was invited aboard a sloop for a day's outing. He showed no elation at being on water. In the coming months Jean Gau faded noticeably into old age. The distressing loss of control over bodily functions, the growing evidence of senility, the loss of recent memory—all were accompanied by lucid moments that, in themselves, lacked grace. But over all were the eternally empty hours in the small trailer, and the inability to provide some satisfying recall, to command sleep, or sometimes even to raise the fallen body.

Feeling that Johnny ought to be nearer the water, Valras officials had the small trailer moved close to the Bassin Jean Gau. But the water tap was fifty yards away, so a friend hauled the trailer to his farm. There, he felt, Johnny would have both comforts and attention. With cows, chickens, and a horse, the sunlit windows of a large kitchen, small children delighted by

"Grandpa's" presence, and the delights of a hand-built fireplace on chilly spring evenings, would not the old man respond? But there were problems.

To shorten the long hours, Gau was given a small television. He quickly became intoxicated with it, preferring it to walking in the countryside, to talking with the farm animals, sitting in the sun on a worn doorstep, or examining the colors and smells of a French spring. "No. Johnny sat in the trailer rethumbing a book with pictures, watching television, or smoking that eternal pipe. It seemed that if he watched, he did not see," his friend wrote. "He neglected to clean his trailer. He did not offer to help with small kitchen chores. . . . No. He was Jean Gau—a very odd but exceptional creature, a real solitary. Tough—both sublime and despicable in his solitude."

But something of his youthful vanity lingered. Once he asked his host to tint his thick silvery hair, saying, "It makes me too old!" Photographs indicate that he may have tinted his hair before arriving in Valras after his second circumnavigation.

Small children seemed to please him. But gone now were the jibes, the merriment, the wonder of his great exploits and stories.

In February, 1976, Jean was a guest at a public lecture in Beziers by a yachtsman named Steinberg. A long ovation greeted the lecturer's dedication of his talk to Jean Gau. When a film of his departure from Valras on his third circumnavigation was shown, Johnny openly sobbed. Letters and money began to arrive, but Jean no longer was able to read his correspondence.

In March he was assessed by a close personal friend: "Jean is a good man. He possesses an amazing strength of character, the grit of a stoic. Because he is so passionately oriented toward one thing, the sea, Gau has a natural purity about him. His natural instinctive goodness is evident in his eyes when watching small children. He does not speak, or only a little, but he is willing to listen to them, something he often would not do with his peers. In his gaze there is an immense bounty. . . . He has never complained. Not once!

"But, increasingly, he gets confused with problems of direction, putting on slippers, making electrical connections. When lucid and if aware of his problems, he shakes that old gray head, makes an ironical bitter remark or seeks refuge in jests. But never does he complain."

"Once, unable to plug in a lamp, unable to strike a match or to locate the flashlight (on a nearby table), he waited in darkness for two hours for the call to dinner. On another occasion, Johnny fell and was unable to stand. He lay in complete darkness for one hour. He swore and cursed heaven, but showed no impatience when rescued. Three days before he entered a hospital he was almost unable to move or to stand. Exerting a great energy and breathing heavily, he tried to get to his feet at the table. Once, he was found on his knees in the bathroom, unable to get up but trying to, unaided. When older people in distress willingly accept an arm, a hand, a shoulder, Gau proudly does his best to manage alone. His breathing at such times were not sighs, according to a close friend, but they were "noble and heartrending."

Gau has no fear of death, caring not a fig for life or skin. Neither money nor glory interest him. After the Steinberg lecture he was questioned but shook his head and said he was used to it. He doesn't like money to be raised in his behalf. There is no fake nor the ham in his attitude. As natural, said a friend, as "Christians and faith."

It was decided to place Jean in an old folk's hospital. It was then, remarked his friend and host, "that Johnny admitted for the first time that he could no longer sail, no longer handle a boat." He was driven the next day to the Beziers hospital where, because of his condition, a nurse had to help remove him from the car. Looking terribly sad, Gau was admitted to a room occupied by two men, "one crazy old grandad who wanted nothing more than to eat, and a lunatic, thin as death, one eye missing and the other staring fixedly at you. My God! I was most depressed. I tried to joke with Jean in English.

"'My boy, what ugly companions you have, eh?'

"I wish that you could have seen Jean's half-laugh, half-grin. There was the horror of death in it . . . Ghastly . . . " His host and friend would say no more. Returning home the man was saddened, feeling that something dear had been lost. "Johnny never spoke much. But every gesture, the look of his eyes, even his presence was enriching. Looking at him I had often reflected how this man had sailed the world, defied storms, had studied stars and visited strange shores. And now this! He was . . . " the host paused to find a suitable word, "an *atom* among so many atoms in life. But he was different. He tried to control, to influence his course where the others zigged and zagged. Life *is* a tragedy. I wish that Johnny could die and be spared more decaying." The large, good-hearted farmer was close to tears.

In April Jean left the hospital after developing an allergy to his medicines which forced him to remain a bit longer. The friend had in the meantime fixed up a small room in his house on the ground floor near the courtyard so that the old sailor had then only to cross the yard to reach the dining room. A chemical toilet was purchased and the electrical fittings in Gau's trailer rewired to eliminate confusion.

As the word of Gau's deteriorated condition spread, others offered help. Among them was France's mariner-philosopher, Bernard Moitessier. His letter to Gau, with its check for two thousand dollars, created widespread interest in the French-speaking yachting community.

August 28, 1976

My dear Jean:

From the newspapers and more recently from letters I've learned of your difficulties. What, my friend, can I say other than to encourage you to stem Life's current as best you can.

It pleases me that I'm able to send you the enclosed sum, hoping that it will in some way help. As others have often helped me it is only proper, Jean, that I now try to help others.

Soon I'll get underway for Ahé in the Tuamotos where I've built a small taré to house my companion and my child.

Before I leave you, my seaman brother, I leave you the wish that you will soon recover.

Bernard Moitessier

Miraculously, Johnny's inability to control his bodily functions actually improved. His loss of recent memory, however, continued to deteriorate. That his mind, which has seemingly lost recall of most of his great sea exploits, still managed to impart some flickering image was evident when he was taken for a recent boat ride to his beloved Valras and the River Orb. As the handsome cutter motored up the swiftly flowing river, Johnny gently raised his hand from time to time to acknowledge the cheers of crowds lining the banks. His host, the boat's skipper, wept. Only a few scattered persons were seen. They ignored the common sight of a boat underway and an old man's waving hand.

July 1976
Annandale, Virginia
Castelnau-de-Guers, France.

Afterword

In the short time allotted to each of us, only a few achieve a destiny almost completely fashioned by their dreams and aspirations. This Jean Gau has done.

Such individuals are identified by tenacity, single-mindedness, staunch determination, and absolute self-confidence. When these attributes are sharply defined in an individual whose sole motivation is the pursuit of adventure, the world, in time, will notice.

But it will notice, too, the flaws that plague these dream-smitten figures. And it will comment on these flaws, which are often as large as the ambitions. An air of total detachment, or of ruthlessness is not uncommon in such individuals.

And the price these people pay? For some—spiritual isolation, the exclusion of love, the absence of sustained friendships. For others—a life lived very much like a lonely voyage, almost desperate in its singleness of purpose. Such people, demanding more from life than it willingly provides, are romantics. In them serious observers detect, though fleetingly, the reality of that

259

elusive and indefinable quality, the human spirit.

The saga of Captain Jean Gau is a timeless one, simply told—of a man and a boat, of two remarkable circumnavigations and eleven Atlantic crossings, of groundings, shipwrecks, a treasure island, and skulls buried in forgotten sands, of almost legendary hurricanes and trying storms at sea. But it is more than this. It is the singular story of a man of simple tastes seeking challenge and adventure in a world that seemingly has little to seek, to admire, to wonder at. And it is the tale of a priceless commodity, of faith in oneself, to achieve whatever the cost. It is a story of spiritual significance, of the worth of the individual. In its simplicity there is a strength and a quality possessed by the oceans, a pristine cleanliness that permits no defects. It is, in its way, a classic.

For most the slippered comforts of old age, a warm seat before the fire, the presence of loved ones, and the sense of having lived a lifetime of quiet desperation are the rewards of enduring. These Jean Gau unequivocally exchanged for adventure. And had not fate intervened, Jean might have achieved his final goal: with his beloved *Atom*, "to sail on or to sail under together."

Serious readers of small-boat literature accord honor to the relatively few who have struggled valiantly against great odds. If Nelson is the epitome of naval courage, it was the Yankee skipper, Joshua Slocum, who alone conquered the waters for small boats; the robust Argentinian, Vito Dumas, who faced alone the rigors of the Roaring Forties; Bernard Gilboy, whom the nautical world has almost forgotten, who managed to cross nearly 7,000 miles of Pacific Ocean in an eighteen-foot schooner-rigged boat. They are great men all.

And the odyssey of Jean Gau—with his level gaze we see the rigorous reality of the world's oceans and breezes as they accommodate the spirit of man. And we are enriched, for it is the pure *spirit of adventure* that emerges in his writings. As mountains were made to be climbed, oceans were made to be crossed. A world jaded with ease and comfortable travel still longs for daring.

Jean loved the sea as he loved adventure. Through this passionate commitment he has provided a model for the sea-thirsty, determined to challenge the distant oceans of this world.

Perhaps, as was suggested by a Gau fan, Richard Hughes, "his life is a symbol of possibility outside the ordinary."

At the age of fifty-one Gau set sail in a thirty-foot wooden ketch, returning four years later from a voyage around the world. At sixty-one again cleared New York for a remarkable second voyage. And in an unadorned description of these voyages he provides possibly the best open-eyed account of the problems, dangers, rewards, and delights such journeys afford. As is evident from his prose, Gau did not employ a ghost writer. Accordingly, one finds in his writings very possibly the most accurate description of what lies beyond the sea's horizon.

If he does not provide lists of foodstuffs and medicines for long voyages, Gau does provide a list of what sailors need in the way of encouragement: patience, good sense, timing, and a unshakable belief in one's ability to survive. Much nautical literature must be pared down, attacked with a scalpel, to find the marrow. Gau's writing needs no knife.

Jean's story could be the last of its kind; fewer circumnavigations are being made today by solitary men in small wooden boats. As today's amenities—iced beer, rapid communications, stereo music—become available to deep-sea sailors, it seems likely that there will be less emphasis in their writings about the immensity of the oceans or the closeness of man to nature. Jean Gau's spirit dwelt simply, with the sea.

And what of *Atom?* On the negative side, she was a sluggish performer in light airs, but this appears not to have worried her skipper. As for her scantlings, a famed French builder of Tahiti ketches, Fernand Pfister, recalls that *Atom* "was far more heavily built than today's boats." And of her design, "A barge!" roars the eighty-six-year-old Cape Horner (by square-rigger), Captain L. Vernette. "So crammed with junk," added this gregarious Gau fan, "she never rode to her lines, proper-like! Her nose was always wet!"

But if the Tahiti ketch design attracted admirers (and still does), it attracted also nautical writers who scoffed at "stubborn skippers who survive more because of their skills than because of their boats." Such writers, to our knowledge, have not grounded on the sullen reefs in Torres Straits or ridden out a severe

Mediterranean gale with the cabin in waters knee-deep, as did the lowly *Atom* and her doughty skipper.

That she was a poor windward sailer is correct — repeatedly Jean offered excuses for not beating to windward to regain lost disances after being hove to or from drifting past a port of call at night; but for this he never criticized *Atom*. Perhaps she could have pointed much higher had her internal ballast been removed.

If beating to windward wasn't *Atom's* forte her sea-kindly motions in a seaway were, for Jean, a joy. The point, however, that true boating pleasure is found in a boat's performance cannot be ignored. If performance means only speed then *Atom* failed. But if it means survival after capsizing, a refusal to sink when rogue waves submerge the deck, or the ability to survive a dismasting, *Atom* was a winner.

Possibly her modest freeboard, low deckhouse, and considerable reserve buoyancy explained her longevity, as perhaps did her small cockpit and long waterline and the fact that her widest beam was aft of midships. Critics say that the Tahiti ketch has too much wetted surface and that her V-shaped bows guarantee that it's a diver — which *Atom* was. Because of a hard turn to her bilge she had good initial stability, a condition augmented by her outside ballasted keel. But, of course, she was a great roller, too.

Whether *Atom's* canoe stern actually broke the following seas, as the literature of round sterns suggests, is not clear. She did survive some pretty horrendous following seas.

That she was undersailed is evident, but at times Jean had a problem getting even these sails down. Her low aspect ratio would make her a poor ship when running before the wind, say the critics, who point out also that the slewing force of the Tahiti design would make her impossible to steer. They may be right. After more than 100,000 miles Gau never found it worth mentioning. *Atom's* clubbed headsail they considered dangerous, and, as for reefing the jib, it little mattered, they said, for it had so little pull. Again, they may be right. Yet without phenolic sheaves, roller-furling headsails, rod rigging, spinnakers, or — believe it or not — winches, *Atom* repeatedly challenged the world's oceans, giving thereby a quick beat to man's pulsing nature.

And *"Johnny"* — his boyhood friend, Henri Sauzet, tears lining his image-filled eyes, spoke softly — *"Johnny only thought about the land when his cigarettes were low."* Henri's remark echoes that of Jean-Charles Taupin, past Commodore of the Slocum Society: "For Gau, the goal is the voyage, not its goal." Of his achievements old friends have said, "Johnny's not a yachtsman or a sailor if the term means a man who insists on maximum performance from his boat." A staunch admirer, Valras mechanic and early Gau fan, René Paletta, explains. "Jean is *not* your typical sailor. He's special. What he's achieved no one else has. Tabarly, Chichester, Blythe, these men are not old sea dogs. They have nice boats that will go to windward." Paletta was silent for a moment. "When Jean decided to go, he went. Anytime, any weather."

The mechanic suddenly looked off toward the Bassin Jean Gau and the quietly flowing River Orb. His head nodded thoughtfully. "What Jean wanted was water, just water. He was happy just to live between the sea and the sky."

And, by so doing, Captain Jean Gau, Windseeker, sailed alone more than any man who has ever lived.

Chronology

1902	17 February	Jean Gau born in Serignan, France.
1914		Youth Gau informs father of intention to become a sailor; his intentions thwarted, Gau quits school.
1915		Gau becomes an apprentice mechanic.
1919		Studies at the Louvre; sells 60 paintings in Spain.
1920		Commits forgery and is imprisoned.
1921		Conscripted for Army, Gau is posted to Blida, Algeria.
1922		Read Gerbault's book. Forays by camel into Saharan wastes.
1923		Discharged, Gau returns to Beziers, France. Works in a distillery.
1926	26 March	Marries Marie Armengaud in Valras, France.
1927		Jean and Marie emigrate to America.
1928		Wife leaves Gau.
1931		Buys schooner *Onda II* near Boston.

1932		Lives aboard *Onda,* where he learns of sunken Pacific treasure.
1933		Studies celestial navigation.
1935		Sails with companion to Nova Scotia and returns (he never again made long voyages with someone else aboard).
1937	7 July	Completes first Atlantic crossing.
1937	31 September	Loses *Onda* on Cadiz shoals. Letters reveal that "that sea has (him) forever."
1938	February	The Anita Affair aboard SS *Roosevelt.*
1939		Begins the *Onda* paintings period.
1945	October	Buys Tahiti ketch, *Lois,* which he renames *Atom.*
1946		Lives aboard *Atom.*
1947	24 May	Completes second Atlantic crossing. Unable to make headway, berths *Atom* in Cartagena. Goes to Serignan by train.
1948	6 May	Departs Cartagena for America, but, unable to pass straits, returns to Valras, France.
1949	10 May	Departs France for America, arriving NYC 11 September, completing third Atlantic crossing.
1950		Pierre Gau dies.
1952	15 September	Marie Louise Gau dies. Gau flies to France.
1953		Sells home place and on 28 April announces plans to sail alone around the world. Returns to America.
	30 June	Departs Montauk for first circumnavigation.
1954	8 June	Reaches Tahiti and meets Taime.
1955	22 April	Reaches "Treasure" (Rose) Island. Dives, finds wreck.
1956	9 February	Departs Durban, S. Africa. Arrives Valras, France late September. (Gau considers this his fourth Atlantic crossing).
1957	13 July	Meets Churchill in Azores. Survives hurricane Carrie 19-20 September 1957.

	3 October	Arrives NYC, completing his fifth Atlantic crossing and first circumnavigation.
1958		Friends note a change in Gau after his great voyage. He reportedly began to neglect *Atom*. Bassin Jean Gau named in his honor. Resumes work at Hotel Taft.
1962	15 May	Departs NYC for Valras, arriving late August: his sixth Atlantic crossing.
1963	26 May	Begins voyage number two from Valras. Makes seventh Atlantic crossing.
1964	9 January	Armed, Gau witnesses US-Panama riots.
1964	9 October	Reaches "Treasure" (Rose) Island.
1965	3 July	Gau, 64, grounds *Atom* on notorious Warrior Reef.
1966	27 February	*Atom* capsized and dismasted off South Africa.
1967	2 February	Reaches Grenada after 120 days nonstop but cannot land.
	10 June	Reaches NYC. Completes eighth Atlantic crossing.
1968	28 June	Departs NYC for Valras and ninth Atlantic crossing.
	9 October	Arrives Valras and completes second circumnavigation.
1970	May	Departs Valras for America. Found adrift two months later near Valras.
1971	June	Departs Valras for America. Makes tenth Atlantic crossing.
	25 October	Reportedly beginning his third circumnavigation, he goes aground on Assateague Island, Maryland.
1972	20 July	Gau departs Ocean City for New York. Resumes chef's work.
1973	June	Gau suffers stroke and is partially paralyzed. Alone, Gau limps aboard *Atom* and departs 22 June 1973 for Valras.
	22 November	Reported lost at sea. After reaching Cartagena in September (his eleventh Atlantic crossing). Gau

		leaves for Valras days later.
	3 December	*Atom* is wrecked on north coast of Tunisia.
1975		Gau returns to niece's home in Beziers, France, ill and destitute. French admirers donate clothing, trailer. American friend initiates call for money and letters for Gau here and in England, and obtains Social Security benefits for him. Gau's mental and physical condition deteriorates.
1976		Admitted to old folk's hospital in Beziers; later is a house guest of close admirer. Only faint recall of his exploits remain. An effort to raise money in France is launched.

Specifications

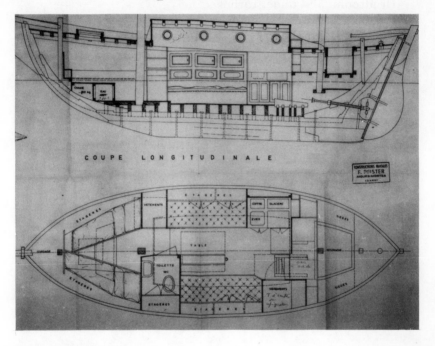

Name: *Atom* (formerly *Lois*)
Rig: Ketch (Tahiti design), gaff
Hull: Double-ended
Length, overall: 29'6"
Length, waterline: 27'
Beam: 10'
Draft: 4'
Engine: Gasoline (Universal), 2-cylinder, 4-cylinder
H.P.: 10-15
Gasoline consumption: 9 miles per gallon
Sails: Canvas; 475 sq. ft.; jib topsail, gaff topsail, mizzen staysail, and
   mainsail.

Construction: White oak frames (2″ x 2¼″), 10″ on center.
Planking of white cedar (1⅛″).
Fastenings are galvanized Swedish iron boat nails.
Keel: 2,700 lbs. iron.
Inside ballast: 4,000 lbs. lead.
Headroom: 5′9″ under carlins
Builder: Bjorne Egeli
Designer: John Hannah
Built: 1938